C000214882

BATTLES
ON THE
TIGRIS

BATTLES
ON THE
TIGRIS

by

Ron Wilcox

Pen & Sword
MILITARY

First published in Great Britain in 2006
Reprinted in 2008 by
Pen & Sword Military
an imprint of
Pen & Sword Books Ltd
47 Church Street
Barnsley
South Yorkshire
S70 2AS

Copyright © Ron Wilcox

ISBN 978 1 84415 430 2

The right of Ron Wilcox to be identified as Author of this Work has
been asserted by him in accordance with the Copyright,
Designs and Patents Act 1988.

A CIP catalogue record for this book is
available from the British Library

All rights reserved. No part of this book may be reproduced or trans-
mitted in any form or by any means, electronic or mechanical including
photocopying, recording or by any information storage and retrieval
system, without permission from the Publisher in writing.

Typeset in Sabon by
Phoenix Typesetting, Auldgirth, Dumfriesshire

Printed and bound in England by
Biddles Ltd., King's Lynn

Pen & Sword Books Ltd incorporates the Imprints of Pen & Sword
Aviation, Pen & Sword Maritime, Pen & Sword Military, Wharncliffe
Local History, Pen & Sword Select, Pen & Sword Military Classics and
Leo Cooper.

For a complete list of Pen & Sword titles please contact
PEN & SWORD BOOKS LIMITED
47 Church Street, Barnsley, South Yorkshire, S70 2AS, England
E-mail: enquiries@pen-and-sword.co.uk
Website: www.pen-and-sword.co.uk

Contents

Maps

Abbreviations on Maps

⎍⎍⎍⎍	Trench lines
Art	Artillery
Cav	Cavalry
CB	Cavalry Brigade
CT	Communication Trench
H/Huss	Hussars
L	Lancers
M.T.	Motor Transport
OP	Observation Point
VP	Vital Point

Acknowledgements
for Portraits and Maps

Burne, Lieutenant Colonel A.H., *Mesopotamia, the Last Phase*, Gale and Polden (nd)

Candler, Edward, *The Long Road to Baghdad*, Vols I & II, Cassell (1919)

Dunsterville, Major General L.C., *The Adventures of Dunsterforce*, Edward Arnold (1920)

Marshall, William, *Memories of Four Fronts*, Ernest Benn (1929)

Moberley, Brigadier General F.J., *The Campaign in Mesopotamia 1914–1918*, Official History, Stationery Office, Vol I, 1923, Vol II 1924

Mousley, E.O., *The Secrets of a Kuttite*, Bodley Head (1922)

One of its Officers, *With a Highland Regiment in Mesopotamia 1916–1917*, The Times Press, Bombay (1918)

Sherson, Erroll, *Townshend of Chitral and Kut*, Heinemann (1928)

Staff College, Quetta, *Critical Study of the Campaign in Mesopotamia up to April 1917*, Government of India, Calcutta (1925)

Tennant, Lieutenant Colonel J.E., *In the Clouds above Baghdad*, Cecil Palmer (1920)

Wilson, Sir Arnold, *Loyalties – Mesopotamia, 1914–1917*, OUP (1929)

General Acknowledgements

I gratefully acknowledge the invaluable help of Bobby Gainher in editing the manuscript and saving me from many errors, and for my son's computer expertise in preparing the maps.

Chapter One

Small Beginnings

(See Map 1)

On the day after Britain declared war on Turkey in 1914, a force of British and Indian troops landed in southern Iraq, a country then usually known as Mesopotamia. Its orders from the Indian Government were to safeguard the Anglo-Persian oilfields leased from Persia at Shushtar in southern Persia and the pipeline that ran from there down to the refinery at Abadan on the Shatt al Arab river close to Mohammera. The Sheikh of Mohammera was friendly to the British, as was the Sheikh of Kuwait on the opposite side of the Persian Gulf, but this attitude was in contrast to most of the tribes in the area.

Shatt al Arab was the name given to the combined waters of the Tigris and Euphrates on their way to empty into the northern shore of the Persian Gulf. Mesopotamia was officially the three Turkish vilayets (provinces) of Basra in the south, Baghdad in the middle and Mosul in the north, but at the time the ancient name of Mesopotamia was used by the British for convenience to describe these particular sections of the Turkish or Ottoman Empire. Its name means 'the land between two rivers', the two rivers being the Euphrates on the west and the Tigris further east whose waters combine near the town of Amara.

In the remote past, Mesopotamia had been a rich and fertile land, the home of some of the greatest civilizations of the Middle East. Four thousand years before, the Uruk culture of the south had invented the earliest form of Western writing on clay tablets and

1

produced the oldest work of literature in existence – 'The Epic of Gilgamesh' – and had first divided the hour into sixty minutes and the circle into 360 degrees. These people were followed by the Sumerians and later by the Babylonians with their great kings Hammurabi and Nebuchadnezzar who defeated Egypt, conquered Syria and Palestine, and captured Jerusalem. Their lands were converted from desert by elaborate networks of canals and channels using the waters of the two great rivers, the Euphrates and the Tigris, but by 1914 the cities and the irrigation systems responsible for creating the agricultural wealth of the ancient world had collapsed, leaving behind a countryside of ruin and poverty that had mainly reverted to primeval desert and marsh.

Mesopotamia had been part of the Turkish Empire from the sixteenth century but it was only after the discovery of oil in south-western Persia that the area became of much interest to European nations, amongst whom Britain and Germany were the most prominent. It was (and is) a Moslem country with the people of the south, from Basra to Kut al Amara (henceforward referred to as Kut) Shia Moslems, professing allegiance to the Sultan of Khalifa, and the people of the north, Sunni Moslems, who used to profess allegiance to the Shah of Persia.

Oilfields had been discovered at the beginning of the twentieth century by an Australian with the most un-Australian name of William Knox D'Arcy. He obtained a concession of 500,000 square miles of territory from the Persian Government to develop the field and with help from Lord Fisher, First Sea Lord, formed in 1909 the Anglo-Persian Oil Company. A year or two later, a British Commission of Enquiry examined the prospects of the company and Fisher's successor as First Lord, Winston Churchill, without reference to Parliament, bought for Britain a controlling stake in it for £2,200,000.

Britain's interest in the area, apart from the oil, was a proposal to develop overland communication between Europe and India through Mesopotamia, a route that would obviate the sea journey via the Suez Canal or around Africa, while Germany was intent on building a railway through Turkey to Baghdad and beyond to achieve a similar link with south-western Asia.

Before the First World War, German influence in the region had been growing, particularly in the Turkish Empire where, at the approach of war, the property of British subjects was being confis-

Map 1. Lower Mesopotamia

cated and plans for blocking the Shatt al Arab were being made so that British steamers in the waterway would be prevented from sailing from Iraq's chief port of Basra, at that time not particularly busy with ocean-going traffic but important for local traffic conveying dates, the chief product of its bankside groves, to the town.

Britain had stationed two warships on the river, HMS *Espiègle* anchored off Mohammerah, and HMS *Odin* at the mouth. In addition, the Royal Indian Marine HMS *Dalhousie* lay off Abadan.

3

The Turks tried to order the British to leave in a letter delivered on board the *Espiègle* by a Turkish naval officer, that read: 'Please you leave the Shat before 24 hours.' In response the ship moved half a mile up the Karun river that joins the left bank of the Shatt at Mohammera where she was indubitably in Persian territorial waters. A few days later the Turks turned up the heat by positioning guns on the river bank opposite Mohammera and telling the British consul that the ship would not be allowed to go back down to the Shatt unless she left within eight days.

A week later the Turkish governor of Basra suggested to the Sheikh of Mohammera that he should allow a large body of Turkish troops disguised as Arab women to position themselves on the housetops on either side of the Karun river alongside the *Espiègle*. At a given signal, two guns on the island of Dabba would open fire on the British warship and when she returned fire the force on the housetops should open fire 'especially at the gunners' and 'there will an unexpected slaughter. When no-one can defend the gunboat they will board it, killing everyone they can find and seizing the vessel.' It was pointed out to the Sheikh that this act of treachery would be a valuable act of service to the Turkish Government. Needless to say, the Sheikh would have nothing to do with the scheme.

In Whitehall it was decided that although some action should be taken it was not necessary to make Mesopotamia the scene of any large-scale operations and the measures required for the defence of British interests there should be left in the hands of the Indian Government. They were told to prepare an Indian expeditionary force to be despatched with the objectives of reinforcing the morale of the Arab sheikhs at the head of the Persian Gulf and protecting the 'oil stores' by occupying Abadan Island where the oil refinery was. These instructions were not received with any great enthusiasm by the Indian Government which was of the opinion that the despatch of such a force was 'provocative'.

So far, the most important military duties laid on the Government of India by the British Government had been to defend the North-West Frontier from incursions by Afghan tribes and maintain internal security in the country. Overseas expeditions of a minor kind might be undertaken but no additional expense was to be incurred. This was a policy suggested originally by the Indian Government itself and approved by the India Office in March 1914. Presumably, the Indian Government was now given to understand that this Mesopotamian venture was an 'expedition of a minor kind' and in this way they were dragged willy-nilly into a war that initially they were not keen on and certainly did not have the resources to support.

Vague instructions given to Brigadier General Delamain, the commander of the Force, by the Indian Government did not make clear how troops in occupation of Abadan could protect both the 130-mile long oil pipeline to the oil fields at Shushtar or the oilfields themselves in country controlled not even by the Persian Government in whose territory the oilfields lay, but by unreliable Persian nomadic tribesmen.

However, despite the Indian Government's misgivings, an Anglo-Indian force, known as 'Force D', landed at Fao on 6 November 1914. It had been despatched from Bombay on 16 October in the utmost secrecy disguised as part of a large convoy destined for Egypt, with sealed orders that were to be opened after three days at sea. These orders told the force commander, Brigadier General Delamain, to detach his command from the convoy and head for Bahrain, there to await further instructions. These came within a few days and informed him that, after the capture of Fao, at the mouth of the Shatt al Arab, and Abadan, he was to move up the river and reconnoitre routes towards Basra in preparation for the advance of a larger force that was being mobilized in India. Basra, therefore, had now become the objective of the expedition. Constant changes of objective became, as we shall see, a recurring feature of the Mesopotamian Campaign.

The Indian Army was by no means a first-rate fighting force – the only thing that was outstanding about it was the character of the soldiers themselves, both British and Indian, who were to demonstrate bravery and endurance of the highest order in the coming years. It was a defensive force that had come into being in 1895 with the integration into one Indian army of the Madras, Bombay and Bengal armies, which had been made up of a number of military formations organized originally by the native princes. In 1903 this army was reorganized and renumbered to virtually create the army that was to fight in the First World War.

Infantry and cavalry were formed into double companies each commanded by a British officer aided by a British junior officer. In the infantry units the senior Indian officer was called the subahdar-major and risaldar-major in the cavalry, whilst to each half company was attached a junior Indian officer called a jemadar. Indian officers issued all orders to the Indian troops. Four double companies formed an infantry battalion commanded by a British officer with a British adjutant, quartermaster, signalling, scout and transport officers. Shortly after the outbreak of the war, a re-arrangement into British-style companies and platoons was adopted, the commands being held by British and Indian officers respectively. Cavalry regiments were organized into four squadrons with sixteen British officers commanding the regiments and squadrons. In addition there were the risaldar-major, three risaldars and nine jemadars.

As mentioned above, the Indian Army was always intended as a defence force, but a suggestion had been made by Sir Douglas Haig, while Chief of Staff in India, that the Indian military establishment might one day have to put together an expedition armed and equipped sufficiently to confront a European army. The enemy he had in mind was Turkey, either alone or supported by Germany, but this idea was pooh-poohed by the Viceroy, Lord Hardinge. His decision was in line with the policy of the British Cabinet who were anxious to restrict expenditure, so nothing was done to modernize the force.

Sir O'Moore Creagh was Commander-in-Chief of the Indian military at the time and he was constantly calling for modern equipment like machine-guns, heavy howitzers and signalling equipment, but his demands were turned down by the Finance Department and the Viceroy and he became so frustrated that he resigned six months before the end of his term of office. He was succeeded by Sir Beauchamp Duff in April 1914 who was a far more complacent individual.

As a result, the Mesopotamian Expedition or 'Force D' as it was officially known, was equipped as though it was going to face a frontier rebellion of tribes armed only with rifles, while the Indian Government acted as though the war was going to be a short one and ordinary peacetime routine could be followed. In no way during the first eighteen months of the war did it rise to the challenge of conquering a whole country, which was what the campaign was soon to become, because it insisted on relying on the agreement that had been made with the India Office earlier in 1914.

Responsibility for the war was divided between the India Office in London who provided the day-to-day policy and the Indian Government who managed the expedition. As a result, the objectives of the expedition were never set out in advance, so that the Commander only knew what he had to do next and not what the long-term aims were likely to be. Advanced planning, therefore, was non-existent.

This lack of foresight is most obvious throughout the whole of the first half of the campaign in the shortage of river transport. There were no roads so the River Tigris was the only practicable route by which men and supplies could be carried to a battlefront that speedily retreated further and further away up an unstable river, yet this was never fully understood by the Indian authorities who, when they were called upon for more river transport, responded with inadequate and unsuitable vessels. General Cowper, senior administrative officer to General Nixon, who sent requests to India in 1915 for additional transport, was threatened with dismissal by Sir Beauchamp Duff, the Commander-in-Chief in India, for being too insistent. Allied to this, the base port of Basra, or more properly Ashur, its riverside suburb, was not equipped for handling the amount of material that had to be transferred from ocean-going ships to those that used the river, and long delays became the norm.

But the most scandalous failure was in the provision of medical equipment and personnel. No river hospital steamers were available, there were few medical personnel, either doctors or nurses, an inadequate land ambulance and a shortage of medical comforts, drugs and dressings. This was apparent from the first days of the campaign, but later on it became one of the blots on its otherwise gallant story.

Composition of 'Force D', November 1914 (16th Indian Infantry Brigade)

> Brigade Headquarters
> 1st Indian Mountain Artillery Brigade
> 22nd Company, Sappers and Miners
> 2nd Dorsetshire Regiment
> 20th Punjabis
> 104th Rifles
> 117th Mahhrattas
> Section, 34th Divisional Signal Company
> 125th Field Ambulance
> 12th Mule Corps

13th Mule Corps
Supply Column (S & TC)

Field Post Office
Ordnance Field Park

91 British officers, 918 British other ranks, 82 Indian officers, 3,640 Indian other ranks, 460 followers, 1,290 animals.

Chapter Two

Ambition is Stirred

(Maps 1, 2 and 3)

After occupying Fao, Delamain made a second landing a couple of days later at Saniya, 2½ miles north of the pipeline terminal at Abadan, where his camp was attacked by the Turks and the first British and Indian casualties occurred.

British troops formed almost a quarter of the force, the contingent comprising mainly the 2nd Dorsets, while the Indians contributed much of the rest, both infantry and artillery, in total, some 4,182, a figure that includes Indian camp followers (non-military personnel attached to Indian regiments). In the force there were nearly 1,300 mules which were the only available transport. With the contingent was a formidable figure as Political Officer, Sir Percy Cox, who had been Foreign Secretary to the Government of India and who had his own very definite ideas as to how the Mesopotamian Campaign should be directed.

It has been suggested that at this juncture General Delamain could have moved up the Shatt al Arab using the naval sloops to escort troop transports. They could have steamed up the river, shelled Basra and landed the soldiers above the town, who could have captured it. It would have been an operation analogous to, but on a smaller scale to what was to be attempted in the Dardanelles. But more cautious advice prevailed, for it was thought the river was blocked and the naval gunfire would have been ineffective against artillery on the banks.

On 14 November the rest of the 6th Division began to disembark at Sanila. In command was Lieutenant General Sir Arthur Barrett who now took over from Delamain, whose force remained intact as the 16th Indian Infantry Brigade in the 6th Division, and continued the advance by attacking the Turkish position at Saihan. This small battle encapsulated two features of the fighting that were to figure prominently in most of the later engagements. One was co-operation with the Navy – in this case the sloops HMS *Odin* and HMS *Espiègle* which fired on the enemy from the river – and the other was the presence of the mirage that bedevilled much of the reconnaissance. Despite this, Delamain, with three battalions and two batteries, enveloped both flanks of the Turks' position and drove them out of it.

The mirage was one of the most remarkable features of campaigning in Mesopotamia. In the open desert, distant troops would appear to come forward, to retreat or suddenly vanish. Small bushes would turn into infantry platoons and a dozen sheep would become a squadron of camelry. At a distance of 1,000 yards large bodies of troops would be quite invisible while at 300 yards it might not be possible to identify objects or even be sure if an object was there at all. Early in the morning the mirage caused things to merge together. A troop of Turkish horsemen would look like a row of trestle tables with elongated legs, but soon everything would be lifted off their feet. Where the troops had been, there was a floating table – the legs had disappeared. The camel of an hour before was a ship suspended in the air. A little mound resembled a burst of shrapnel with a clear streak of horizon under it. (Candler)

Two days later Barrett advanced and defeated another Turkish force of some 4,000 Turks and 1,000 Arabs with twelve guns at Sahil. Barrett didn't at first realize how complete this victory was but as a result of it, the Turks decided to evacuate Basra. This news reached the British commander by way of the Sheikh of Mohammera whose Arab spies in the town passed the news downstream.

Ships were immediately despatched up the river with a small advanced force and the rest of the army set out on the long, tiring march along the river bank and through the date groves that lined it. In the river the flotilla came upon a barrier that the Turks had placed across the Shatt al Arab just below Basra, consisting of a sunken German liner and three other ships tied together by cables. Fortunately the Turkish attempt was inept – as the seacocks were

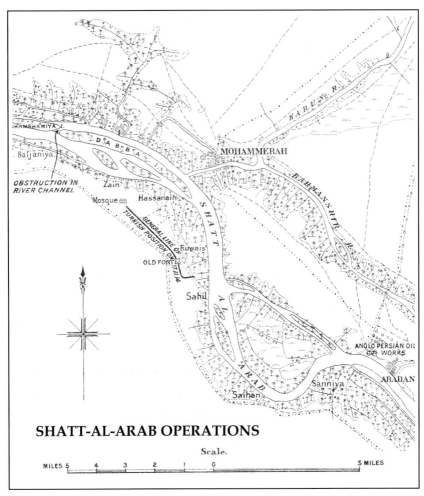

Map 2.   Shatt-al-Arab operations

opened the German liner swung in the current to the Persian bank
and sank there, leaving a clear if narrow passage in the middle of
the river which became known as Satan's Gap and remained the
only water entrance to Mesopotamia throughout the campaign.

The advance guard of *Espiègle* and *Odin*, the two Royal Navy
sloops, arrived off Basra to find that the Turks had made off and the
Arabs were looting the town. Order was restored and next day
General Barrett arrived with the main force. In order to impress the
natives, he made a ceremonial entry and hoisted the union flag. Sir

11

Percy Cox read a proclamation in Arabic which carried the imperial flavour of the times:

> The British Government has now occupied Basra, but though a state of war with the Ottoman Government still prevails, yet we have no enmity or ill-will against the population, to whom we hope to prove good friends and protectors. No remnant of Turkish administration remains in this region. In place thereof the British flag has been established, under which you will enjoy the benefits of liberty and justice, both in regard to your religious and secular affairs.

One might almost draw a parallel with similar promises made to the Iraqi people by another great power nearly ninety years later.

Percy Cox and his small staff now came into their own. It was their job to set up a civil administration, a task complicated by the loss of most of the Turkish records, by the need to make a clear distinction between the Turk and his government and the Arab population, and by the fact that the Arabs with whom we wished to be friendly were legally enemy aliens, being Turkish subjects. As such, in law, they could not be traded with or negotiated with, nor could they be issued with passports. The civil administration got round this by providing a form of passport that described the bearer as an inhabitant of the Occupied Territories of Mesopotamia and entitled as such to British good offices.

A further complication for Cox was the attitude of the military to the Arabs, with whom they were not always friendly. Many of the members of the Turkish forces ranged against them were Arabs, so they were the enemy, while those Arab tribes they came across further upriver proved themselves adept as pillagers and murderers of the wounded on the battlefield and determined thieves of anything they came across that was not nailed down. This conduct was encouraged to some extent by the Turkish commander, Lieutenant Colonel Suleyman Askati Bey, a highly educated and enthusiastic soldier, who sent letters to Arab chieftains to suggest that they rise up and fight the infidels, but the Arab tribesmen preferred to operate unorganized as unofficial predatory guerrilla bands.

Meanwhile, the Turks divided their forces into two 'wings': the Euphrates wing under Suleiman Askeri Bey with orders from the War Minister, Enver Pasha, to advance on Basra via Nasiriya;

and the Tigris wing commanded by Mehmet Fazil Pasha who led the 35th Division and Arab cavalry units.

The population of Iraq at that time was approximately 2½ million, thinly scattered apart from the few towns. Half led settled lives while the rest were wandering nomads or semi-nomads using temporary pasturage and water sources for their herds. About a million and a quarter were Arabs, the rest a mixture of Turks, Kurds and Persians. Most were Moslems but there were a few Christians, Jews and Devil worshippers, the Yezidis, amongst them.

Now that the British were established in Basra the expedition seemed to have run its course. After a rapid and successful campaign, British prestige was high in Arab bazaars throughout the delta, and the oilfields had been saved.

But political ambition began to rear its head. Sir Percy Cox sent a private telegram to the Viceroy of India urging that the force should not rest on its laurels since he was sure that Turkish resistance was certain to continue to be slight and he followed this up with the following passage:

According to general reports Turkish troops recently engaged with us were completely panic-stricken and very unlikely to oppose us again. Arab element in Baghdad is already friendly and notables here volunteer opinion that we should be received in Baghdad with the same cordiality as we have been here and that the Turkish troops would offer little if any opposition. There remain the tribes between here and Baghdad. From among this element the well-known Muntafik Shaikh, Ajaimi, who was ostensibly co-operating with the Turkish troops, has just sent an emissary to covey his submission and intimate his wish to come in and hand over four thousand rifles received or seized by him from the Turks and it is hoped that the neutrality if not the active co-operation of the tribes can be secured by judicious diplomacy. *Effect of the recent defeat has been very great, and if advance is made before it wears off and while the cool season lasts Baghdad will in all probability fall into our hands very easily. After earnest consideration of the arguments for and against I find it difficult to see how we can well avoid taking over Baghdad.* (Author's italics)

This may sound like a breathtaking piece of advice, albeit with a familiar ring, and perhaps could only have come from a political officer. Baghdad, the chief Turkish political and military town in the region, was 500 miles away up a shallow and difficult river, and the British force consisted of only a single division. Cox had spent six earlier years in the Indian Army as a career officer and, one thinks, should have known better. But it is probably fair to say that no sooner was this idea mooted than it became an obsession with several influential people that was to represent a permanent menace to sound strategy in the Mesopotamian Campaign.

In the political departments in the India Office in London and in Delhi the idea was eagerly welcomed and soon even the military minds, as they contemplated the suggestion, began to be dazzled by the early prospect of a triumphant entry into the heart of the enemy's country.

Although the Military Secretary in the India Office in London, General Sir E. Barrow, rejected an advance on Baghdad, he was sufficiently seduced by the prospect to suggest a move upriver to the town of Qurna which sea-going ships could reach and which controlled all the rich cultivated land along the river. He also pointed out that Persian Arabistan, where the oilfields were, would be more adequately covered by the advance and the project would have a good moral effect on the Arab tribes.

It is difficult to know how much the authorities, either in London or India, knew of climatic conditions in Iraq. Between May and October temperatures could reach as high as 134 degrees F (57 degrees C) in the shade, but in November and April it is cool, while between December and March it is decidedly cold. The winter season was plagued by a biting wind that drove a cold rain across the desert. After a couple of hours of this the country became a sea of glutinous mud which made movements of troops and animals almost impossible and aircraft could not take off. Not that there were any aircraft in the country at this juncture. When they did arrive, they found that in extreme heat they could not fly between 0900 and 1700 hrs because the under-powered machines of the time could not rise through the super-heated air.

During the flood season huge areas of the desert were converted into stretches of open water or impassable morasses. In all directions there was a limitless plain with a horizon as level as the sea, while depressions turned out to be swamps with bays and inlets. At right angles to and closer to the river banks ran canals and cuttings with hard ridges as banks while deep irrigation channels complicated the movement of wheeled vehicles. Here and there, to give what little variety there was, palm groves straggled along the banks of the rivers.

The Tigris became the main means of carriage of troops and equipment. Baghdad could be reached by river craft but at all times of the year navigation was difficult – boats drawing 5 feet of water could get there in the flood season but in the dry season the journey was restricted to smaller vessels of 3 feet draught, the journey in both cases taking at least five days.

Basra was the key to the door of Mesopotamia but it had no facilities that fitted it as a base for a military expedition. It had no quays, harbour facilities or areas on shore where troops could be assembled, or places where stores could be piled. Shipping had to be unloaded in mid-stream into mahellas, the common sailing craft on the Tigris, or into rowing boats called *bellums*. Railways were non-existent south of Baghdad. If roads were to be built the material would have to come from abroad for Mesopotamia boasted no stone; nor, indeed, any firewood for cooking purposes, so along with the roadstone, coal would have to be imported.

Later, Basra was improved in several ways: the streets were kept clean, the river frontage at Ashur was updated to cope with a dozen ships unloading at one time and new roads were constructed. The provision of a native police force proved more difficult. Recruitment was very slow, the young Arabs, fearing the return of the Turks whom they had seen boiling malefactors alive outside the town, brutally hanging them or quietly sewing them into sacks and dropping them into the Shatt al Arab by night, being reluctant to sign up with the new administration. However, Indians were recruited from India and they proved very efficient.

Meanwhile, accommodation had to be found for the troops in Basra. There was none outside, where the Arabs lived in reed huts surrounded by refuse dumps, the date groves were fetid morasses and the desert was a sea of mud in what was a particularly wet winter. Billeting was the only answer which meant that the Military Governor had to take over large numbers of houses by expelling the inhabitants, and install an efficient sanitary system. Fair rents were paid to house-owners but the Arabs to the last considered this their principal grievance against the occupying power.

At the end of November General Barrett, having been reinforced by the rest of the 6th Division, made up his mind to occupy Shaiba, a few miles from Basra, 'as an outpost to the west', and make Qurna his next objective. He knew that the Indian Army was not properly equipped for a modern war since it was deficient in artillery, small arms, clothing, boots and equipment, in up-to-date machine-guns and signalling equipment, wire-cutters, grenades and flares, but he reasoned that a small advance of some 30 miles was within the capabilities of his force. Later, these deficiencies, that could only be made up by Britain, were to become serious and the medical service even more so. For a long time it had no motor transport for the wounded. Instead it was equipped with the standard transport vehicle – the AT cart – a two-wheeled, springless conveyance drawn by two mules at the customary speed of 2½ miles an hour.

This paucity of equipment was due to the attitude of Lord Kitchener when he held the dual posts of Commander-in-Chief and Military Member in India between 1903 and 1909 – despite modernizing army training and establishing a Staff College, he had deliberately and repeatedly refused to spend money on army medical supplies, or even on up-to-date military equipment. This, with the encouragement of the British Government, became the policy in India in succeeding years.

Qurna, on the western bank of the Tigris, stood at the junction with the Euphrates that drains the western half of Mesopotamia. On the east bank, a smaller river, the Shwaiyib, joins the Tigris about 5 miles south of the town which was defended from an approach on that side by Turkish entrenchments amongst the palm groves planted along the riverside.

On 30 November a British force disembarked on the northern bank of the Shwaiyib. It consisted of two field guns, half a company of Royal Engineers, one company of the Norfolk Regiment and two Indian battalions (the 104th Rifles and the 110th Mahratta Light Infantry). Strangely enough, they were from two different brigades under the command of a senior battalion commander instead of a brigade under its brigadier. It was to be a combined operation and this force was accompanied by two warships, two armed river steamers each with field guns mounted on board and three armed launches. Towing the lighters that carried the troops were the river steamers and two other vessels.

The warships steamed a couple of miles upriver round a bend and within sight of Qurna. There the *Espiègle* and the *Lawrence*, a Royal Indian Marine paddle steamer, armed with the same 4-inch quick-firing guns as the sloops, came under fire from Turkish guns and a gun battle developed that ended as the troops began their advance, and the armed river steamers which had carried the troops were released from their duties of towing the supply lighters and could join in the bombardment alongside the warships.

A mirage came down as the troops advanced towards the Turkish entrenchments that when they got closer turned out to be only a line of trenches rather than the substantial fortifications they had appeared through the mirage. These were cleared by the 119th Mahrattas, the Norfolks and the Royal Engineers, taking over sixty prisoners and capturing two field guns in the process. The Turks then took cover in the palm groves that fronted the river but did not stay there long, hastily evacuating across the river to Qurna where they lined the bank and fired across the 200-yard-wide river into the palm groves that they had just left.

Without more artillery cover the launches could not transport the British troops across the Tigris in the face of Turkish rifle fire that was later augmented by field guns, so the British withdrew to their landing place by the River Shwaiyib. Taking advantage of this, during the night the Turks recrossed the river and went back to their original entrenchments on the left bank.

It was decided that the best plan was to clear the Turks back across the river and to march futher up the left bank and make a crossing of the Tigris out of sight of Qurna. With the help of the ships and some reinforcements under General Fry this was done on 7 December. A detachment marched a couple of miles or so further on to a spot out of sight of Qurna where a flying bridge was built that allowed a couple of battalions and section of mountain guns to cross and bivouack on the right bank with the intention of advancing on Qurna next morning. But no further operations were needed.

At midnight, the main force below Qurna sighted a steamer, blazing with lights, coming down from the town. On board, a messenger from Colonel Subhi Bey, the commander of the 38th Division, brought an offer of surrender. Next day, 45 officers, 1,000 men and 7 guns were in the bag, although a number of the enemy, including the crack Osmanjik battalion, had already made off towards the north.

The Turkish commander in Mesopotamia was now Lieutenant Colonel Sulaiman Askari, who commanded the Osmanjik battalion. He seems to have been a stout-hearted man and had enjoyed an adventurous career chasing and rounding up Bulgarian

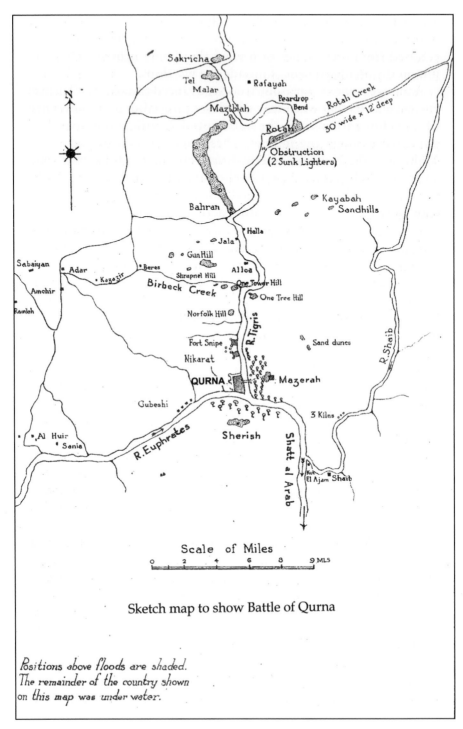

Scale of Miles

0   2   4   6   8   9 MLS

Sketch map to show Battle of Qurna

Positions above floods are shaded.
The remainder of the country shown
on this map was under water.

Map 3.   Fighting near Qurna

brigands before the Balkan War. Although serving in the Balkan War with distinction, at the beginning of the European war he had fallen out for some reason with the ruling Committee of Union and Progress in the capital, and as was usual with those not in favour, he was sent as far as possible from Constantinople – hence his appearance in Mesopotamia. When he was subsequently severely wounded in the knee during an attack at Ruta, the Turkish War Office sent down another officer to command in his place, but Sulaiman Askari refused to hand over and proceeded to Nasiriya on a litter. He continued to command till after the Battle of Shaiba, still confined to his litter, and ended his career by shooting himself after the battle.

The Indian Army was now firmly ensconced in Qurna at the confluence of the two great rivers of Mesopotamia. According to Mohammedan legend Qurna was the site of the Garden of Eden and the Tree of Knowledge, but the collection of filthy lanes and mud-and-reed hovels hardly lived up to that reputation. The Official History records the remark of a disgusted English soldier who declared that it would not have required a flaming angel with a flaming sword to keep him out of the place.

What to do next? Some advised staying put, emphasizing that the seasonal floods that were just beginning would place difficulties in the way of river movement and, of course, there were no roads apart from the tracks along the river banks that were beginning to disappear underneath the floodwaters.

Others suggested a move forward to Amara further up the Tigris, or an advance up the Euphrates to Nasiriya, an important tribal centre. Sir Percy Cox was in favour of both advances on political, administrative and commercial grounds but his advice on this occasion was not accepted.

General Barrett was undecided but early in 1915 he opted for a solution that many commanders did in that situation – he asked for reinforcements. India was not impressed and a discussion began between the Commander-in-Chief in India and the India Office in London. It was proposed that if Indian reinforcements were to be sent, they could be replaced in India by Territorial Battalions from England.

While the argument raged, the British position in Mesopotamia began to change for the worse. During January the prospect of a Holy War – a jihad – against the unbelievers was being raised by the

Turkish Government. It was widely taken up and preached in every mosque in Syria and Mesopotamia, and emissaries were busy amongst the tribes and in the towns urging them to do battle in the name of the Faith. The effect of this campaign was greatest amongst the Shia tribes of southern Mesopotamia and amongst the tribes in southern Persia who had no love for their overlord, the Sheikh of Mohammerah, and the revolt spread like wildfire. They even breached the oil pipeline belonging to the infidel. The rising culminated in Shustar where a German agent, Wassmuss, a Moslem convert, arrived and began to foment trouble amongst the tribes around the oilfields. Germans at this time were assiduously cultivating Moslem countries. Wassmuss announced that the Kaiser himself had made a secret pilgrimage to Mecca and was styling himself 'Haji' Wilhelm Mohammed, protector of all Moslems.

In Persia there were already 1,000 Persian mercenaries on the German payroll plus a number of Indian Army deserters and captured sepoys who had joined the Turco-German cause. So complete was Berlin's penetration of central and southern Persia that no fewer than seven out of the seventeen branches of the British-owned Imperial Bank of Persia were in German hands, their vaults having been plundered to help fund the Holy War. Telegraph offices, too, had been seized in many places by Germans for their exclusive use and to deny them to the British. Virtual anarchy, deliberately fomented, now reigned throughout much of the country with the pro-German gendarmerie doing little or nothing to stop it. (Hopkirk)

Wilhelm Wassmuss had originally been a member of a combined Turkish and German Expedition to Afghanistan but had broken away from the party to engage in an expedition of his own in southern Persia. Before the war he had been the German consul at Bushire (now Bandar-e Būshehr) and he had put himself out to impress the local dignitaries and tribal leaders and create a pro-German party in an area which had been described as a sphere of British influence in the Anglo-Russian Convention of 1907. This was possible because after the signing of the Convention, many Persians saw Germany as their natural protector against the British in the south and against the Russians, whose sphere of influence had been designated as the north of Persia. Wassmuss intended to preach the Holy War that the Kaiser was determined to unleash on the Middle

East. Speaking Persian like a native, posing as a Moslem convert, familiar with every detail of Persian habits and customs and with plenty of gold, his self-set mission was to stir up the local tribes against the British communities and the oil concessions there.

At the beginning of the Mesopotamian Campaign a German agent had been arrested by the British in the British protectorate of Bahrain. His description of the strength of Brigadier General Delamain's force was to have been sent to the German Consulate at Bushire which had a radio set. The British thereupon raided the Consulate, found and destroyed the radio set, and arrested and sent the Consul to detention in India. Amongst the documents that Sir Percy Cox, Chief Political Officer with the force, read with interest was the news that Wassmuss was on his way down from Baghdad.

He had known Wassmuss of old and knew that he would be as difficult to deal with as an enemy as he had been as a consular colleague. Messages were therefore sent out to the Persian tribesmen along Wassmuss's route saying that the British would like to speak to the gentleman. A party of tribesmen managed to intercept the German and a British officer was sent to take him into custody, but before he got to the meeting-place, Wassmuss had escaped, although his two companions were captured along with Wassmuss's baggage and weapons .The most important item in his baggage was his code book that was swiftly was sent to London.

Wassmuss managed to get to Shiraz, north-east of Bushire, where he set up his base of operations amongst the Tangistanis who controlled that area. His attempts to subvert the Bakhartiaris, further north, had been unsuccessful, but he was amongst more fertile ground with their neighbours in the south. He was fairly safe since the Persian authorities were too lax to bother him and their gendarmarie were officered by Swedes who were generally pro-German.

Cox offered a reward for his capture, a move that earned him a rebuke from the Foreign Office which described the offer as abhorrent and detestable and ordered him to drop the idea. However, Cox got his revenge later on when the Foreign Office asked his advice as to what should be done about Wassmuss's increasing activities in southern Persia and Cox was able to reply: 'Fear of exciting the abhorrence and detestation of His Majesty's Government prevents me from offering any further suggestions.'

Wassmuss had his eye on the British Residency at Bushire. He now had most of the leading Tangistanis on his side and they were ready to strike a blow for the jihad and fell in with his suggestion that the Residency would be a good place to start.

He had numbers on his side too. He divided the Tangistanis into two detachments that were both larger than the the garrison of the Residency and planned an attack from two sides. A small scouting group was sent ahead but were spotted by the British who despatched a patrol to investigate. Behind the Tangistanis was their main force which opened fire on the Indian soldiers and killed several before the remainder got back to the entrenchments around the Residency. From these positions the Indian soldiers found the charging tribesmen an easy target and many were shot down before the others turned tail. A second attack on the same flank the following morning was equally unsuccessful; the other group who were supposed to attack from the east never appeared.

In reaction to the strongly anti-British attitude of the Tangistanis and the soporific reaction of the Persian Government, the British decided to occupy Bushire for a time. In order to punish the tribesmen, they despatched some Royal Marines and Indian troops to land on the coast south of Bushire, destroy the Tangistanis' main settlement and cut down the groves of date palms, their main source of income. In September a second attack was launched on Bushire by the tribesmen, but after some hard fighting the British drove them off with artillery fire and with heavy casualties.

Wassmuss was also a thorn in the flesh of the British in Fars, the Persian province that stretches along the northern shore of the Persian Gulf. In the capital, Shiraz, he found that the Persian Governor-General was strongly pro-German. Equally friendly, again, were the Swedish and Persian officers of the gendarmerie who became unofficial German agents throughout the province.

By the autumn of 1915 Wassmuss, acting as German Consul, was continuing the anti-British agitation in Shiraz with the aid of these men and in October the honorary British Vice-Consul, a Persian, was murdered in broad daylight. The representatives of the so-called 'National Committee for the Protection of Persian Independence', acting under the instructions of the German Consul and backed up by the gendarmerie armed with quick-firing Schneider guns, cut the telegraph wires and, stationing their guns in commanding positions, called on the British consul, Colonel O'Connor, either to surrender or be bombarded. There was no alternative and the whole British colony was taken under guard to the coast, where they were subsequently split up, the ladies being sent to Bushire and the men interned by the Tangistani; they were exchanged seven months later.

In the middle of March 1915 the situation in Bushire became so acute that it was necessary to divert troops from Mesopotamia for its protection, and a battalion of Indian infantry was sent there shortly after the Battle of Shaiba. In June, the force's responsibilities were enlarged to include Bushire and its defences were reinforced by two captured Turkish guns. The garrison was eventually expanded into a brigade which, under Brigadier General Brooking, fought a series of actions against the Tangistani tribes, who were also engaged by landing parties of the Royal Navy. These events added to the constant anxieties of the Commander-in-Chief in Mesopotamia and his political advisers.

In 1916 Sir Percy Sykes landed at Bandar Abbas with a small number of British and Indian troops. He raised a body of 11,000 Persians to take the place of the gendarmerie, the greater part of which had for all practical purposes joined the Germans or dispersed owing to lack of pay. This force came to be known as the South Persian Rifles and was designed solely for the restoration of law and order, and for the maintenance of Persian neutrality in southern Persia.

Germans were active in other parts of Persia. The German Consul at Kermanshar attacked and drove back the British and Russian consuls when they attempted to return to the place under Persian escort. A merchant named Pugin, disguised as a Persian, professing Islam, succeeded in persuading many of the leading citizens of Isfahan that the whole German nation had converted to Islam under their Kaiser 'Haji'. Assassination was a favourite weapon. The Russian Vice-Consul in the town was murdered, the British Consul was wounded and his Indian orderly killed. Isfahan became so dangerous that the European community left for Ahwaz.

Elsewhere, bands of levies, with a nucleus of Germans and Austrians, visited the chief towns of western, central and southern Persia. At Yezd they looted the bank treasury and drove away the European colony. At Kerman, in association with the gendarmes, they assassinated a cousin of the Aga Khan and demanded the expulsion of British and Russian subjects who could do nothing else but quit and escape to safety in Bandar Abbas.

Wassmuss and the other Germans in Persia were adept at persuading gullible Persians to believe their stories and support their cause. On one occasion Wassmuss had induced a wealthy merchant of Shiraz to become a German agent, telling him that the Kaiser would send him a personal message by wireless. Entering the room where Wassmuss had rigged up a fake arrangement of wires and a telegraph instrument attached to a pole, the Persian was told that the Kaiser was indeed present in the Berlin telegraph office and he was told to kiss the ground thrice as a mark of respect. Then he was informed that the German leader was asking after his health and that such a compliment from the All-Highness was usually returned in the form of a donation, in this case £10,000 in Persian currency. After thanking the merchant graciously, the Kaiser departed, promising to send a portrait to him by wireless. Two days later it arrived at his house!

It was in the autumn of 1915 that Russian troops landed in Persia to defend the Allied legations from the tide of German activity that seemed to be sweeping the country. This display of force was successful in stemming it in northern Persia but in the south German influence continued to remain strong.

Composition of 'Force D' (6th Division) on 1 December 1914

Headquarters (21 all ranks)

CAVALRY:
33rd Queen Victoria's Own Light Cavalry

ARTILLERY:
HQ, Divisional Artillery
10 Brigade, Royal Field Artillery:
   76th Battery RFA
   82nd Battery RFA
   63rd Battery RFA
   6th Ammunition Column RFA
1 Indian Mountain Artillery Brigade:
   23rd Indian Mountain Battery
   30th Indian Mountain Battery

ROYAL ENGINEERS:

HQ, Divisional Engineers
17 Company, 3rd Sappers and Miners
22 Company, 3rd Sappers and Miners
No. 34 Divisional Signal Company
No. 3 Troop, Wireless Signal Squadron (later No. 41 Wireless
  Signal Company)

PIONEERS:

48th Pioneers

INFANTRY:

16 Indian Infantry Brigade:
  2nd Battalion Dorsetshire Regiment
  20th Duke of Cambridge's Own Infantry
  (Brownlow's Punjabis)
  104th Wellesley's Rifles
  117th Mahrattas
17 Indian Infantry Brigade:
  1st Battalion Oxfordshire and Buckinghamshire
  Light Infantry.
  119th Infantry (the Mooltan Regiment)
  103rd Mahratta Light Infantry
  22nd Punjabis
18 Indian Infantry Brigade:
  2nd Battalion Norfolk Regiment
  110th Mahratta Light Infantry
  120th Rajputana Infantry
  7th Duke of Connaught's Own Rajputs

MEDICAL SERVICES:

No. 16 British Field Ambulance
No. 17 British Field Ambulance
No. 125 Indian Field Ambulance
No. 126 Indian Field Ambulance
(the above combined later into 1, 2, 3 and 4 Combined
Field Ambulances)
No. 19 Clearing Hospital
No. 57 Indian Stationary Hospital
No. 3 (a) British General Hospital (2.5 sections)

No. 9 Indian General Hospital (6 sections)
No. 2 X-Ray Section
Advanced Depot Medical Stores

Naval Forces

ARMED VESSELS:

HMS *Espiègle* (sloop) – six 4-inch QF, two 3-pdr guns and two Maxims
HMS *Odin* (sloop) – four 4-inch QF, two 3-pdr guns and two Maxims
HMS *Lawrence* (paddle steamer, Royal Indian Marine) – four 4-inch QF and four 6-pdr guns
Comet (steam yacht) – one 3-pdr gun and three old Nordenfeldts
Lewis Pelly (small steam yacht) – two 3-pdr Hotchkiss guns and one Maxim
Miner (small river steamer) – one 12-pdr (8 cwt) gun, one 3-pdr and one Maxim
Shaitan (steam tug) – one 12-pdr (8 cwt) gun and one Maxim
Sirdar-i-Naphte (steam tug) – one 12-pdr (8 cwt) gun and one Maxim
Mashona (steam tug) – one 3-pdr gun
HMS *Ocean* (pre-Dreadnought battleship) – off bar of Shatt al Arab
HMS *Dalhousie* (Royal Indian Marine) – four 6-pdr guns – off Bushire

UNARMED VESSELS:

Mejidieh, *Blosse Lynch* and *Malamir* of the Euphrates and Tigris Steam Navigation Co. (Lynch Bros)
Sumana, *Shibab* and *Shurur* of the Société de Transports Flaviaux
The *Salimi* and six small launches taken up locally.

Chapter Three

Townshend's Regatta

(Maps 1 and 3)

Back on the Tigris, Qurna had been converted into an island as the floodwaters from both the Tigris and the Euphrates reached their confluence, while the troops at Shaiba, west of Basra, were cut off by floods that covered the desert. To complicate the situation, a Turkish and Arab force was gathering further up the Euphrates in the vicinity of Nasiriyeh which lay to the west of the British position, and the oilfields were also being threatened. These events ended the argument between Simla, the Indian headquarters, and London and another Indian Division, the 12th, was mobilized in India for service in Mesopotamia.

At the end of January, a gunboat, the *Comet,* and the *Shaitan,* an armed launch, were sent up the River Karun to Ahwaz, followed by an Indian infantry battalion. Ahwaz was a small town on the river through which the oil pipeline passed. This detachment was to support the Sheikh of Mohammerah who had warned that a Turkish force was advancing south from Amara towards Ahwaz. This force set up camp about 10 miles north-west of the town and the British commander marched towards it only to find that the Turks' allies, the Arabs, began to gather around his flanks in large numbers. He decided to retreat and the enemy were not finally driven off until they were back in Ahwaz. The British lost 189 killed or wounded; the enemy was estimated to have lost 900.

Meanwhile, on the same day a detachment was sent out from Shaiba to reconnoitre towards the north-west in the direction of

27

Nukhaila. Followed by the infantry, the cavalry got to within 4 miles of the town before they had to withdraw as the enemy was hanging around their flanks. The cavalry were already being outnumbered by Arab horsemen when a fresh body of the enemy charged up and attacked. The infantry, who by this time were close by, up to their knees in heavy sand and hampered by poor visibility caused by clouds of dust, had difficulty in distinguishing the Indian cavalry from the Arab horsemen, until the Arabs were so close that they stumbled into them and charged. Rapid fire from the British guns, machine-guns and rifles drove them off and the British force was able to withdraw to Shaiba.

Both these skirmishes ended unsatisfactorily for the British which persuaded the British Cabinet that more reinforcements were needed and they told the Indian Government to send another brigade to Mesopotamia. Accordingly, on 7 March, 33 Infantry Brigade and a howitzer battery were ordered to embark for the front, arriving in Basra on the 25th. Back in India another infantry brigade was being made up to meet possible eventualities. The initial 'minor expedition' was growing rapidly.

Barrett was still concerned about the situation on his left flank on the Euphrates. Close to its confluence with the Tigris, the Euphrates became a large flooded area which was deep enough at its western end to warrant the name of Hammar Lake. On the Euphrates, beyond the far side of this flooded area, was the town of Nasiriya, where the Turks were concentrating troops. News came from Arab spies of activity that suggested that this force was preparing to advance and attempt to recapture Basra. To forestall this, Barrett despatched an armed flotilla consisting of three stern-wheeler river steamers on which were mounted either field guns or 3-pounder naval guns, the tug *Sumana*, a motor boat and a barge equipped with a 5-inch gun, plus detachments of both British and Indian infantry to delay the Turkish advance. The Turkish advanced camp was shelled and the route south from Nasiriya was blocked, delaying the Turks' preparation for their attack and allowing the British to strengthen their forces at Shaiba.

By this time the British force in Mesopotamia was almost up to two divisions and the Government of India decided to reorganize it by forming II Indian Army Corps, with a new, more senior officer in command. This turned out to be General Sir John Nixon.

Sir John Nixon arrived full of enthusiasm from his previous post in northern India. As most senior officers were at the time, he was getting on towards the close of his career, and he saw this appointment as his final opportunity to make a name for himself in what promised to be an important and brilliant campaign. A cavalryman, a polo player and a pig sticker, he had earned a reputation in manoeuvres for 'ginger' and he seems to have thought that he had been selected on account of his dash and his reputation as a natural leader. He was not a hide-bound commander in the field, regarding war as a job for the practical man who used his common sense and who should not be hampered by administrative constraints or be afraid of using unconventional methods.

In his instructions from the Commander-in-Chief in India, beside the repetition of the ones already issued to General Barrett, he was told to submit plans for an advance to Baghdad. Not unnaturally, he saw this as a change in policy and he began to formulate a vigorous plan of action, a process on which his inexperienced and untrained staff had very little restraining influence. This keen desire to push on at all costs was fully encouraged by Sir Percy Cox, his political adviser.

Meanwhile, the Secretary for State in London had been taking stock of the campaign. He came to the conclusion that its aims should be limited to its original objectives to safeguard the Basra vilayet and the oilfields, and that General Nixon should 'play a safe game in Mesopotamia'. But he unfortunately added a qualification that he should not seek to extend the sphere of operations unless a purely local offensive up the Tigris towards Amara was perhaps useful in adding to the security of the oilfields and pipeline. This gave Nixon his opportunity.

Shortly after he arrived at Basra, the expected Turkish offensive from Nasiriyeh began. Almost 4,000 enemy troops advanced on Shaiba where the British had constructed a fort on the edge of a flooded area that separated them from Basra, some 10 miles away to the west. The Turks came forward and began a rather ineffectual investment of the eastern side of the British encampment. Reinforcements from Basra were called for and they either waded waist deep or were poled across the inundation in Arab *bellums*. The struggle swayed backwards and forwards for three days in the area between the British fort and the Turkish trenches in front of Barjisiya Wood, east of Shaiba, until the British and Indian infantry were in sufficient strength to mount a determined advance in the intense heat close up to the Turkish trenches where a firefight broke out.

The commanding officer of one of the Indian battalions noted that the heat and the situation had a strange effect on those of his officers and men who had never been under fire before – they were overcome by sleep for periods of ten or fifteen minutes so that alternate men were sleeping while their next-door neighbours fired with slow deliberate aim. There was a complete absence of rapid fire and a sense of unreality that he had never experienced before.

At about 1600 hrs on this last day of the engagement the British got up and charged forward to overrun the Turkish first line; they were preparing to attack the second line when the enemy began to put up white flags. From the wood behind the enemy lines a mass of Turks could be seen leaving the trees and making off; these were followed by the second-line troops but the exhausted British were far too tired to chase them far. The Turks fled north-west towards Nasiriyeh in great confusion with scarcely a halt until they were 90 miles away, being attacked en route by their Arab irregulars who turned upon their erstwhile comrades-in-arms, slaughtering stragglers and stealing their very clothes. The Turkish commander committed suicide in his litter, denouncing the faithlessness of his Arab allies.

The battle had been a confused one, had been bedevilled by the mirage that made observation very difficult and by the heat, but it was a victory, albeit very narrow, and as a victory it was claimed by Sir John Nixon as the first of a string of expected successes.

Having regained the initiative, the next step could be contemplated – what it would be was hardly in doubt. But before Nixon could undertake the advance up the Tigris he had to restore the oil supply through the broken pipeline. In contrast to the attitude in September 1914, Winston Churchill had already dismissed Mesopotamia from his volatile mind and his eyes were turning to an attack on Constantinople by way of the Dardanelles. He minuted in a disparaging comment on a note urging the despatch of troops to defend the oilfields that they should buy oil elsewhere and not bother with Persia, but the Admiralty was becoming anxious about the shortage of fuel and was looking again to Abadan.

Meanwhile, the oilfields were the objective for a Turco-Arab force that was slowly approaching from the north. It was a sizeable column, consisting of eight infantry battalions with eight field guns and some 7,000 mounted tribesmen, who formed the irregular complement to Turkish armies in Mesopotamia. They were extremely mobile and effective when the Turks were winning, but were a liability and indeed a danger when defeated and in retreat since, as we have seen, they were liable to turn on their erstwhile companions-in-arms.

Major General Gorringe was in command of a force that set off in heavy rain to improve the situation in Arabistan where the oilfields were. He reached Braika, 60 miles north-east of Basra on 27 April. Soon after he had started off, although some local Arab tribes sent envoys to offer their co-operation, others were hostile and in one incident two squadrons of Indian cavalry were attacked and three officers killed. General Gorringe decided to try to bring to action the Turkish force that had invaded the north of Arabistan and aimed for Illa, the mud-built town on the Karkha river, a stream that rose in the mountains of Persia and finally dwindled into nothing in the marshes along the Turco-Persian frontier, east of the River Tigris.

At Illa, after a struggle with the full flood and the strong current, Gorringe managed to build a bridge and cross the Karkha river. Sappers had problems with the unusual width of the swollen river, now some 250 yards, and the consequent steep banks and sticky clay soil. In addition a gale blew all day. Once the bridge was completed, Gorringe led a column along the north bank while on the south side General Lean remained to command a smaller force that kept pace with the main body.

Few signs of the enemy were discovered along the river towards the north, until a large number of Arabs were discovered at Khafajiya, a collection of mud huts that straggled along the southern bank of the Karkha river. This was a village belonging to the Bani Tamin tribe who had mutilated British wounded after the action near Ahwaz on 3 March. In order to attack and punish them, Gorringe's column had to recross the river. This was accomplished with difficulty but without any casualties and the Arabs were driven out of their tumbledown refuges; their grain stores were destroyed and about a thousand of their sheep and cattle seized as a fine for their previous behaviour. The fugitives fled to the west so that Persian Arabistan was clear of the enemy as the Turkish force had retreated to the Tigris, leaving the Arabs to face the British. The British had not seen a single Turk.

31

General Gorringe and his column returned to Basra, exhausted by heat and thirst, driving their four-legged prizes before them, having restored the supply of oil to Abadan and ensured the safety of the pipeline.

General Nixon, meanwhile, was considering the situation. If he was to advance to Amara, he would have to capture Nasiriyeh on the Euphrates and this would mean he would be holding a line extending from Ahwaz in the east to Amara on the Tigris, and across to Nasiriyeh in the west. But the hot weather was starting and he had a force that, due to the parsimony of the Indian authorities, was not well equipped, lacking transport, tents, medical equipment and other supplies, and was about to campaign in difficult desert country without adequate communications. It is clear in deciding on this plan General Nixon was displaying neither lack of enterprise nor fear of accepting responsibility, but rather a degree of rashness that would appal a modern commander in his position.

India seemed to be in favour of a further advance but awaited a final decision from London that came on 24 May. In his telegram the Secretary of State sanctioned the proposal but only on the clear understanding that General Nixon was satisfied that he could install a large enough garrison at Amara to withstand any attack from Baghdad during the summer. This condition was added as, owing to the lack of water in the Tigris, it would be difficult to move up reinforcements from Basra.

Major General Townshend, with his dog 'Spot' and banjo, had arrived in Mesopotamia a few weeks before to command the 6th Division that would advance and capture Amara. The dog is self-explanatory but the banjo needs an explanation. Townshend was an enthusiast for what nowadays we would describe as 'show business'. He had theatrical friends both in Paris and London, and fancied himself as a performer on the banjo – indeed, he gave impromptu recitals to whatever audiences he came across during the campaign. However, he was to prove to be a successful choice as commander since he was a man of great energy and initiative, with a readiness to accept responsibility and the ability to face unexpected situations with courage and resource that made him an admirable adjunct to General Nixon's impetuous temperament. Together they achieved tactical success despite the absence of clearly defined strategic objectives, the problems presented by the unpredictable and unfavourable climatic conditions, and by the unusual situations that the campaign threw up. He explained that his success was due to his study of the campaigns of Napoleon, volumes of whose works he always carried with him.

Unusual conditions were evident at once. At Qurna, the small garrison was entirely surrounded by floods which were actually two feet above the level of their camp. The Turks were equally encircled by water on four small islands which had appeared some 3 miles to the north on the right bank of the river while their other outpost sat in solitary state on One Tree Hill on the left bank. Norfolk Hill was closest to Qurna, north of which was One Tower Hill, then Shrapnel Hill and finally Gun Hill, the most northerly, on which the Turkish artillery was positioned. Floods were generally some 3 feet deep but over the irrigation canals they could be as much as 20 feet. In this large expanse the only cover was given by areas of reeds but none were more than 5 feet high and usually nearer 2 feet, so that in most places they provided few hiding places, surprise was out of the question and any outflanking movement would be seen at once.

General Townshend had already decided that he would have to make a frontal attack across this lake and had been organizing a special force, training his troops to manoeuvre in native *bellums*. Ungainly looking vessels out of the water, being long, heavy canoes weighing half a ton, on the water they could be surprisingly graceful although not very easy to manoeuvre. Each battalion was allotted sixty of these craft and some 500 soldiers were set to practise punting them along. As can be imagined, the sights on the stretch of the river where the sweating and sulphurous sergeant-majors were attempting to train their men in the new technique attracted a considerable number of off-duty troops and licentious comments. The operation was nicknamed 'Townshend's Regatta'.

Covering fire for the advance across the flood was to be given by the river gunboats and by field guns mounted in barges in the main river channel, keeping pace with the bellums to the east. Alongside the armada some machine-guns were carried on rafts while the Field Ambulances travelled on covered rafts that were nicknamed 'Noah's Arks'. A few *bellums* were earmarked to carry cooking pots for the Indian troops whose religion forbade them to use other people's pots. Each infantry *bellum* carried ten men with an NCO, 125 rounds of reserve ammunition and two sandbags per man, a day's rations and a waterproof sheet.

With the sloops HMS *Espiègle* and *Clio* out in front in the river,

33

Townshend's Regatta set out across 7,000 yards of flooded open desert on 31 May. It was an intensely hot day with temperatures of over 100 degrees F (38 degrees C). Townshend was in the *Espiègle* together with General Nixon, who typically could not be kept out of the action and was present during the advance, even though he had announced that he would not interfere in the main operations, but would be in charge of demonstrations that were to be carried out on each flank.

Punting through the reeds was hard work. In some places the soldiers had to climb out of their boats and push them along since the water was so shallow and the reeds so thick that they obstructed the poles. On the left-hand side of the Tigris, Norfolk Hill was the first objective and this was captured in fine style by a company of the Ox and Bucks Light Infantry who leapt out of their boats when they were still a hundred yards short of it and splashed ashore. The garrison of 135 troops were all Arabs with a Turkish officer; about seventy-five were killed and the rest demoralized by the gunfire from the ships and from Qurna. A guard was left on them and the punters, refreshed by their immersion in the flood, returned to their boats.

On the other side of the river, the garrison of only twenty on One Tree Hill was easily taken prisoner by the 22nd Punjabis. The Punjabis settled themselves on the hill and opened fire with their machine-guns on One Tower Hill across the river. At this point the generals were surprised to see the first British aircraft in Mesopotamia flying over the *Espiègle*. It was one of two that had arrived in packing cases and had quickly been assembled, but it had taken two weeks for the Royal Flying Corps to find a strip of ground dry and long enough for the aircraft to take off.

The re-embarked Ox and Bucks Light Infantry advanced on One Tower Hill with the 119th Infantry in support. From the river the two ships, now joined by the sloop HMS *Odin*, the Indian Marine steamer *Lawrence* and the launch *Miner*, bombarded it. As before, the punters splashed ashore and this time the whole garrison on the island was taken prisoner together with a 16-pounder field gun and a Turkish officer in charge of an electrically operated switchboard that was meant to explode mines in the river.

Shrapnel Hill was the third objective and by 0930 hrs the 103rd Mahrattas had pushed through thick reeds and were approaching it under fire from the garrison, who could see their punt poles match-sticking above the reeds. The garrison surrendered as the bellums grounded on their island. On Gun Hill, the garrison had been under bombardment from naval guns and, as the armada approached, all other guns were concentrated on it as well. The Turkish fire gradually decreased as the force got close and eventually all firing ceased, the Turkish soldiers surrendered and at noon General Townshend suspended operations for the day.

On the eastern side of the river, Nixon's demonstration involved the *Comet* and a horse-boat carrying a 4.7in naval gun moving up the River Shwaiyb until they were within range of Ruta, a settlement further up the Tigris, and bombarding it in order to disrupt the Turkish retreat. On the other flank, two river steamers moved up the al Huwair, a tributary of the Euphrates that flowed into the river from the north. They diverted some of the marsh Arabs from the main attack but navigation was too difficult for them to go far and they soon rejoined the main force.

Next morning the objective was Abu Aran, the village on the river on the way to Ruta. After a bombardment, minesweepers preceded the naval ships as they steamed up the Tigris. On board one of them was the Turkish mine officer who pointed out the approximate position of some of the mines in the main channel. Alongside but hidden in the reeds were the *bellums* of 17 Indian Infantry Bde, moving slowly and making heavy weather of the thickets of vegetation. When the enemy did not reply to the gunfire this was soon explained by one of the British aircraft that dropped a message alongside the *Espiègle* informing Townshend that not only was Abu Aran deserted, but so were Ruta and Muzaibila, the next villages to the north, abandoned by the Turks who were fleeing northward in anything that would float.

Before 1100 hrs the flotilla had assembled at Abu Aran and Townshend set off in a launch with the Senior Naval Officer to investigate an obstruction across the river at Ruta that was supposed to close the channel. Fortunately, it had not been completed and, after cutting the leads of three large mines, the channel was marked with buoys. Two armed minesweeping launches were despatched through the gap with orders to chase after the enemy shipping whose smoke could still be seen in the distance rising above the mirage.

After a hasty lunch and a quick consultation with General Nixon, Townshend issued orders for a further advance to Ezra's Tomb with 17 Brigade, the 82nd Field Battery, the Norfolks, the 'river section' of the heavy artillery and an improvized hospital steamer. Soon afterwards, the *Espiègle*, carrying Townshend and the Senior Naval Officer, led HMS *Odin* and *Clio* through the obstruction and followed the minesweeping launches upriver. Bends and twists in the river made navigation difficult since, with the floods obscuring the river banks, it was not always easy to know where the river was.

The first sighting of the enemy was by the steamer *Marmaris*, and shortly afterwards the naval vessels were able to open fire on a gunboat and another Turkish steamer. Townshend's 4-inch guns were clearly having some effect for the Turkish ships began to discard the lighters and *mahailas* they were towing. These, full of troops and military stores, were discovered at Ezra's Tomb, where the flotilla paused for breath.

Ezra's Tomb or 'Uzair' was a domed shrine amongst the palm trees, but was probably misnamed since it may not have been Ezra's tomb at all – the scribe was buried beside the Tigris a thousand years before and the river had changed its course several times since. Of course, his bones could have been moved each time to keep them out of its reach.

Townshend left the *Odin* at the shrine to take care of the prisoners and keep off the Arab marauders who circled like vultures around any disaster where there was a chance of plunder, while his staff left on board were told to concentrate the British troops there as they came up the river and send them forward in military sections and in good order.

He pushed on in *Espiègle* in the gathering darkness through the Narrows, the stretch of river between Ezra's Tomb and Qala Salih, which was one of the most difficult parts of the Tigris to navigate. After a short distance the *Shaitan* in the lead came upon a *mahaila* full of Turkish troops who had been left to fend for themselves. It was now almost pitch dark and the rest of the enemy ahead could no longer be seen. At eight o'clock the Senior Naval Officer decided in the interests of safety that his ships should anchor and wait for the moon to rise.

Shouts could be heard along the river as soon as the racket of the engines died away. The searchlight was turned on and revealed more Turkish lighters packed with troops a few yards off, while beyond them, just visible in the beam, a half-sunken steamer could be seen. It was the *Bulbul*, sunk by one of the shells from the *Shaitan* earlier in the day. These discoveries brought the total of Turkish troops captured during the advance to around 200, together with three field guns and stores, explosives and mines.

After the moon had risen at 0200 hrs on 2 June, the chase was taken up again, but navigation difficulties were increasing and the *Espiègle* went aground. Both she and the *Clio* drew too much water and could go no further. By this time, they had come up with the Turkish steamer, the *Marmaris*, which was also aground and abandoned, having been hit by a number of British shells and on fire, bathing the landscape with a flickering eerie glow. Near her was a lighter with thirty Turkish soldiers aboard. Marooned in the next reach of the river the steamer *Mosul* was making signals that she was ready to surrender. In her and packed in a lighter and seven *mahailas* were 140 soldiers, two 15-pounder field guns and a large quantity of rifles and ammunition.

By this time General Townshend was convinced that the Turks were no longer conducting an orderly retirement, but were a demoralized rout. Clearly he should continue the pursuit in order to prevent the Turks regrouping and making a stand, so he transhipped to the lighter-draught vessels. Captain Nunn transferred his pennant to the *Comet* and with Townshend and Sir Percy Cox aboard chugged off, followed by the *Sumana*, *Shaitan* and *Lewis Pelly*, each towing a horse-barge mounted with a 4.7 inch gun. They pushed on all day without meeting any more Turks and at about 1900 hrs anchored for the night.

It was fine evening and the atmosphere was pleasanter and much less sultry now that they had left the marsh behind. The moonlight revealed a new landscape, an apparently endless plain on both sides of the river, covered with low scrub. It had a desolation about it that they were later to find characteristic of much of the Mesopotamian desert. After the noise of the boats' engines had died away, the deep silence was disturbed only by an occasional bird call and the quiet conversation of the crews of the other vessels.

Yet the landscape was not as empty as it seemed. Later in the evening there was a guttural hail from the bank – it was the local sheikh with a small entourage.

Townshend invited them on board and served coffee; during the conversation he revealed to the sheikh 'secret' information of the imminent arrival of 15,000 British troops and asked him to keep the information to himself, but to collect supplies for them. The sheikh went away most impressed, with Townshend's injunction ringing in his ears, leaving the General confident that the news would be all over the country before dawn.

After they set off early next morning this was confirmed by the sight in each mud village of the unhabitants lining the banks, waving white flags and uttering shrill cries of welcome as they passed. It seemed that the sheikh had got up early to spread the news that only he was privy to of a great invasion. When they were 12 miles short of the town of Amara, Townshend called a halt so that they could discuss the situation. He debated whether they should push on and enter Amara, which was a considerable town with several thousand inhabitants and housed several hundred Turkish troops. This intelligence had just been received by the *Comet*'s radio that could receive but not send messages – aircraft flying over Amara had apparently seen the soldiers. In fact, what they had seen was not the enemy Tigris force but the one retreating from Gorringe's demonstration in Arabistan, but they were not to know that. The news, as well as a report of the presence of three river steamers embarking the troops in the town, had been taken back to General Nixon and was relayed by him up the river to Townshend.

Townshend and Nunn had with them on the *Comet* 3 sailors, 2 marines and 12 soldiers, while the *Shaitan* and the *Sumana* could provide 8 sailors, the *Lewis Pelly* 4 sailors and one marine, and the launch 2 sailors and one marine, a total of 41 men and officers, not a very impressive invasion force to enter a hostile town.

Whereas Captain Nunn and Sir Percy Cox were sure that they should push on despite the odds, Townshend had a frightening vision of himself, the Divisional Commander, being captured in a ludicrous exploit that would undoubtedly end his army career. He could already visualize the newspaper headlines. But his natural inclination to make a name for himself spurred him on and he finally told the others that he 'would go on and chance it'. 'Hare-brained' is the adjective that comes to mind but Townshend's character would not allow him to pass up a chance that could lead to glory – in any case he was the last man to sit still and wait for others to catch him up.

At about 0945 hrs the ships set off again with the *Shaitan* and a small launch being sent ahead to act as scouts. The *Shaitan* was under the command of a young Royal Navy officer, Lieutenant Mark Singleton.

When he entered the long straight of the river below the town,

Singleton could see ahead a bridge of boats with a column of enemy troops crossing it to embark on a barge attached to a steamer lying along the bank. As the *Shaitan* was sighted the steamer hurriedly cast off, the bridge of boats was opened and the steamer made frantic efforts to get through.

Shaitan fired a warning shot, Singleton rang down for full steam ahead and the troops scrambled out of the barge and up the right bank. The young captain set a course for the gap in the boat bridge and shot through. Beyond, the river takes an abrupt bend to the west; they skidded round it. On the left bank, Amara was full of troops who hurriedly retreated in confusion as the *Shaitan* appeared like magic in front of their eyes. North of the town more troops were seen, about a thousand on the left bank making off, and on the right bank about 500 yards distant another 1,500 moving in a more orderly fashion. No one fired a shot.

The Navy vessel didn't wait to fire on the troops in the town but steamed through at full speed for about half a mile, before she tied up to the right bank of the river and accepted the surrender of six officers and about a hundred soldiers, all fully armed. The officers and all the rifles and ammunition were taken on board, while the men were turned round and marched back towards Amara, the ship keeping pace with them. A few hundred yards closer to the town 150 more soldiers appeared out of the palm trees and threw down their rifles. They too joined the procession beside the boat. When they reached the boat bridge they were ordered to sit down outside a coffee shop on the right bank.

The *Comet* was still a mile away. Singleton had precipitated the rout of over 2,000 Turkish soldiers, and had captured 11 officers and 250 men. For this exploit he was later awarded the Distinguished Service Order, while two of his eight crew were decorated with the Distinguished Service Medal.

General Townshend and Sir Percy Cox, with the rest of the minute force, arrived at 1339 hrs and landed at the Custom House where they were met by the Civil Governor, the Commandant and a number of Turkish officers who surrendered the town. Orders were given to arrange supplies for 15,000 men who were soon arrive and the Union Jack was hoisted.

On the water front Lieutenant Palmer RN with two sailors, one marine and twelve soldiers of the Royal West Kents and the 1/4th Hampshires were posted to keep order. Shortly afterwards they received a message sent down from the barracks in the town where a battalion of the Constantinople Fire Brigade Regiment, a crack formation, were waiting to surrender. Lieutenant Palmer with a seaman, a marine and an interpreter strode up there through the crowded streets with as much aplomb as they could muster, and found a battalion of about 400 Turkish soldiers with their officers, all fully armed, drawn up in the courtyard.

Palmer gravely accepted their surrender from the commanding officer, their arms were piled, and he marched ahead of the battalion through the street down to the quay, with the seaman and the marine bringing up the rear. There he led them directly onto a big lighter moored at the bank; full of some 800 prisoners, this was then anchored in mid-stream under the guns of the flotilla.

During the afternoon, Turkish soldiers kept coming into the town to surrender, afraid of falling into the hands of their erstwhile allies, the Arabs. At one time about 2,000 troops approached from the north-east. Townshend, with his tiny force, could not cope with this number so the *Shaitan* steamed to that end of the town and fired a few shells at them – they fled in confusion to the north-west. However, the advance guard persisted in coming on so they were made prisoner – about fifty of them – and these were marched back to join their comrades in another barge on the river. Meanwhile, some of those who had fled, in fear of the local tribe, the Beni Lam, kept turning up to beg to surrender.

It was an anxious time. Townshend now had nearly a thousand prisoners on his hands in the middle of an Arab town of some 10,000 inhabitants. These were warned that they would be shot if they appeared on the street. Night came on, but not the reinforcements, although the rays of a searchlight of a steamer coming up were seen – she came no closer and was evidently stopped.

The night was nerve-wracking but uneventful until close to dawn when the Arab inhabitants seemed to have woken up to the situation and began looting. They were too late, however, for an hour after daybreak a steamer arrived with the Norfolks and they restored order with a few shots over the heads of the townsfolk. Further troops arrived during the day and General Nixon himself, in high good humour, in the evening.

In the Turkish barracks there were seventeen field guns and a large quantity of arms and ammunition, plus on the river were a Turkish gunboat and some smaller craft. Altogether there were 2,000 prisoners. The British had lost four killed and twenty-four injured in the whole operation of Townshend's Regatta.

Amara was a good supply centre, drier and healthier than Basra and later became the medical centre for the campaign. The town itself was comparatively modern, having been built with wide streets (for Mesopotamia) in 1866. It was soon the most popular military station in the country.

'Force D' was reorganized on 1 April 1915 as II Indian Army Corps

6 CAVALRY BRIGADE:

'S' Battery RHA
Lancers
6th Cavalry

INFANTRY:

6th Poona Division:
   16 Infantry Brigade comprising:
      2nd Dorsetshire Regiment
      20th Punjabis
      104th Rifles
      117th Mahrattas
   17 Infantry Brigade comprising:
      1st Ox and Bucks Light Infantry
      22nd Punjabis
      103rd Mahrattas
      119th Infantry
   18 Infantry Brigade comprising:
      2nd Norfolk Regiment
      7th Rajputs
      110th Mahrattas
      120th Rajputana Infantry
   Divisional Troops:
      33rd Cavalry (less 2 squadrons)
      10th Brigade RFA (18 guns)
      Divisional Ammunition Column
      1st Indian Mountain Artillery Brigade (12 guns)
      17th Field Company Sappers and Miners

22nd Field Company Sappers and Miners
34th Divisional Signal Company
48th Pioneers
12th Indian Division:
  12 Infantry Brigade comprising:
    2nd Queen's Royal West Kents
    4th Rajputs
    44th Merwara Infantry
    90th Punjabis
  30 Infantry Brigade comprising:
    24th Punjabis
    76th Punjabis
    2/7th Gurkhas
  33 Infantry Brigade comprising:
    1/4th Hampshires
    11th Rajputs
    66th Punjabis
    67th Punjabis
  Divisional Troops:
    2 Squadrons 33rd Cavalry
    56th Heavy Battery RGA (4 guns)
    104th Heavy Battery RGA (4 guns)
    1/5th Hants Howitzer Battery (4 howitzers)
    12th Field Company (Sappers and Miners)
    Sirmur Imperial Service Coy (Sappers and Miners)
    12 Divisional Signal Company.

DETACHMENT IN ARABISTAN ON 1 MAY 1915

6 Cavalry Brigade:
  'S' Battery RHA
  7th Lancers
  33rd Light Cavalry
  No. 131 Cavalry Field Ambulance
  Supply Column
30 Infantry Brigade:
  1/4th Hampshire Regiment
  24th Punjabis
  76th Punjabis
  2/7th Punjabis
  2/7th Gurkha Rifles

12 Infantry Brigade:
    2nd Queen's Royal West Kent Regiment
    4th Rajputs
    44th Merwara Infantry
    90th Punjabis
    67th Punjabis
Divisional Troops:
    10th Brigade RFA (less one gun)
    No. 6 Ammunition Column
    Maxim Gun Battery
    12th Company Sappers and Miners
    11th Rajputs
    66th Punjabis
    1 Company 48th Pioneeers
    2 Sections No 31 Signal Company
    2 Sections No 34 Signal Company
    Wireless Signal Troop Company
    No. 3 Combined Ambulance
    No. 108 Combined Ambulance
    2 Sections No. 19 Combined Clearing Hospital
    Divisional Supply Column.

Chapter Four

The Repulse at Ctesiphon

(Maps 1, 4 and 5)

While General Nixon was planning what he hoped to do next, a fresh commander was appointed for the Turkish forces in Mesopotamia. Nureddin Bey was an experienced, prudent and capable soldier who was expected to turn the tide of the British advance up the river. The British general might well be facing a more innovative opponent than he had previously.

With the capture of Amara on the Tigris and the securing of the oilfields, the area that could still prove to be a hindrance to British suzerainty over southern Mesopotamia was the left flank, the lowest section of the Euphrates river, occupied very largely by marshland and Hammar Lake.

Nixon proposed to the Commander-in-Chief in India, Sir Beauchamp Duff, that he should occupy Nasiriya at the far end of Hammar Lake, and also advance up the Tigris to Kut. He considered that the capture of the latter place would enable him to control the Shatt al Hai, a river that was thought to link Kut with Nasiriya and which would enable the Turks, if Kut was not taken, to ferry troops down it and attack a garrison at Nasiriya. The General Staff in India agreed with Nixon on this, although it later turned out that the river was too shallow for such a scheme to be carried out even in the rainy season. But he was only instructed to advance to Nasiriya since the Viceroy and Sir Beauchamp Duff, and Mr Chamberlain at the India Office in London, were not persuaded that there was a strong enough reason for taking over Kut, which was a sizeable town and would be another burden added to the commitments of the campaign.

The Turks had seven battalions and a few guns at Nasiriya, which was the headquarters of Turkish administration in the area, situated about 80 miles north-west of Basra and only accessible through country that was mainly either a shallow lake or a swamp. By midsummer the heat was at its most extreme – 120 degrees F (nearly 50 degrees C) in the shade, and the area of the drying lake was alive with biting insects. It was the worst time of the Mesopotamian year to launch a campaign but it is a measure of Nixon's impatient nature and Sir Percy Cox's urging that it was undertaken. Cox's chief argument was that Nasiriya was the headquarters of the powerful Munyafik tribes who were hostile to Britain and were soon likely to cause trouble.

Under General Gorringe, the advance took six weary weeks, setting off on 27 June from Qurna. The *Odin* and the *Espiègle* led the naval flotilla, followed by two armed launches, three stern-wheelers and two horse-boats, each mounted with a 4.7 inch gun. At the start, the convoy was flanked on both sides by thickets of tall reeds extending as far as the eye could reach. To the west was the broad expanse of Hammar Lake, dotted here and there with islands, some of which were covered with mud huts. Buffaloes up to their necks in mud moved slowly out of the water like prehistoric beasts as the ships approached, while the side channels were encumbered by fish traps made out of date stalks and reeds. Arabs in their graceful *mashufs* – canoes made of reeds and covered inside and out with pitch, with long, raking prows – made off more speedily than the buffaloes, but also sought sanctuary in the narrow channels within the reeds, peering out fearfully as the column steamed majestically by.

The *Odin* and the *Espiègle* were left at Kubaish and shortly afterwards the rest of the flotilla reached the Akaika channel, the only navigable route out of the lake that led up to Nasiriya. It was blocked by an irrigation dam, a solid barrage built by the local Arabs out of mud, date logs, an old *mahail* or two, stones and a few bits of stout timber. The sappers worked all night to breach it and by the next morning a channel had been cleared through which came a great rush of water, too strong for the stern-wheelers to push through unaided.

General Gorringe, a sapper himself, then took charge, standing on a small island in the middle of the dam in the blazing sun, directing through his megaphone tug-of-war teams on either bank, hauling the ships through by brute force. On 30 June the flotilla was assembled above the dam.

There were no maps of the area, whose watery landscape changed at the whim of the weather, and small reconnaissance parties had to work in advance of the force. The British were not alone in this deficiency – the Turkish High Command in Istanbul had no proper maps of any part of Mesopotamia either. After attempts to produce their own, they bought two German maps at a scale of 1:50,000 and used those.

It became clear that the British force was being harassed by two enemies – the Turks, of course, but in this area the Arabs were hostile as well, not only to the British, but to the Turks. This was illustrated by an incident involving the only political officer with Gorringe's force, an Arabic speaker, Arnold Wilson, who led some of the reconnaissances. His small party had had a skirmish with two Turks, both of whom were shot, one in the back and the other in the shoulder. They were left where they lay and the party pushed on. On the way back, when they reached the spot where they had last seen the wounded Turks, they found them, both stripped naked and with their throats cut. Their allies, the Arabs, had got to them.

Most of the officers and men regarded the Arabs collectively as faithless and mercenary, and as thieves and murderers, but the political officers had to try to take a more favourable view. This was in spite of the numerous incidents of wounded being slaughtered and the dead dug up for the sake of their clothes and left to jackals.

Clearly, the political officers were not always sympathetic to the Arabs either. It is worth illustrating this point by quoting verbatim from Arnold Wilson's book (*Loyalties – Mesopotamia, 1914–1917*, page 55) in which he describes another incident in this advance when he needed a boat to convey his small party across a creek:

> covered by the rifles of a party of the 48th (Pioneers) I swam the creek and accosted a greybeard. 'Salam 'alaikum' – 'Allah yasellimak'. 'Are there any Turks near here?' 'I am not a Turk, I am an Arab.' 'Have you a bellum in which we can cross?' 'I am an old man, I am poor, I have no bellum.' 'I see bellum poles and paddles against the wall – I am sure you have a bellum.' 'The Turks have taken all the bellums, I am an old man . . . &c.,&c.' Something had to be done; I

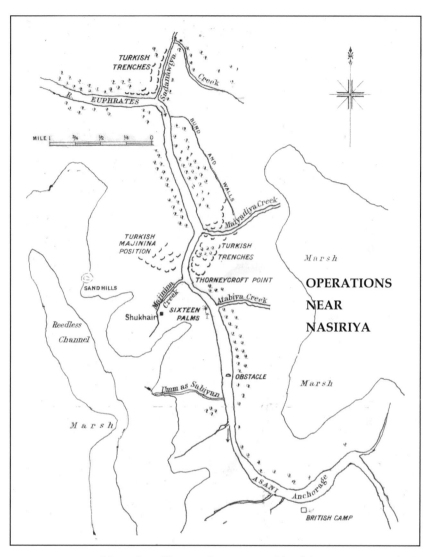

Map 4.   Operations near Nasiriya

seized a stick and beat him. 'Quwa, Quwa,' he groaned, 'ana abak.'
'Force, Force, I am your slave, there is a mashuf close by, I will get
it.' I feared a ruse and continued to beat him, simulating wrath but in
fear lest the bluff be called. Out ran two sturdy men: 'He is our father
– he is old – he is mad – leave him and we will bring a canoe.' I held
my hand and a few minutes later one was provided. 'Ferry me across

47

in it,' I said, 'and ferry the troops too, lest by leaving it to them they claim it as spoil.' The argument appealed to them and in half a dozen trips we had the ammunition across.

By 6 July the town of Suq ash Shuyukh was occupied, the inhabitants flying white flags as the force approached. It was an important centre of local Arab trade with a population of around 12,000 and some 15 miles from Nasiriya. Further movement was made cautiously for Arab informants suggested that 2,000 Turkish troops with four field and two mountain guns, two launches and large numbers of Arab irregulars were lying in wait further up the river. The British had only 1,900 soldiers.

Six miles south-east of Nasiriya the Turks had entrenched themselves on both sides of the Euphrates just below the great right-angle bend in the river where there were further fortifications. As the British advanced up the river on both sides lay impassable marsh, with beyond on the left date groves intersected by walls that gave every indication of concealing riflemen; with the approaching force restricted entirely to the river it would be impossible to escape any ambush should one be arranged for them.

If the Arabs they passed had combined behind them the British might well have been surrounded, with their communications back to base cut, not only by Arabs but also by a falling river level. This had already made it necessary to send back the gunboats to the deeper water of the lake. They were in an unpleasant position which threatened to become far worse. Climatic conditions did not help – temperatures in the shade were now even higher at 110 degrees F (44 degrees C); the bully beef swam out of the tin; and the mosquitoes were as ubiquitous and virulent as the Arabs.

Gorringe determined to make a carefully planned attack on the first Turkish entrenchments, a place the British named Thorneycroft Point, where they encountered a couple of Thorneycroft launches supplied to the Turks before the war. An officers' patrol had discovered that about half a mile to the west of this place was a group of sandhills that could, by virtue of the floods, be reached by *bellum*. An attack from here would outflank the Turkish trenches at their western end and it could be co-ordinated with a frontal attack up the Euphrates.

On the night of the 14th the operation began. The journey by *bellums* across the desert to occupy the sandhills turned out to be extremely exhausting – in places the floodwaters were unexpectedly shallow and the unwieldy craft had to be pushed a great part of the way. Guns were carried on rafts and these were left in a position about a mile short of the objective. As the Indian infantry advanced and got closer to the objective, they opened a brief bombardment at 0500 hrs.

The soldiers waded forward as soon as the guns fell silent through water up to four feet deep, to be met by a spirited response, as Arabs fired on them from the flank and Turkish guns to the north also opened up.

It was clear that the situation was untenable as the Indians were unable to advance fast enough to rush the defenders so their commander ordered a retreat. It was a slow business, encumbered as they were by their wounded, whom they could not leave to the mercy of the Arabs. Eventually they covered the mile back to the guns and concentrated there, but Turkish infantry had followed them up and the second half of the withdrawal with the guns continued to be hazardous. *Bellums* kept grounding on unseen shoals, as did the gun-rafts, and it was not until nine and a half hours after the start of the operation that they reached the safety of the Euphrates. One hundred and fifty men of the 400 who had set out had been killed or wounded.

As a result of this debacle, General Gorringe decided to abandon his frontal advance up the river for the time being. Instead, he began harassing attacks and waited for reinforcements that arrived on 19 and 20 July. They included the 110th Mahrattas, the Norfolks, some Royal West Kents and artillery. Two BE2C aircraft also appeared overhead and gave General Gorringe his first intelligence about the general lie of the land by dropping sketch maps to him.

On 24 July the battle was rejoined. Turkish resistance again was very stubborn but the British artillery worked well, with several guns mounted temporarily on the river craft able to be move forward at a moment's notice when required. They were augmented by fire from smaller naval ships whose role, along with the barges, was invaluable, carrying troops swiftly upriver and landing them where they would do the most good.

The confused fighting went on all day until during the afternoon the Turks began to waver and then broke entirely, fleeing northwards across the marshes. Captain Nunn in the *Shushan*, accompanied by the *Sumana* and the *Mahsoudi*, pushed on towards

Nasiriya, demolishing one of the Thorneycraft launches with a single shot on the way. White flags appeared over the rooftops but there were still Turks in the town and when they opened a heavy fire on the ships, Captain Nunn pulled back below the town and anchored for the night.

Next morning a deputation of leading citizens appeared on the bank and informed him that the Turks had made off during the hours of darkness. After conferring with General Melliss, encamped not far away, the Senior Naval Officer entered Nasiriya with a hundred Gurkhas. It was not a sanitary place and included a hospital full of wounded Turks from the recent engagement, lying in their own filth. The Arab inhabitants received the newcomers with a sort of philosophic courtesy, but without enthusiasm.

After the battle, the Force's medical arrangements proved to be inadequate. When the wounded were evacuated they were crowded onto the iron decks of the barges that had not been cleaned since horses and mules had stood on them for a week; there were few mattresses. It was a foretaste of what would happen in the future.

Sir John Nixon – whose motto, according to Arnold Wilson, was 'l'audace, toujours l'audace', Danton's exhortation to the defenders of Verdun in 1792 – was still considering a further advance up the Tigris to Kut and still arguing for it. Sir Percy Cox was enthusiastic in support of this notion and, with the influence that he could exercise with the Indian Government, he was a powerful ally. Arnold Wilson has this to say: 'To his [Cox's] in-fluence more than to that of any other man must be ascribed the successive decisions which culminated in the occupation of Baghdad.' We have already recorded that Cox had telegraphed this advice to the Viceroy in India on the day that Basra was captured. Wilson recalls this and comments: 'The logical and inescapable sequence of events was clear to him from the first, but it was long before he was able to induce successive Commanders-in-Chief in Mesopotamia or authorities in Simla and Whitehall, to face the inevitable implications of a forward policy in terms of men and material.'

After his successes on the Tigris, Townshend was in India on sick leave. He found that the Foreign Department in Simla was against any further advance which they thought might have the aim of occupying Baghdad unless more forces were available. So was Sir

50

Beauchamp Duff, the Commander-in-Chief of the Indian Army, whom he found overworked and tired. 'What I want,' he said to General Townshend, 'is a senior general in whom I can have absolute confidence as regards loyalty and ability, who can be a sort of deputy Commander-in-Chief and carry on the work for me at times while I have a short holiday.' Townshend commented, 'He had no-one answering to this description' (from Townshend's account of the campaign). This confession by Duff encapsulates also very neatly his attitude and that of others in the Indian Army HQ to the Mesopotamian Campaign.

Duff's powers were failing. He never moved from GHQ and lost touch with other senior generals in the Indian Army. His staff protected him from all outsiders so that even the Viceroy did not know the true situation. He clung to office as long as he could and died in January 1918. Meanwhile, Townshend found some staff at GHQ enthusiastic for an advance, suggesting that for a few months a brigade could be borrowed from Aden as reinforcement.

In London it was felt that from the administrative point of view Nixon's arguments were not convincing, for an advance would mean in increase in length of communications up a depleted River Tigris of 150 miles at a time in late summer when it was still hot. The number of men sick, suffering from the various complaints that affected troops in hot, marshy conditions, was already very high (the 1/4th Hampshires were only 115 strong at the time) and reinforcements were not available as there had been no increase in the number of ships able to operate on the shallow summer river.

The argument dragged on. The Viceroy (Lord Hardinge) had made up his mind that Kut, at least, was essential to British prestige and affirmed that in the opinion of 'the man on the spot' (Nixon) the advance was 'strategically desirable and will have a quieting effect on Persia and the Bakhtiaries'. So on 20 August, the Secretary of State allowed himself to be persuaded and three days later General Townshend was ordered to occupy the place.

By adopting Kut as the objective the defensive policy was definitely changed to an offensive one that saw the occupation of Baghdad as the political coup de main. This was the turning point of the campaign. But, as the Home Government had argued, there was neither the reserve of troops available nor the administrative machinery in place to cope with a new, enlarged situation. Originally, policy and strategy had worked together, but now policy – seeking to acquire prestige by a spectacular occupation of Baghdad – leaped ahead of strategy.

But nothing succeeds like success. So far the campaign had been an almost unbroken succession of victories in the face of great hardship and difficulty. One can see this clearly by comparing it with the progress that had been made at Gallipoli. But this situation was not to continue and it was the decision to advance to Kut that was the cusp and would lead to the nadir of the expedition. Of course, neither Nixon nor anybody else connected with the Tigris force could have foreseen this at the time, although less spirited commanders might have been more cautious.

Before he left for Amara, Townshend had an interesting conversation with General Nixon in which he told his superior that if he routed and stampeded the Turks in the coming battle he might follow them into Baghdad. He would take the responsibility even though he knew that the Home Government did not want him to enter the city, but he assumed that his orders would allow him to pursue at least. General Nixon raised no objection to this piece of speciousness and even told Townshend to telegraph him so that he could enter Baghdad with him.

Townshend had also wanted six months' reserve of stores to be placed at Amara, but this demand had been turned down by Nixon who said it was out of the question. Six weeks' stores was the reserve authorized by Headquarters in India for the whole of the Mesopotamian Army. Nevertheless, Townshend was so sure that it was necessary, before he left, he ordered his staff on his own responsibility to purchase the six months' supply from India and store them at Amara. This purchase turned out to be fortuitous since the stores were subsequently taken by him to Kut where they helped to eke out the food supplies there and proved to be invaluable in prolonging the siege.

It was thought that the British advance up the river would be opposed by 5,000 to 6,000 troops, with twelve guns positioned on both sides of the unfordable Tigris. Townshend therefore decided to take advantage of this disposition that effectively cut the enemy force in half, by disposing of the one half of the enemy force on the left bank after making a demonstration to distract the Turks on the other side.

He started to concentrate his three brigades of the 6th Division at Ali Gharbi. The naval flotilla consisted of the *Comet, Shaitan,*

Sumana and four 4.7-inch guns in horse boats towed by two small naval launches. The Senior Naval Officer was away at this juncture and his place was taken by Lieutenant Commander Cookson who kept pace with the soldiers marching along the river bank.

It was still intensely hot but the nights and early mornings were comparatively cool, and by marching from daybreak to 0830 hrs the force was able to make good progress. The Turks they encountered appeared reluctant to fight and fell back as the 6th Division advanced. At Sannaiyat, Townshend had to halt and send back the ships to Amara to pick up howitzer batteries and supplies. Meanwhile, General Nixon received a definite order from Sir Beauchamp Duff, C-in-C in India, not to operate beyond Kut without permission, which he somehow neglected to pass on to his subordinate.

Townshend had aircraft with him that reconnoitred the Turkish positions below Kut. Between two marshes on the left bank – the Suwacha Marsh some 6 miles from the river and the Suwada Marsh within a couple of miles of it – there was a gap of firm ground. At the further side of this gap the Turks were hurriedly digging trenches. They had already dug trenches between the Suwada Marsh and the river, and constructed a boom across the Tigris that joined these trenches with those on the right bank that were built along and in front of an ancient disused canal which ran between banks 20 feet high. It was known to the British as the Es-Sinn banks, from the top of which there was an excellent view and field of fire.

The construction of the defences on the left bank was reminiscent of those on the Western Front. The front line was well traversed and concealed with a good field of view over the flat and empty desert before it, an area that was provided with adequate wire entanglements and land mines, while in the rear were miles of communication trenches and underground bunkers. Covered ways were made to the river banks where ramps and landing stages facilitated the landing of supplies, while pumping engines were installed there that filled the water channels that carried drink to the soldiers in the trenches. Guns were placed in brick and mortar emplacements connected by broad communication trenches along which guns could be trundled.

On 25 September General Nixon arrived in the *Malamir* with his usual assurance to Townshend that he would not interfere with his arrangements.

Townshend advanced from Sannaiyat to Nukhailat, about 4 miles from the Turkish position, and there established his HQ on the left bank with a scaffolding observation tower and boat bridge across the river. Here, on the day of the advance, he was joined by General Nixon. General Delamain's column bivouacked at Chahela Banks on the right bank to give the impression to the Turks that it was the main British force, and the 103rd Mahrattas marched 2 miles further forward as though they were taking up positions for an attack.

Next day a further demonstration was made on that bank but all the troops involved returned under cover of the early darkness to the Chahela Banks and crossed the boat bridge in time to concentrate for the real attack on the opposite side of the river. A demonstration was also carried out on the left bank during the day but again the troops retired to join the concentration by midnight on the 27th.

At 0200 hrs on the 28th General Delamain and his column set off to circumnavigate the Suwada Marsh and attack the right wing of the Turkish entrenchments. The column was headed by Brigadier General Hoghton with cavalry and six infantry battalions, who marched in silence through the night over a surface that was soft and spongy and raised considerable clouds of clinging dust that hung in the damp, heavy atmosphere. They halted close to the edge of the Suwada Marsh and General Hoghton led the cavalry off to the north to get round the end of the Turkish entrenchments and attack them from the rear.

When the sun rose at 0600 hrs he was surprised still to find marsh on his left and it was clear that he had missed the gap between the Suwada and the Ataba marshes, was too far north and was now marching between the Ataba and Suwacha marshes. He had been let down by the lack of accurate compass bearings in his orders which had been prepared after reconnaissance by an aircraft. At that time the aircraft compasses in Mesopotamia were not totally reliable.

Rather than turn back he decided to march round the Ataba Marsh and having reached the northern edge by 0700 hrs he changed direction to the west. Soon, however, the guns of the 76th Field Battery found the going too soft and the line of march had to be adjusted further to the north. By this time General Delamain, waiting where he had left him to the south, was getting rather impatient to attack and telephoned Hoghton to urge him not to stop on any account.

When the march resumed Hoghton immediately ran into a

Turkish battalion and had to charge their entrenchments which the 104th Indian Regiment did in great style, capturing one Turkish officer and 111 men. A group of about 500 reinforcements, sent by the Turks to the relief of this force, were caught in the open by the British machine-guns and driven back with many casualties.

By 0820 hrs General Delamain could at last see General Hoghton's leading troops on the horizon and ordered his force to advance, again urging General Hoghton on. This was the last communication between the two commanders as Hoghton's force outran the 7 miles of telephone cable that they were unrolling behind them.

Delamain's attack was on the strong point at the northern end of the Turkish line, called by the British the Northern Redoubt. The Turks resisted strongly but eventually the position was carried at the point of the bayonet by both British and Indian troops with the aid of an attack from the rear by Hoghton's force.

Moving south the two forces overran another strong point called the Centre Redoubt with its associated trenches. But the artillery was being made ineffective by a strong wind that had got up, raising clouds of dust that combined with the usual mirage to make accurate observation almost impossible.

The third redoubt, the Southern, was more difficult to overrun due to the lack of artillery support, but eventually, by about 1245 hrs, another combined Indian and British assault carried it.

Delamain ordered Hoghton to regroup his column and march south behind the Suwada Marsh to the River Tigris, where the centre section of the Turkish position was located. But by now the troops were very tired and thirsty after their long march, their water bottles had been empty for hours and ammunition was running low. By 1530 hrs the dust completed their discomfort and when they halted for a rest about 2 miles from the river, they almost at once came under heavy fire from Turkish guns dug in by the Tigris.

South of the Suwada Marsh the advance was under the command of Major General Fry, his leading troops being the 7th Rajputs, 120th Infantry and 110th Mahrattas, with the Norfolks in reserve. They were escorted by artillery and the guns of the naval flotilla which bombarded the Turkish positions on the right bank.

At 10.40 hrs an aeroplane fired a Very light over General Townshend's HQ to signal that General Delamain's assault had been successful. Shortly afterwards the telephone cable between

Townshend's and Delamain's HQs ran out and communication between the two was by aeroplane or the seaplanes that were able to use that stretch of the river. No wireless set was available for Delamain, the two in use being with Townshend and Nixon.

By noon Delamain had arrived behind the Turkish centre section trenches south of Suwada Marsh but was hampered by the wounded. Could General Fry press his attack home on the Turkish front-line positions? Fry replied that he was not yet in a position to do so. At 1730 hrs Delamain's slow southern movement was brought up short by a Turkish force that had crossed the river from the right bank, a fight developed and the Turks took up position in a dry nullah (watercourse) running north from the river. Despite the heavy Turkish fire and their exhaustion, the British infantry, fixing bayonets, charged and drove the Turks headlong from their position. With this final effort, Delamain's force was finished for the day and despite the extreme cold they dropped where they stood and spent the night on the bare ground. Fry's force also bivouacked on the other side of the Turkish centre position.

During the night the Turks evacuated all their positions and began a retreat that took them past Kut and up towards Baghdad. Early that night Townshend suggested to the acting Senior Naval Officer that he might make an attempt to clear away the Turkish boat bridge. Lieutenant Commander Cookson in *Comet* and two other armed tugs crept upstream in the dark but as they neared the bridge they were detected and came under very heavy rifle and machine-gun fire from both banks.

Cookson discovered that the obstruction consisted of a *mahaila* and two iron lighters tied together with wire hawsers. The best method of clearing the way would be by releasing the *mahaila* in the middle and allowing it to be swept downstream by the current. Cookson manoeuvred the *Comet* against the *mahaila* so that the hawsers could be cut with an axe. In view of the risk involved he decided to do the job himself, but as soon as he went over the side he was riddled with bullets and died ten minutes after his crew managed to drag him back on board. He was later posthumously awarded the Victoria Cross.

A day later these Turks made off upriver leaving two men firing an old muzzle-loading gun to guard the obstruction. Their gallant though futile resistance was soon disposed of.

General Townshend hastily embarked a force on the steamers and set off in pursuit of the disappearing Turks. After passing the boat-bridge obstruction and pausing for the night just below Kut, he passed the town and pushed on after the fleeing enemy. But the river was not easy to navigate and, although the enemy rearguard was overtaken, conditions in the British line of communication were so chaotic that the pursuit had to be abandoned when they reached Aziziya.

Nixon's force was now very much split up. At Kut and in the vicinity he had eight squadrons and a horse battery, 6th Divisional HQ, and three infantry brigades with a complement of field artillery, engineers and signals. 30 Infantry Brigade, less two battalions, was doing line-of-communication duties. At Ali Gharbi there was half a battalion with one gun; at Amara was 12th Divisional HQ and one and a half battalions of 30 Brigade; at Qala Salih there was a platoon; at Qurna there was half a battalion; at Nasiriya there were a squadron, 12 Infantry Brigade and a mountain battery; at Basra was the headquarters of the Line of Communications and two battalions of 33 Infantry Brigade; at Fao were fourteen riflemen; at Abadan were one officer and twenty-five riflemen; at Ahwaz were a squadron and half a battalion; at Bandiqir was a regiment less one squadron; at Bushire were a squadron and two battalions.

But to Nixon, one thought only filled his mind and that was of the fabulous city of Baghdad just over the horizon and within his grasp. All he had to do was to stretch out and take it. By now he was convinced that his army, having once again triumphed over extreme difficulties, was invincible. He told the Secretary for India: 'I am confident that I can beat Nureddin and occupy Baghdad without any addition to my present force.' He laid stress on the military value of Baghdad, which seemed to be essentially much the same as that of Kut or Nasiriyeh, namely that Baghdad, unless it was captured, could be used as an advanced base for a hostile counter-offensive. One wonders where this process of depriving the enemy of advanced bases was to stop. If Kut, why not Baghdad; if Baghdad why not Tikrit and so on. The weakness with this argument was that the further the British went into the enemy's country in order to deprive him of his advanced bases, the longer, more difficult and vulnerable the British line of communication would become.

Townshend, unusually for him, had lost his earlier enthusiasm for advancing further. He had now reached far enough up the Tigris for the seriousness of his situation to have a sobering effect on even his mercurial nature. He was 380 miles from the sea up an unstable river, 'teeming,' as he describes it, 'with Arabs at present more or less hostile', with a solitary division. He suggested to Nixon that either he should be given another division or he should retreat to Kut and occupy that strategic position in strength. Nixon was at Kut, as usual breathing down Townshend's neck, otherwise, as Townshend says in his book, he would have taken the responsibility on himself and returned to Kut without reference to him. But Nixon had the bit between his teeth and was determined to push on.

This decision chimed in with political thinking in India, where the Viceroy, in constant anxiety about internal Indian security, was looking for any military success which might be used to heighten British prestige in Asiatic eyes and compensate for British failures in the West, where recently we had lost ground north of Ypres, and in Turkey where the Dardanelles venture had definitely and obviously failed. In short, the purely local significance of the campaign in Mesopotamia was becoming inflated into a major feature of worldwide British prestige.

In London, enthusiasm did not run high with everyone. Lord Kitchener and the War Office thought that the most Nixon could accomplish was a raid on Baghdad, but the Cabinet was of another mind. The Secretary of State telegraphed to India that they were so impressed by the political and military advantages of the occupation of Baghdad that every effort should be made to spare the necessary forces. He asked if one division was sufficient.

The War Committee of the Cabinet now considered the matter after having taken soundings from various sources. After discussion they came to the conclusion that if it was decided that Nixon should advance he would need two extra divisions, but they eventually passed the buck and announced that the decision as to whether to advance was to be left to India.

On 24 October General Nixon was authorized by India to move on to Baghdad. He had by now learnt that the enemy was not as disorganized as he had first thought and that they were entrenching their position at Ctesiphon just below Baghdad; he commented later: 'It was advisable to smash him [the Turk], and nothing could justify letting slip such an opportunity.'

In his mind, the difficulties of river transport did not appear to represent an insuperable obstacle. Nor did they to the General Staff in India who also knew how little had been done to improve the administrative and ancillary departments of the Force, yet they seem to have expected that by some miracle an expedition whose system of maintenance up an unreliable river with too few vessels was already at best precarious, could double in size, add a hundred miles to its communications and still be successful.

In reply to a long telegram in which he described his unsatisfactory position, Townshend received the following:

> Everything points to your having to turn the Turks out of the Salman Pak (Ctesiphon) position. Please report from Azizieh whether you propose to concentrate your division and, if so, where. Azizieh would be quite suitable from our point of view, as our machines (aircraft) could then visit Baghdad. It is reported that they already had a most disturbing effect on the enemy. It seems desirable to form an advanced depot wherever you concentrate and return all ships and barges to Kut to refill.

He was also told that another Division was actually on its way from France but of course, as Townshend remarked, it was not going to be much good to him in his present advance. However, it was useless to argue any further.

On the night of 27/28 October 1915, the larger part of General Townshend's force made a night march of 8 miles across the bend in the river above Aziziya and attacked the Turkish advanced detachment at Kutuniya. The combined Turkish and Arab force were rudely awakened in the early morning and immediately retreated in disorder, leaving their camp and thorn-bush strong point to be destroyed before the British force marched back to Aziziya.

An interesting footnote can be provided at this point that illustrates the ambivalence of the public and private attitudes of the politicians in London to the campaign. It is demonstrated by the speech that Mr Asquith, the Prime Minister, made in the House of Commons on 2 November: 'General Nixon's force is now within measurable distance of Baghdad. I do not think that in the whole war there has been a series of operations more carefully contrived, more brilliantly conducted, and with a better prospect of final success.'

Yet in his diary (*Memories and Reflections*, Vol ii, p. 69) he says on 25 March 1915:

Grey and I . . . both think that in the real interests of our own future the best thing would be if at the end of the War we could say that we had taken and gained nothing, and this not from a merely moral and sentimental point of view. Taking Mesopotamia, for instance, means spending millions in irrigation and development with no immediate or early return. Keeping up quite a large army in an unfamiliar country, tackling every kind of tangled administrative question worse than we had ever had in India, with a hornets' nest of Arab tribes, and even if that were all set right having a perpetual menace on our flank in Kurdistan.

The War Office now became aware of Turkish reinforcements. Both the 45th and the 51st Divisions, plus a howitzer battalion had already arrived and Nureddin could now field 20,000 men, 19 machine-guns, 52 artillery weapons and some cavalry. The 38th and 45th Divisions were in the front line with the 51st Division in the second line.

On 16 November, the War Office wired to Nixon that another 30,000 Turkish troops under Halil Bey, uncle of the War Minister, were on the way from Anatolia, and General von der Goltz, the renowned German general attached to the Turkish army, was soon due in Mesopotamia to take command. Nixon refused to believe the news and did not pass it on to General Townshend – in any case he was sure he would be in Baghdad before they arrived – but he did repeat a request for more river transport.

Nureddin was not happy with the imminent arrival of the German general. He wired to the Turkish High Command: 'The Iraq Army has already proved that it does not need the military knowledge of Goltz Pasha . . . The idea of sending a non-Muslim general to Iraq, which has a Muslim population and where we declared a Holy War, is remarkable.'

Time was then lost while reinforcements were ferried upriver to Townshend, although the river was becoming shallower and the larger ships were unable to venture safely too far. It was not until 18 November that Townshend's force moved to Zor, 15 miles above Kutuniya where a bridge was built across the Tigris, and on the 20th to Lajj where the force was concentrated.

Townshend called for reconnaissance and the commander of the Royal Flying Corps detachment, Major Reilly, took on the duty himself. In those days it would have been called a long reconnaissance, a journey of some 80 miles there and back, the object being to see what was going at Baghdad. But the aircraft did not get that far. The straight course to Baghdad passed 4 miles east of Ctesiphon where the Turkish trenches were and it was there that Major Reilly noticed that there were some distinct changes in the Turkish dispositions – their second line had been considerably reinforced. He immediately abandoned the flight to Baghdad and flew over the section to examine the new defences. As he changed course a Turkish rifleman fired up at him and by a stroke of luck hit the engine, putting it out of action. Reilly turned with the intention of landing further east in the desert and hiking back to the British lines, but he was unlucky. Although he landed safely he was captured by Arabs. On him was a sketch map showing the course of the Tigris below Baghdad and the British positions. The Turks were delighted for they had no reliable intelligence, but the greatest disaster was that Reilly was unable to carry the news of the Turkish reinforcements back to Townshend. Further bad luck befell the RFC on the same day when two other aircraft were put out of action, leaving the force with just two.

The centre of the Turkish fortifications was the Arch of Ctesiphon close to the left bank of the River Tigris. Further south were the ruins of another ancient building known to the British as 'High Wall'. Both monuments were the remains of the Susanian capital of the fourth century AD.

Two lines about 6,000 yards apart formed the Turkish defences with the Arch of Ctesiphon situated midway between them. Considerable work had been put into constructing the first line that consisted of fifteen redoubts linked by a continuous trench line starting just west of the river at a point where the Turks had cut off an unnecessary bend in the river, leapfrogged the Tigris and continued north-east for nearly 12,000 yards to low mounds on which the final two redoubts were placed. Townshend designated this place 'Vital Point' (or VP). High Wall was situated halfway along and just in front of the front line.

The second line was much less strong. The southern half of the line was covered by the Tigris which flowed parallel to and in front of it about a thousand yards away. The northern half of it was where the Turks expected the British attack would be made across an open plain covered in a few places by scrub about 3 feet high. Between the two Turkish lines were emplacements for field guns

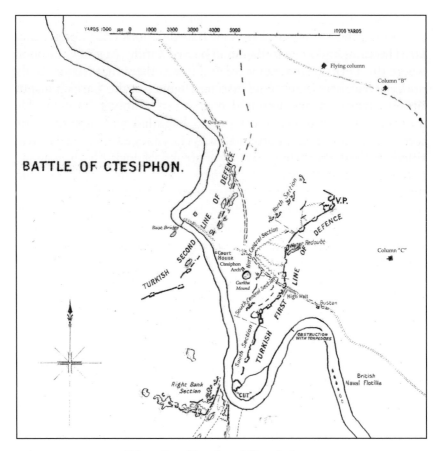

Map 5.   Battle of Ctesiphon

and a heavy battery. As with the defences at Sanniyat the Turks had installed a pump on the river bank that supplied water to the emplacements.

At Ctesiphon the Turkish force consisted of about 18,000 infantry, 400 cavalry, 2 regiments of camelry, 52 guns, 19 machine-guns and a few thousand Arabs. General Nixon's staff, however, computed them to number about 13,000 with 38 guns, while Townshend, in his optimistic fashion, announced them to be 10,000 to 11,000 with 30 guns. The situation on 20 November was that General Townshend was about to attack with 13,700 riflemen, 5 batteries and 11 squadrons of cavalry.

62

He anticipated an early success and was so confident that he committed the whole of his force to the battle without making any arrangements for a reserve, and also gave orders that the wounded were to be evacuated forward into Baghdad after its capture.

He intended to attack the Turks on the left bank of the Tigris with three columns advancing 4,000 yards apart. The left one (Column C) was to march towards the enemy front line and contain them there while another (Column A) was to attack VP. To the north, Column B and the cavalry were to envelop the enemy's rear.

In his account of the campaign after the war Townshend wrote in his characteristic style, mixing 'dash' with pedantry, that he

hoped to make up for want of numbers by exploiting the principle of economy of force . . . hoped to paralyse a great part of the forces of the enemy, extended along a large extent of front by the use of an inferior fraction of my troops, acting as a minimum force, disguising its weakness by audacity, or in forcing it to undertake an enterprise which will cost heavily, while I hit the hammer blow on the enemy's flank and rear with my principal mass.

This, no doubt, was a principle that he had absorbed from his study of the campaigns of Napoleon Bonaparte.

The first movement of the Battle of Ctesiphon was at 1430 hrs on 21 November as a preliminary to the attack launched at dawn on the 22nd. The advance of Column C towards the Turkish front line drew no response from the Turks. Column B and the cavalry soon after commenced their advance but were brought to a halt after about 1,200 yards by continuous rifle and heavy gunfire. Column A, heading for VP, started its advance at 0900 hrs with about 5,000 yards to cover under artillery fire, which it soon managed to do despite suffering heavy casualties, until it was brought up short by wire entanglements in front of the Turkish trenches.

But the Indian infantry, undeterred, forced their way through the wire and shortly after 1000 hrs, had driven off the Turks and captured VP. To the south Column C had just got close enough to the Turkish front line to be able to mount an attack, but to the north Column B and the cavalry were still bogged down.

This was the situation when at about 1045 hrs Townshend decided to see for himself what was happening in the Turkish front line. With his staff strung out behind him he galloped under brisk

Turkish artillery fire across the 2 miles of open plain to VP. It was time for unorthodox methods so he sent an order to General Hoghton, in command of Column C, to move left at right angles to the previous advance in front of and about a mile from the Turkish trenches. This movement of moving to the flank in front of an entrenched enemy was certainly not recommended in military text-books and they suffered considerable losses from rifle, machine-gun and shrapnel fire.

Some reinforcement were sent from VP to Hoghton's aid and after heavy fighting an attack on two of the Turkish front-line redoubts was successful, most of the Turkish garrisons being killed. General Nixon now turned up at VP with his staff to add his support to Townshend, although whether Townshend was genuinely grateful for this gesture is a moot point.

At about 1300 hrs the Turks abandoned the rest of their front line. During the afternoon, the British, now seriously short of men, there being no reserve, collected together what ancillary troops and strag-glers that they could and with a party of some 250 men from General Hoghton, mounted an attack against the Turkish second line, but after hard fighting they were unable to make any progress.

Shortly after 1700 hrs Townshend gave orders for his troops to concentrate at VP and a roll call revealed that of C Column only 700 men were on their feet, while the others could only muster 1,000 and 900 men respectively.

It was clear to the General that he was in no shape to resume the offensive the next day. Instead he proposed to occupy the southern half of the Turkish front line where he could easily be resupplied with water, food and ammunition from the river. His casualties amounted to some 4,500 but the enemy had also suffered badly and remained quiet in their second line all night.

Generals Townshend and Nixon spent the night at VP where the wounded were collected from all over the battlefield on the beds of nails that were the antique AT (Army Transport) carts. Four field ambulances were present with equipment to deal with some 400 casualties. In the event they coped with over 3,500 Indian, British and Turkish wounded.

But the Turkish commander was aware of the perilous position of the British and at 1500 hrs next day he launched an attack that lasted through the afternoon and all that night, and was so vigorous that Townshend realized that the Turks had been strongly reinforced.

Meanwhile, a tragic situation had arisen. Hospital ships with accommodation for 500 lay at Lajj about 10 miles downriver from Ctesiphon but these were soon filled with the casualties that came trickling back across the desert even before the main battle was joined. When the main battle casualties arrived on the night of 22 November, their thin clothing soaked through from the rain that fell that night, and their bodies almost flayed by the bitter wind that was blowing, no room could be found for them. These men were jolted over the rough desert in the springless, cushionless AT carts improvised as ambulances that were so unbearable that men threw themselves out to crawl across the desert on hands and knees rather than endure the agony of the shaking, or used dead bodies as cushions between themselves and the iron bars that served as the bottoms of the carts. They were stuffed into ships to endure the voyage hundreds of miles down to Basra, most without any further treatment.

Small steamers carried 600 cases and took up to thirteen days to reach Basra as they had to run the gauntlet of hostile Arabs on the river banks. But even before that it was taking two days to get the casualties to the waiting steamers on which they were crowded, unmurmuring, as Arnold Wilson says, like cattle. The four field ambulances that did the work were now running out of medical supplies and also finding it difficult to find sufficient food for the wounded.

Horses were being watered in the river covered by a detachment of Indian troops on Gurkha Mound just to the south of Ctesiphon Arch, but they had to retire in the face of the Turkish gunfire that heralded their attack at 1500 hrs. The most desperate fighting took place at VP and along the line to the south of it. Townshend and Nixon were with this part of the force and as they actually took part in the fighting it soon became clear to both of them that the Turkish reinforcements they were facing were of a considerably higher standard than the troops they had defeated earlier in the campaign. While the struggle was going on in the front line, the evacuation of wounded was continuing from the rear. Next morning, as the attacks died away, General Nixon returned to Lajj where the *Malamir* was moored.

Townshend was reconsidering his position. At first he thought that he had no option but to follow Nixon and retire to Lajj, but less than an hour later he had changed his mind. He wired to General

Nixon: 'This [to have the ships brought up to Bustan just below the Arch of Ctesiphon where he intended to stay] I have arranged with the SNO. Thus I get rid of any retirement whatever – I remain on here on the field of battle . . . It will have a much better political effect not to retire, both here, India, and at home.' To this Nixon agreed.

But this decision was not to stand. The ships could not get up the river and on the 24th Townshend decided to move back to Lajj next day. Any movement forward was obviously out of the question until there were reinforcements, so Sir John Nixon travelled downstream to expedite them, mulling over Townshend's latest decision. His instinct was always to push on and he made a further attempt to prevent the retirement. He telegraphed to Townshend: 'I do not like your proposed retirement on Lajj for military reasons . . . You should of course prepare a fortified position at Lajj on which to retire in case of necessity and to cover your advanced base but for military reasons I do not consider retirement desirable at present . . . Remember the moral is to the physical as five to one.'

Townshend, with understandable exasperation, replied from Lajj on 26 November:

> I received your telegram this morning on arrival with the force. I adhere very stongly to my [decision] of the 25th. I consider that with 4,300 casualties – which is the total – and when the brigades are reduced to little more than a full strength battalion, it would have been madness to have remained at Ctesiphon a moment longer than I did. At 4 p.m. yesterday two large columns of Turks estimated at 5000 each by air service were advancing from their entrenched line covering the Diyala north of Qusaiba . . . I waited till darkness and moved off in the dark to Lajj where I am now entrenching and going to make myself comfortable. [In his anger, he repeats himself] From a military point of view it would be madness and nothing else to remain at Ctesiphon. Remember you agreed before to my Lajj reasons . . . I hope you will approve of what I have done to the best of my judgment. Nothing will alter my opinion that I have acted for the best.

With this comprehensive telling off of his commanding officer, Townshend ended the Battle of Ctesiphon in which both British and Indian troops displayed outstanding gallantry and which was skil- fully handled by Townshend who gained tactical success with dispositions that had brought him success in previous battles. In this one the repulse of the Turkish counter-attack of 23 November was an outstanding achievement. But he had just run out of shots in his locker.

Nixon sent a magnanimous reply: 'I quite agree with the action you have taken.'

Composition on 14 November of Townshend's column advancing on Baghdad

CAVALRY:

HQ 6 Cavalry Brigade
'S' Battery R.H.A.
7th Lancers (4 squadrons)
16th Cavalry (3 squadrons)
33rd Cavalry (3 squadrons)
One squadron, 23rd Cavalry (Divisional cavalry)
Total: 11squadrons and 6 guns

ARTILLERY:

10th Brigade RFA (63rd, 76th and 82nd Batteries)
1/5th Hampshires Howitzer Battery RFA
86th Heavy Battery RGA (one section in barges)
104th Heavy Battery RGA (less one section)
One post gun, Volunteer Artillery Battery
Total: 29 guns, of which 3 guns were left at Aziziya

INFANTRY:

16th Brigade (2nd Dorsets, 66th Punjabis, 104th Rifles, 117th Mahrattas)
17th Brigade (1st Ox and Bucks, 22nd Punjabis, 103rd Mahrattas, 119th Infantry)
18th Brigade (2nd Norfolks, 7th Rajputs, 110th Mahrattas, 120th Rajputana Infantry)
30th Brigade (2/7th Gurkhas, 24th Punjabis, 76th Punjabis)
48th Pioneers.
Total: 18 battalions, half a battalion as garrison at Aziziya

DIVISONAL TROOPS ETC.:

Maxim Battery
17th Field Company, Sappers and Miners
22nd Field Company, Sappers and Miners
Bridging Train
Searchlight Section
Divisional Ammunition Train
34th Divisional Signal Company
One Brigade section, 12th Divisional Signal Company
One section, Army Corps Signal Company
One wagon wireless station
Two pack wireless stations
Field Ambulances
Clearing hospitals on the *Blosse Lynch* and *Mosul*

AIR SERVICE:

Five aircraft of the Royal Flying Corps (including two converted naval seaplanes). Two more aircraft arrived on 17 November. Seaplanes could often not take off because the wind was in the wrong direction, and they suffered from shifting sandbanks and other obstructions on the Tigris.

Chapter Five

Medical Scandal

The military achievement has always been overshadowed by the scandal of the treatment of the wounded, and in March 1916 the Vincent-Bingley Commission was set up to review the breakdown of medical arrangements for the campaign. This was prompted by what happened after the Battle of Ctesiphon and they found that the responsibility lay initially with the Indian Government for not providing sufficient equipment, and subsequently with Surgeon-General Hathaway, the Senior Medical Officer with the force, for not making sure that the original deficiencies were made up. Some responsibility rested also, to a lesser extent, with General Nixon who, as C-in-C of the force, did not sufficiently consider the seriousness of the medical situation.

One of the principal witnesses to the Commission was Major Carter of the Indian Medical Service who was in charge of the hospital ship *Varela* waiting at Basra for the wounded being evacuated from Ctesiphon. He describes the arrival of one of the river convoys bringing the wounded downriver:

> I was standing on the bridge in the evening when the *Medjidieh* arrived. She had two steel barges, without any protection against the rain as far as I remember. As this ship, with two barges, came up to us, I saw that she was absolutely packed, and the barges, too with men. The barges were slipped, and the *Medjidieh* was brought alongside the *Varela*. When she was about 300 or 400 yards off it looked as if she was festooned with ropes. The stench when she was close was quite definite, and I found that what I mistook for ropes were dried stalactites of human faeces. The patients were so huddled

and crowded together on the ship that they could not perform the offices of nature clear of the edge of the ship and the whole of the ship's side was covered with stalactites of human faeces. This is what I saw. A certain number of men were standing or kneeling on the immediate perimeter of the ship. Then we found a mass of men huddled up anyhow – some with blankets and some without. They were lying in a pool of dysentery about 30 feet square. They were covered with dysentery and dejecta generally from head to foot. With regard to the first man I examined, I put my hand into his trousers and I thought he had a haemorrhage. His trousers were full almost to his waist with something warm and slimy. I took my hand out and thought it was blood clot. It was dysentery. The man had a fractured thigh and his thigh was perforated in five or six places. He had apparently been writhing about on the deck of the ship. Many cases were almost as bad. There were a certain number of cases of terribly bad bed sores. In my report I describe mercilessly to the Government of India how I found men with their limbs splinted with wood strips from 'Johnny Walker' whisky boxes, 'Bhoosa' wire, and that sort of thing.

The Indian Government should have been aware of the situation themselves but to some extent they were being hoodwinked as to the full extent of the tragedy. After the dreadful evacuation from Ctesiphon described above, Surgeon-General Hathaway sent a detailed report on the operation to the Director of Medical Services that made no mention of anything untoward having taken place. In addition, General Nixon, presumably as a result of what he had seen at Lajj and Hathaway's reports to him, wired to India ten days later describing the same operation as being extraordinarily well carried out in the circumstances.

The military authorities in India knew that the original Expeditionary Force had been sent to Mesopotamia without a British Stationary Hospital and that the reinforcing division which arrived in the spring of 1915 was also unaccompanied by hospital staff or field ambulances for two out of three of its brigades. Sir Beauchamp Duff, the C-in-C in India, explained to the Commission that, owing to the shortage of doctors in India, they were forced to send them in that condition.

Later, when the advance to Kut in 1916 was sanctioned, but with the deficiency not yet made up, Mr Chamberlain in the India Office asked the Viceroy whether more doctors, nurses, medicines or hospital comforts were needed. Lord Hardinge replied, presumably on advice from the military, 'My Government arranged for doctors and medicines.' However, a fortnight later Surgeon-General Hathaway informed India of a deficiency of seventeen medical officers and fifty sub-assistant surgeons

Two months afterwards, Mr Chamberlain telegraphed again, anxious about the health of 'Force D', the risk of malaria and the state of hospitals in the country. Lord Hardinge replied:

> Preventives adopted are purification of water by clarifying and boiling and chlorination, prophylactic issues of quinine, treatment of mosquito breeding places, supply to all troops, British and native, of mosquito nets. A sanitary committee has been formed . . . British and Indian General Hospitals at Basra are provided with electric lights and fans and each bed has a mosquito net, but buildings are not suitable for use of gauze netting.

Actually, the water supply was far from being satisfactory, nor were there the number of electric lights, fans and mosquito nets as many as suggested.

On 14 October Mr Chamberlain voiced the same disquiet in a private letter, and a few days later on 29 October he wrote again. In this letter he said: 'I continue to receive from Members of Parliament and others anxious enquiries about the health of the troops in Mesopotamia and the provision made for them. Inter alia, I have been sent a letter from some officer there in which he incidentally observes that my statement as to ice and other comforts provided at the hospital "was all eyewash".'

On 3 December Mr Chamberlain wrote again: 'I beg you not to be content with easy assurances. On your advice, comforts, &c, are not being sent from here, and we shall have no defence at all if all that is possible is not done.'

There is little doubt that Lord Hardinge passed on this unease to Beauchamp Duff about how little progress was being made in improving matters. One might think that it was strange that he himself did not already know about the gravity of the situation but it seems he was being kept in the dark.

The Commander-in-Chief, complaisant as always, was of a different stamp to the Viceroy. He did not take notice of complaints unless they were accompanied by the name of the complainant. This was his response to a question from the Mesopotamian Commission:

> The reports come in. In every campaign I have seen in my life there are complaints. A large number of complaints come in, many of them extremely frivolous. When such reports are sent to you anonymously and the names of the people who make the complaints are refused you attach little weight to them. The moment I get a report with a name I pay strong attention to it. I find going into these anonymous reports is simply a waste of time.

But he must have been aware of the sufferings after Ctesiphon. Major Carter, in charge of the medical staff on the hospital ship plying between Basra and Bombay, sent a report on the situation on 14 December to Surgeon-General MacNeece, the Director of Medical Services in India. He speaks of casualties he took on board his ship at Basra.

> These were all serious stretcher cases that had lain on the *Medjidieh* for thirteen days after their first dressing on the field of battle. Their condition was grave and the result of an unfortunate train of circumstances the most serious of which was that there is no distinct river service of hospital steamers used alone for the conveyance of the sick and wounded in Mesopotamia. On the *Medjidieh* alone 28 had died on the journey . . . Deaths during the voyage total 14. It is now necessary to explain the markedly increased death-rate on this the third journey. In the first place, we carried a high proportion of the most serious cases of gunshot and shell wounds brought by the *Medjidieh*, the P.5, the steel boats and smaller steel barges from the front.
>
> Unless one had actually seen the condition of the wounded on arrival, one could have had no accurate standard by which to judge the extraordinarily difficult position in which the medical personnel have been recently placed in Mesopotamia. For example, on the *Medjidieh*, a small river steamer, it was necessary to crowd over 600 sick and wounded from November 24th to the evening of December 6th, 1915. The equipment of the field hospitals at the front had to be abandoned to the enemy, and there was practically nothing left with which to dress wounds or treat medical cases.
>
> Everyone seems to consider that it was extremely fortunate that they got away at all. The men were loud in their praise of the devotion

to duty shown by many of the medical officers under heavy fire, both in the field and at the point of attack on the Tigris. There is but little chance of recovery for men with severe gunshot fractures, who lie on the bare decks of boats and barges for 13 days, amid septic discharges, diarrhoea and dysentery, swept at night by a wind that dropped nearly to zero, without any protection against the cold, save their clothes and country blankets, which in the cases of total cripples were sodden with their own discharges and dejecta.

I write this to protect from hostile criticism by the laity the members of the medical services, who in these primitive boats and cattle barges have struggled for 13 days against the difficulties of a task that is happily exceptional in the war history of our Imperial forces. There is no shadow of doubt that the medical staff who accompanied these sick and wounded from Ctesiphon did all that lay in their power to help and tend their patients, but it was attempting to make bricks without straw.

Surgeon-General MacNeece referred this to Sir Percy Lake, the Chief of the General Staff, asking that it was brought to the attention of Sir Beauchamp Duff.

When the Viceroy pressed him to have a full enquiry made, Duff wrote back on 30 December:

I will certainly have the whole matter enquired into and reported on.

I am quite sure that in India itself and between India and Basra everything is right. The flow of stores, supplies and comforts is regular and as complete as we can make it, any deficiencies that may exist being confined to articles for which we are dependent on England and the prompt supply of which we cannot always ensure. As to what happens beyond Basra I am dependent on official reports. The private complaints which Your Excellency mentions do not reach me. It is one of the drawbacks of military discipline that officers will not mention such matters to me or my Staff lest they should be looked on as throwing blame on those under whom they have been serving directly. My official reports indicate nothing wrong except the shortage of river transport which we are straining every nerve to supplement, and even that has only become a burning question since Force 'D' began to grow larger. I feel sure that everyone in Mesopotamia is doing his best but our very long river line is necessarily a great handicap and we cannot reproduce there these

French conditions which are due to good railways, good roads and abundance of motor transport.

But though I will leave no stone unturned to get at the actual facts, I would ask Your Excellency to remember that the experience of previous campaigns shows that such complaints are very often exaggerated by officers making general statements which are really based only on one particular incident.

The enquiry referred to was carried out by Surgeon-General MacNeece who went to Mesopotamia or, to be exact, to Basra, where he conferred with General Nixon. While he was thus engaged at Basra, matters were getting worse upriver. The sufferings of the wounded after the January battles, which were part of the attempt to relieve Townshend, were worse than those endured after Ctesiphon and rumours about the medical conditions became so loud and insistent that even Sir Beauchamp Duff was able to hear them. On 22 February he telegraphed to Sir Percy Lake, who had relieved Nixon in command of the Mesopotamian Force: 'Terrible stories are being received here as to treatment of wounded after Sheikh Saad and later battles and total want of proper medical arrangements. I fear a serious scandal is impending and I shall be compelled to send out a commission to enquire. It is imperative that all this should be improved before the next fight.'

This threat of a serious scandal had at last forced Sir Beauchamp Duff to act firmly and thus the Sir William Vincent and Major General A.H. Bingley Commission was born on 2 March. The results of this enquiry were swept up with those of the Mesopotamian Commission Enquiry of August 1916 and so brought to public attention.

This aspect of the medical situation – the tendency to cover up – went right down the chain of medical command, and as suggested above, Surgeon-General Hathaway was the chief culprit in this regard. In his relationship with the Director of Medical Services in India he either did not reveal the true state of affairs in certain instances, or his reports were misleading. He did not let him know about the conditions in the hospital in Amara and Orah, and he made out that there was a plentiful supply of vegetables and fresh meat in the rations. In a report on the water taken from the river he said: 'The water is absolutely safe, the only precaution being necessary is the sedimentation. The 'Wadi' water is precisely the Tigris water so is correspondingly safe.' Barely a month later, the Vincent-Bingley Commission condemned the measures taken for purifying the water from the rivers.

Wounded soldiers who had been evacuated from Ctesiphon were accommodated in the camp at Sheikh Saad, which was visited by the Vincent-Bingley Commission.

After the occupation of Sheikh Saad on the 9th January, about 2000 of the wounded were moved to the camp there, the remainder, numbering 1,200 being left in a camp on the left bank of the river at Musandaq in charge of a small medical staff. The conditions of the camps at Musandaq and Sheikh Saad have been described to us by various witnesses, and we are constrained to find that the arrangements for the accommodation and treatment there were very defective. The medical staff was so small that the wounds of many remained undressed for days. The camps were in a very insanitary condition. The supply of surgical stores and appliances ran short, and there was practically no subordinate staff to see to the welfare of the patients. The suffering and discomfort endured by the unfortunate wounded in these camps were very great, and even up to the 18th January, when the Meerut Stationary Hospital took over charge at Sheikh Saad, this condition of affairs continued there. The officer commanding the hospital describes the condition of that camp in the following words: 'On arrival here we found about 195 British and 800 Indian sick and wounded in an irregular camp situated on filthy muddy ground behind the village . . . There was one Indian temporary I.M.S Officer in charge of the Indians and he was ill. He had two sub-assistant surgeons and some of the personnel of an improvised cavalry field ambulance to help him. He had no dressings left, and many cases still had on the first field dressings which had been applied on the battlefield. About 200 of the patients had dysentery, and there were no proper latrine arrangements. The state of the camp was indescribable. Near the middle of the hospital tents was a pile of bags of atta etc., mostly ruined by the rain, which I was told represented 10 days rations.

A month later Surgeon-General Hathaway presented a report to the Indian Government in which he makes no mention of conditions that had previously existed at Sheikh Saad, but says: 'The Meerut Stationary Hospital is under canvas here [at Sheikh Saad], under

Major Goodbody, I.M.S. in excellent order, accommodating 607 cases, including 19 British; 277 of these are suffering from dysentery of a mild type. This hospital is worked in a thoroughly efficient manner.'

As described above, Major Carter tried to let the Indian authorities know about the situation after the Battle of Ctesiphon. Nixon intervened and ordered the Surgeon-General to deal with him with reference to his objectionable remarks. As a result, General Cowper, Assistant Quartermaster-General of the Mesopotamia Force, threatened to put him under arrest and get his hospital ship taken away from him for a meddlesome, interfering faddist.

Earlier, Colonel Hehir, who had been principal medical officer in Mesopotamia up to April 1915, was asked by the Director of Medical Services to give the benefit of his experience to Surgeon-General Hathaway when he arrived to take over, but the resentful reception his suggestions received was so unpleasant that he gave up.

Chapter Six

The Beginning of the Siege

(Maps 6, 7 and 8)

Townshend commenced his retirement down the Tigris at 1930 hrs on 25 November 1915, his rear being brought up by the naval flotilla, and reached Lajj five hours later. There he received news from the aircraft and cavalry of the approach of some 12,000 Turkish infantry and he decided on a further retreat to Aziziya some 22 miles further south. Here he halted for two days in order to complete the evacuation of the wounded and stores. By now the Arabs were becoming a nuisance. When the *Shaitan* went aground and was being unloaded she and the other ships came under fire at close quarters from Arabs on both banks. In response from a request from the Senior Naval Officer, Townshend sent out a section of field guns with the Cavalry Brigade who drove them off, leaving a hundred dead behind them, speared and shaken off the lances of the Indian cavalry like ripe fruit.

The retirement continued to Umm-ut-Tubul, the weary soldiers reaching it late on 30 November and spending the night there. But Townshend got little rest, being woken up to be told of the proximity of the body of Turks earlier estimated at about 12,000 men. How they had managed to catch up with the British force is a mystery. According to Turkish accounts, their cavalry, whose duties included reconnaissance in advance of their infantry, had spent the night in drunkenness amongst the plunder left behind by the British at Aziziya, and, setting out in the morning, were behind their main body, reporting its movements as those of the enemy. But the

Turkish infantry still managed to bump into the British.

The British Commander ordered his transport column to move out at 0630 hrs and as the characteristically sudden eastern daylight appeared, the British artillery and gunboats saw a host of white tents on the higher ground behind them 2,000 yards off. The field guns were in the process of packing up but they could not miss such a target and within two minutes they were in action, cutting great gaps in the tents and in the columns of panic-stricken Turks. But it wasn't long before the Turks replied.

Captain Mousley of the Royal Field Artillery gives us a picture of General Townshend as the carts and the rearguard were hastily packing up around him:

> One could not but feel the keenest admiration for General Townshend, so steady, collected and determined in action, so kind, quick and confident. There, totally indifferent to the shell fire, he stood watching the issue, receiving reports from the various orderly officers and giving every attention to the progress of the transport. Some shells pitched just over us, one, not fifteen yards away, killing a horse and wounding some drivers . . . More than once I caught a humorous smile on the General's face as some shell just missed us.
>
> (From his book *The Secrets of a Kuttite*)

One Turkish regiment with two mountain guns had gone astray during the night and at daybreak found itself at the river bank south-west of the British camp. It opened fire on the *Comet* and *Shaitan*, setting them on fire. Both had to be abandoned. HMS *Firefly* was hit in her boiler and was likewise left to the Turks who subsequently used her to pelt shells into Kut. She might have been sunk by the *Sumana*'s 12-pdr gun but aboard the *Firefly* lay a poor fellow in the engine room, still alive but terribly scalded by the escaping steam. His state was so dreadful that it was impossible to move him so he was given a merciful dose of morphia and left where he lay. The *Firefly* was later recaptured in the advance to Baghdad and returned to the Royal Navy, one of twelve Admiralty gunboats built for the shallow Tigris. They were extremely handy vessels since they drew only 2 feet 9 inches and were described as the 'Fly' class.

About nine o'clock, General Melliss' Cavalry Brigade, having set out in advance of the main body appeared through the dust to the south-east and threw back the Turkish infantry who were mustering

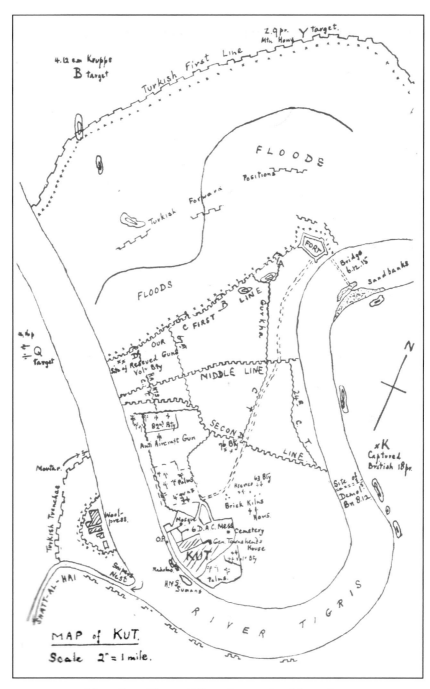

Map 6.   Plan of Kut drawn by Mousley.

to attack. The British batteries were limbering up one by one and following the transport before gradually outdistancing the Turks who were being kept off by the cavalry.

Townshend was thus able to commence his retirement at 1930 hrs. He was determined to shake off pursuit by marching the 26 miles to Qala Shadi, which his troops accomplished, half awake and shambling with Mousley acting as guide and losing his way twice. The march became a nightmare in ten hours of cold and darkness. They arrived in the early hours of the next morning at a place called Monkey Village where they bivouacked on the sandy soil, scraping hollows for their bodies and making sand pillows for their heads. The cold was intense and it was by no means quiet for Arab snipers were active and sections of the force had to take turns crossing a tiny stone bridge over a deep nullah.

Mousley described the operation: 'The scene was of the wildest confusion. Camels were being thrashed across, kicking mules hauled across, troops trying to cross at the same time. Several overturned vehicles complicated matters. The whole force had to cross the tiny bridge. After all had crossed the sappers blew it up.'

The *Sumana* and the other craft were having difficulties in coping with the low water in the river, every vessel repeatedly running aground. After abandoning the *Shaitan* and the *Comet* they came across more of the transport craft aground. While the *Sumana* managed to get some of them going again, a launch, a motorboat and a barge containing sick and wounded had to be abandoned. A few days later the Turks sent these men into the British camp, saying that as they had so many of their own wounded to attend to, they could not look after them.

At daybreak on 2 December, the retirement was resumed All were hungry and exhausted, and transport carts behind the column picked up stragglers as they fell out. After 18 miles they bivouacked 3 miles short of Kut and some bread was sent out to them. It was colder than ever and the weary soldiers were faced with another night in the open. No lights could be shown as Arabs swarmed on the opposite bank of the river. On 3 December the retirement of 44 miles in thirty-six hours was completed with very little food and water, and Kut was reached.

On the same day, Townshend telegraphed to General Nixon: 'I mean to defend Kut as I did Chitral.' Chitral was a fort in the state of that name on the north-west frontier in what is now Pakistan, which he had successfully defended in 1895. Townshend went on to say that he would make Kut into an entrenched camp, but typically he was soon reviewing the situation after he received a telegram from Nixon that told him that a force would be concentrated at Ali Gharbi and hoped to effect relief within two months. Townshend was taken aback by this timescale and concluded that if he was not relieved for two months the whole Turkish army would be round him and he would be forced to surrender. He felt that his position was insecure, as he was confined in a narrow peninsula, but now that his troops were rested, he still had time to withdraw to Ali Gharbi.

Nixon replied that he did not approve of the decision to fall back again, and that Townshend was fulfilling the duties of a detachment by holding up superior numbers of the enemy. He was counting on receiving the reinforcement of two divisions by the end of the month and then would immediately begin the relief. He was also hopeful of some co-operation from the Russians who had increased their forces in north-west Persia and might be persuaded to march on Baghdad. So he considered that by standing at Kut the British would be materially assisting the Russian commander, General Baratov, in his advance since he would have less ground to cover. After this tirade, Townshend seemed to become resigned to staying where he was and reported a couple of days later that he was already practically surrounded.

In subsequent weeks there was a flurry of telegrams between Nixon, India and the Secretary of State in London about reinforcements, the situation in the oilfields and at Nasiriya, and the policy in regard to Mesopotamia. Eventually Mr Chamberlain made the following points to the Viceroy in India that sum up clearly the British Government's attitude to the situation in the Middle East. At this time Gallipoli had been evacuated without any loss but that did not make the picture any less gloomy:

From the point of view of the Empire, France and Flanders are the main theatres of war, so that every effort must be made to concentrate maximum strength there but adequate force must be maintained in Egypt for its defence.

The mission of the Mesopotamia force was to be of a defensive nature and for the present you must rely on the existing garrison in India reinforced by twelve more garrison battalions for its defence.

Under existing conditions no hope can be held out that the two additional divisions that Nixon had asked for can be spared.

After relieving Townshend, Nixon's policy should be to act on the defensive so defensive positions should at once be prepared in the Qurna and Shaiba areas in case withdrawal from Kut should become necessary.

By this time, Nixon was becoming ill and this disappointment must have contributed to his state of mind. He was still optimistic, still anxious to push on, and, typically, his strategy was still purely opportunist. Although the decision to stand at Kut – a matter on which the whole safety of the campaign depended – was originally made by a subordinate commander, Townshend, it was backed by him even though he knew the General Staff in India favoured further withdrawal and thought he was overreaching himself in the usual way by deciding to hold a position so far in in advance of his main force. In the event he was still neglecting sound military principles because of the fatal attraction of Baghdad and of the fancied necessity for upholding British reputation in the Middle East by refusing to give up ground. He must have been aware that to attempt to bolster prestige by risking General Townshend's division 300 miles from its base was simply unsound from the tactical point of view.

On 6 December, the General Staff in India, after calculating that by the middle of January the Turks might be able to concentrate sufficient men and guns in the vicinity of Kut to contain Townshend's force and at the same time have some 20,000 men to oppose the relieving force, and taking into consideration the various advantages and disadvantages of holding on to Kut, arrived at the conclusion that the risk of holding Kut outweighed the advantages. They therefore considered that Kut ought to be evacuated if it were still possible to do so. But it was too late, even if they could bring themselves to order Nixon to carry out the withdrawal.

So by 7 December, although Townshend was shut up in Kut and reinforcements were slowly approaching, pushed up the river piecemeal and without organization, Nixon was still left to manage by India, without adequate administrative staff to cope with the new situation.

The town of Kut stood on a peninsula about 2 miles long and one mile wide. It was situated in the south-western corner alongside the Tigris with a river frontage. Opposite it across the Tigris at that time was the village of Yakasub which was occupied by the British and

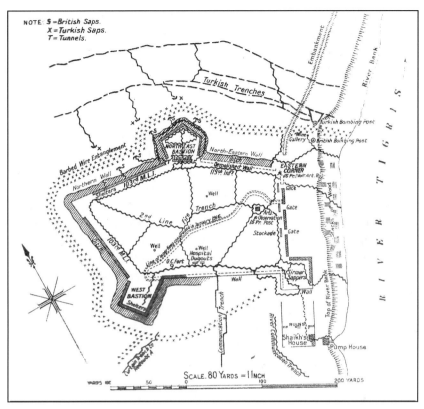

NOTE: **S** =British Saps.
X =Turkish Saps.
T =Tunnels.

Map 7.   Plan of fort at Kut

surrounded by a trench and barbed wire. This place was more commonly referred to by the British as the Woolpress Village or the Liquorice Factory after the two principal establishments there. Around Woolpress Village the Turkish sapping eventually brought them right up to the British wire but their main trench line was some 1,600 yards to the south-west.

At Kut the narrow peninsula was defended by three sets of British trenches fronted by barbed wire and linked by communication trenches. The front line crossed at the mouth of the peninsula and cut it off from the desert to the north-west. Some of the advanced Turkish trenches were eventually 500 yards from the British front line, although their first line was at least 800 yards off and their third line over 2,000 yards away. From the advanced trenches the Turks sapped up to the British wire, especially around the fort which lay at the north-eastern extremity of the British front line 2,000 yards north of the town and was the scene of the most dangerous attack of the whole siege. The town consisted of a dense collection of about 650 buildings and huts, built more or less haphazardly. There were some better-built two-storey houses, about 200 shops, several cafés and a few wool storehouses, some built of fired brick but most of mud brick. Many of the shops and cafés were in a covered bazaar, consisting of a series of inter-connecting colonnades with roofs and a large number of small stalls. Roads inside the town ran east–west, the main one joining another running north–south near the river frontage.

Most of the 6,000 inhabitants were Arabs but there were some Jews, Sabians and Nestorian Christians, practically all living in squalor, with no drainage system and no sanitation. Rubbish and other unmentionable things were just piled in the streets and alleys, on the water-frontage and around the perimeter, so that the place stank.

The fort had been built by the British during the preceding weeks and from it a line of four redoubts, holding ten or twelve men each, ran south-westwards across the mouth of the loop of the river, joined by barbed wire – it was this line that became the British front line. Like the redoubts the fort was mud-built. It had a north-eastern and a western bastion (see Map 7) opposite which, on the right bank of the Tigris, was a line of Turkish sniping posts that were later extended down to the Sand Hills at the most easterly part of the bend of the river.

According to the strict military principles that General Townshend tried to adhere to as far as his mercurial nature would allow, the native population should be turned out of the place but Townshend was uneasy on this point and asked Sir Percy Cox for a view. Cox, as Chief Political Officer, was not happy with the effect that it would have on the Arab population of the Middle East by sending out into the desert in the wintry weather and bitterly cold nights, men, women and children, most of whom were likely to perish. Townshend thereupon decided to allow all authentic house-holders to remain with their families. His staff calculated that there was sufficient food in the town to feed the 6,000 people that were left for three months. Supplies for the troops, both for the British and the Indians, would last for two months on full rations. But as a reserve, the military governor and supply officer were told to buy up whatever grain and other supplies that they could find in the town.

All the sick and wounded and Sir Percy Cox were sent down to Amara along with the river transport, and the cavalry departed on 6 December leaving as a garrison about 7,000 combatant infantry, together with gunners and a few technical troops. The gunners had forty-three guns including quick-firers, howitzers, and naval guns.

After they had gone the bridge across the Tigris below the town was destroyed in a gallant action by two subalterns from the Royal Engineers and the 2/7th Gurkhas. They crossed the bridge with charges strapped to their backs to ensure that the explosion would happen even if they were hit, with the Turks in force at the other end. Both got back safely.

Townshend had taken up his quarters in a two-storey building in the centre of the town. It had a courtyard and a flat roof used for observation where he spent a lot of his time with his telescope. From there his signallers sent instructions by heliograph to the perimeter of the enceinte. The heliograph, an ancient device, worked by reflecting sunlight in flashes from a movable mirror using morse code.

On 9 December the Turks heavily shelled the town and the defences that were still under construction, and kept it up during the two following days. Stacks of fodder and food were destroyed by a fire in the town and nearly 200 men were killed on the first day, although casualties declined after that. On the 10th the Turks attacked the north-western side of the defences by sapping up close to the wire and slinging bombs, but they were so close that the Indians of 16 Brigade calmly drove them off with accurate rifle fire. Meanwhile others advancing close to the fort at the north-eastern corner of the enceinte occupied irrigation channels adjacent to it and started digging and sapping forward all round the northern and eastern walls.

In response, a trench raid was arranged by the British on the night of the 17th which killed forty Turks and took eleven prisoner. The British had only one man slightly wounded and they discovered that the Turks had not got as far as tunnelling to undermine the walls as they had feared. But, next morning, the Turks returned to the spot and continued to sap forward, confirming that this heralded an imminent attack on the fort.

Having been hastily built of mud brick by the British after their capture of the town, the walls of the fort were not sturdy enough to stand much in the way of bombardment, so low-level loopholes were cut through them and trenches dug inside. Across the entrance to the north-eastern bastion where the Turks had been digging, a blockade was built in case it collapsed and was rushed by the enemy.

Before first light on 24 December the Turks opened fire on Woolpress village with a heavy gun and this bombardment continued until 0830 hrs, but no assault followed. Meanwhile at 0700 hrs an even heavier bombardment was opened on the town, the northern defences and the fort, when it became clear that their main interest was in the fort which had the fire of twenty-two guns directed at it from positions in a half circle stretching from the north-west to the river on the south-east.

Bit by bit the mud walls crumbled until great gaps opened up and the defenders could see the Turkish trenches through them. The north-eastern bastion was soon made indefensible. Some time between eleven o'clock and noon the Turks scrambled out of their trenches and charged, the larger numbers making for the crumbled bastion until it was surrounded by a mass of yellow jackets and long Turkish bayonets. The Ox and Bucks bombarded them with their home-made 'jam-pot' bombs, while four machine-guns poured bullets into the screaming mass. The Turks continued to send forward reinforcements and were able to force their way into the bastion but after half an hour they began to waver in the face of the determined resistance and finally turned and ran.

On the north-eastern wall the enemy was engaged by the infantry of the 119th but, as elsewhere, the attack died away. The afternoon was fairly quiet but the garrison of the fort knew that it was a quiet that preceded a storm and at 2000 hrs, with the moon just rising, the Turks came again. As they charged at the bastion, smoke, dust and the difficult light produced by the flares made it impossible for the defenders to see clearly. In the confined space, the noise of rifles, machine-guns and bombs was deafening, with the Turkish war cries adding an unearthly touch to the scene.

A bomb landing behind the right-hand end of the stockade across the entrance to the bastion killed or wounded most of the defenders on that side, and for a short time the situation was extremely threatening, but reinforcements were gathered together and rushed up so that the moment passed.

At eleven o'clock further reinforcements in the shape of the 48th Pioneers joined the defenders of the stockade and they finally settled the matter. The Turks withdrew and at 0230 hrs they launched a final, desperate assault but the Pioneers held and the last serious attempt during the siege by the Turks to take Kut by assault was at an end. Norfolks from the town arrived to take over from the Pioneers while the attacks on the northern and north-eastern walls were repulsed finally by the 103rd Mahrattas and the Ox and Bucks. Thus Christmas Day 1915 dawned.

The Turks suffered at least 2,000 casualties while the garrison had 382 killed or wounded, most in the north-eastern bastion.

New Year 1916 began with the town encircled by the Turkish XVIII Corps, made up of the 45th and 51st Divisions, and the British relief route blocked by XIII Corps with its 35th and 52nd Divisions about 18 miles further downstream. Nureddin was still not happy with the arrival of a German general especially after the repulse of Townshend's force from Ctesiphon. However, despite this success, on 20 January he was replaced by Halil Bey as commander of the Turkish forces in Mesopotamia.

In Kut it was very cold, made worse by the shortage of food and continual Turkish shelling and rifle fire, although some of the Turkish shells were so old that they ended up in one piece rather than exploding – in one small area, some sixty of these were lying amongst the shell holes of those that had made a more successful landing. Mousley describes how one 40-pdr shell ended up in an artillery mess, having ploughed a path through several feet of soil, beams and iron girders, before being reinserted in the hole it had made above the door of the dugout with its nose pointing directly at the table.

Lieutenant General Aylmer had come from India to take over the command of the Tigris Corps and was faced very soon by a demand from Townshend – who had at first estimated that he had rations for one month for British troops and two months for Indians – to be relieved by the middle of January. Aylmer estimated that by 3 January, the date by which he would have to start to advance to comply with Townshend's request, he would have only the 7th Division, the Cavalry Brigade and one infantry brigade ready to set off. The rest of the Tigris Corps would not be ready until three weeks later. However, Nixon, still impatient, ordered him to advance from Ali Gharbi, where Aylmer had concentrated his force, with Sheikh Saad as his objective.

On hearing that Townshend had repulsed the Turks on Christmas Eve, Aylmer decided that the position was now less critical and he had a little more time in hand, so he ordered Major General Younghusband, commanding the 7th Division, not to make a decisive attack on the Turks at Sheikh Saad but merely to pin them in their positions until he himself could bring up the rest of the Tigris Corps.

Aylmer was relieving Townshend for the second time in his career, having been part of the force that had raised the siege of Chitral. He had won the VC in a frontier war in 1891 by blowing in the gate of Nilt Fort despite being severely wounded. Clearly a brave man, he was an uninspiring leader with a dreary personality. Gertrude Bell met him in 1921 and commented in a letter: 'How he got to be a Lt. General is a mystery to me. The more I see of him the more colourless, indecisive and nervous I think him. The only fixed opinions he holds are violent prejudices, under the fostering influence of which I am rapidly becoming pro-German and pro-Bolshevik.'

His force was a heterogeneous one, being a mixture of units that had arrived from the Western Front and from India. The soldiers from the Western Front were not happy about their transfer far from home, were used to very different fighting conditions and felt that they were being transferred from a major theatre of operations to a sideshow. In the 7th Division, 35 Brigade was from India but had recently been formed and had little training and experience as a brigade. The other Indian brigade, 28 Brigade, was of longer standing and had served as a unit in Egypt. 19 Brigade was an improvised formation and only one unit, the 1st Seaforth Highlanders, properly belonged to it. In fact, the British soldiers stood up better to the Mesopotamian conditions than the Indian troops and far fewer of them fell ill.

Land transport was allocated to the force. High-explosive shells were scarce, there were too few aircraft for proper observation, telephone equipment for the batteries was old and inadequate and many of the guns and howitzers themselves were of ancient pattern and inefficient. As we have seen, medical equipment was totally inadequate. Calculated on the pre-war Indian frontier scale, the medical personnel and field hospitals were only sufficient for roughly one-third of the force which began its advance from Ali Gharbi. At least the force was accompanied by four newly built gunboats of the 'Fly' class, the *Gadfly* being the flagship of the Senior Naval Officer – once again Captain Nunn, back from leave.

General Younghusband started his advance on both banks of the river on 4 January with the river transport moving abreast of the two columns and three gunboats in the lead. At 1430 hrs the next day they reached a point about 12 miles from Sheikh Saad where they bivouacked. About 2½ miles from the town the Turks had constructed trenches on both sides of the river and it looked as though they were determined to make a stand there – they were a different class of troops from those faced by the British in previous battles. These were Ozmanlis, well organized and led and, what was more important, they came flushed with success from their recent victory at Gallipoli.

The next morning's advance was delayed by dense mist. Younghusband's main body was on the left bank with a smaller force opposite on the right bank. When they were 800 yards away from the Turkish trenches, the 37th Dogras, the leading battalion, came under fire from both rifles and field guns – and the mirage had now come down. Together with the 97th Infantry who had come up to their support, the Dogras began to dig in.

On the other side of the river, the advance of 6 Cavalry Brigade was upset by irrigation ditches which eventually brought them to a halt and they opened fire on the other impediment to the British advance – Arab attacks from the flank. By now the infantry were coming under heavy rifle and machine-gun fire, made worse by the length of the Turkish trench line which extended much further from the river than they had expected. But by 1530 hrs they were within 300 yards of the enemy trenches whose actual positions were often difficult to locate, owing to the mirage and the Turkish skill at disguising them even in that absolutely flat, desert landscape. Turkish fire was not interrupted by the mirage since it was simply a matter of firing in the general direction of the advancing troops – there was a good chance of hitting someone as long as they kept their fire low.

At this point General Younghusband decided that no further progress was possible that day and ordered his forward troops to dig in and take up battle outposts for the night in the positions they had reached. These proved to be vulnerable even after dark for the Turks kept up a heavy fire throughout the night hours, which also interfered with the carrying parties sent back to fetch ammunition and water from the rear area. They were not helped, either, by the heavy rain.

The river transport anchored further downstream where

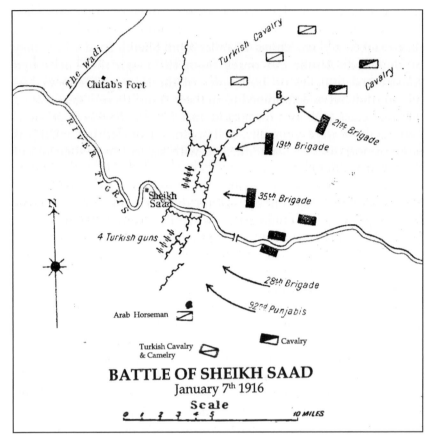

Map 8.   Battle of Sheikh Saad

Younghusband had ordered a boat bridge to be built. Hampered by the rain and wind, the sappers were not able to complete it until after noon the next day.

On this day, 7 January, General Younghusband issued orders for a fresh attack to begin at 1100 hrs on the left bank of the river. The troops, both British and Indian, moved forward doggedly with the Buffs, the Black Watch, the Seaforths and six Indian battalions leading. Turkish fire was heavy but the British artillery was not very effective as the mirage and the sun made it very difficult to locate the Turkish trenches precisely. This patient advance continued all day and by dusk the leading troops were within three or four hundred yards of the enemy, having suffered very badly from the shelling and,

90

as they got closer, the haphazard but still dangerous rifle fire. They dug themselves in at last light while the rain fell and a bitter wind sprang up to add to the discomforts of the night.

On the right bank of the Tigris, the cavalry spent the day fending off the Arab horseman to their left using machine-guns while the infantry advanced aided by the fire from the 28th Battery, the only field guns available to support the advance. It was a dour struggle inching forward under heavy fire but a fine bout of madness suddenly seized the leading troops. Together the Leicestershires and the 51st Sikhs stood up and, followed by the 53rd and 92nd Infantry, carried the Turkish front line in one storming rush. The second line was quickly overrun together with two mountain guns 400 yards behind. Over 300 Turks were killed. Further movement was prevented by the honeycomb of irrigations cuts that fanned out from the river and the heavy Turkish fire which had the range of their own trenches now occupied by the British and Indian soldiers.

Next day, the 8th, the exhaustion of the troops prevented any further advance. During that night, the wounded were removed and ammunition, water and food were brought up in the continuous heavy rain.

On the morning of the 9th it was still raining, finally stopping at 0845 hrs. Early morning patrols came back with the news that the Turks were turning their backs and making off, whereupon General Aylmer gave the order to advance. Sheikh Saad was occupied while the Turks retired upstream to Ora (Wadi), some 35 miles by river from Kut. The heavy rain had turned the sandy ground into glutinous mud, making effective and continuous pursuit impossible.

At this point, General Nixon's health, which had been uncertain for some weeks, completely broke down and he asked to be relieved. Up to the battle of Ctesiphon, when luck had been with him and the Turkish resistance was not as strong as it was later to become, he had achieved an unbroken series of successes. It might be said that self-confidence had carried him through although others have suggested that this often strayed onto the side of over-confidence. But by his ability, determination and the confidence he inspired in his force he had overcome to a large extent the problems brought about by limited means. He has been described as a great commander and to the extent that no commander in history has been great without a large measure of good luck, it is perhaps partly true.

Lord Hardinge's tribute is probably just: 'It is by men of his grit and stamp . . . that the British Empire has been built up.'

His successor was Lieutenant General Sir Percy Lake who came from the office of Chief of the General Staff in India. General Townshend, in his book, tells of the arrival of the new Turkish commander, Field Marshal von der Goltz, with his staff, in front of Kut on an inspection of the Turkish lines. One of the British guns in the fort fired on the group who dived into a trench. Townshend says that he was very annoyed with the officer who ordered the gun to be trained on the Field Marshal without his orders for he had a great respect for the man whom he considered to be the leading strategist in Europe. He ordered the fire to cease at once. Later, he learnt that the Field Marshal had been lucky to escape being hit.

Meanwhile, Kut was being bombed by German planes. Mousley describes one such experience:

> The first indication of his visit comes from the alarm gong which hangs near the river front observation post. All eyes strain skyward and a little black speck scarce distinguishable from a bird dots the blue sky. It approaches and our improvised air-gun, a 13-pounder worked on a circular traverse at high angle, has a pot at it. This gun was set up by Major Harvey, R.F.A., our adjutant, a most efficient gunnery expert from Shoeburyness. He worked out the mathematics, too, with schemes of ranging in the two planes, perpendicular and horizontal. A little white puff of cloud appears near the plane and one hears the report. Then another shot is fired and the plane mounts or swerves and still comes on. His propeller and engine are heard quite distinctly as he gets within range. A fierce burst of rifle fire and the still sharper Maxim gun's staccato music is the signal for all to take cover. One sees him now directly over the Gurkha regiment bivouacs and hears a faint hissing noise as of rapidly spinning propellers. The hissing increases for several seconds until it becomes quite loud and terminates with a crashing explosion. One bomb has dropped. The air is full of other hissing things in various stages of their careers. A creepy feeling suggests that the bomb with its tiny propellers rapidly spinning, is going to pitch on top of one's head and blot one out of existence, like stamping out an ant. It strikes a building a hundred yards off and the resounding smash of falling timber is caught up by another smash which has struck earth, a third has landed in the hospital,

scattering death all around, a fourth has splashed pieces of horse-flesh and hair on the surrounding walls and trees.

All these are captured bombs. A Tommy today observed that the Turks were flinging our bombs around as if they belonged to him. Another wag suggested Fritz was merely returning them.

Troops trapped with Townshend in Kut el Amara

Infantry:
    16 Infantry Brigade comprising:
        2nd Dorsetshire Regiment
        66th Punjabis
        104th Rifles
        117th Mahrattas
    17 Infantry Brigade comprising:
        1st Oxfordshire and Buckinghamshire Light Infantry
        22nd Punjabis
        103rd Mahrattas
        119th Infantry
    18 Infantry Brigade comprising:
        2nd Norfolk Regiment
        7th Rajputs
        120th Infantry
    30 Infantry Brigade comprising:
        Half Battalion, Queen's Own Royal West Kent Regiment
        One company 1/4th Hampshire Regiment
        24th Punjabis
        76th Punjabis
        2/7th Gurkhas
        Half Battalion, 67th Punjabis

Pioneers: 48th Pioneers

Cavalry comprising:
    One squadron, 23rd Cavalry
    One squadron, 7th Lancers

Royal Engineers comprising:
    Bridging Train

17th Company, Sappers and Miners
22nd Company, Sappers and Miners
Sirmur Company, Imperial Service Sappers
Engineer Field Park

Artillery comprising:
10th Brigade RFA comprising:
63rd Battery
76th Battery
82nd Battery
1/5th Hants Howitzer Battery
86th Heavy Battery RGA (5-inch guns)
One section, 104th Heavy Battery (15-pdr)
One spare 18-pdr gun
6th Divisional Ammunition Column
Two 13-pdr guns of 'S' Battery, RHA

Miscellaneous comprising:
Maxim Battery (6 machine-guns)
Detachment, Army Signal Company
34th Divisional Signal Company
One Brigade section, 12th Divisional Signal Company
Wireless section (two wagon and one pack set)
A few details, Royal Flying Corps
Supply and Transport personnel, including details of the Jaipur
    Transport Corps and of the 13th, 21st, 26th and 30th Mule
    Corps
No. 32 Field Post Office
Three Chaplains comprising a C of E, a RC and a Methodist

Medical Units comprising:
No. 2 Field Ambulance
No. 4 Field Ambulance
No. 106 Field Ambulance
No. 157 Indian Stationary Hospital
No. 9 Indian General Hospital
Half No. 3A British General Hospital
Officers' Hospital
One section, Veterinary Field Hospital

Naval Detachment comprising:
  HMS *Sumana* (gunboat, one 12-pdr and two 3-pdr guns. Two
    guns later mounted ashore.)
  Four steam launches. Three sunk when bridge was pulled down.
  Two motor launches
  Six barges
  Four 4.7-inch guns in horse-boats
  One 12-pdr gun mounted ashore

Relieving Force

6 Cavalry Brigade comprising:
  'S' Battery RHA (four guns)
  14th Hussars
  7th Lancers (less one squadron)
  33rd Cavalry (less one squadron)
  4th Cavalry
  Cavalry Brigade Ammunition Column
  Cavalry Brigade Signal Troop

Infantry comprising:
  28 Infantry Brigade comprising:
    2nd Leicestershire Regiment
    51st Sikhs
    53rd Sikhs
    56th Rifles
  35 Infantry Brigade comprising:
    1/5th Buffs (East Kent Regiment)
    37th Dogras
    97th Infantry
    102nd Grenadiers
  19 Infantry Brigade comprising:
    1st Seaforth Highlanders
    28th Punjabis
    92nd Punjabis
    125th Rifles

Three Brigade signal sections
13th Company Sappers and Miners, and Bridging Train
128th Pioneers

No. 20 Combined Field Ambulance
Half No. 3 Combined Field Ambulance
Artillery comprising:
  9th Brigade RFA
  20th Brigade RFA
  28th Battery RFA
    (together eighteen 18-pounder guns).
  1/1st Sussex Battery RFA (four 15-pounder guns)
  Heavy Artillery Brigade comprising:
    72nd Heavy Battery (four 5-inch howitzers)
    77th Heavy Battery (four 5-inch howitzers)
    One section 104th Heavy Battery (two 4-inch guns)

Other Units under Corps Commander comprising:
  16th Cavalry (less one squadron)
  107th Pioneers
  1/4th Hampshire Regiment (less one company)
  One company, 67th Punjabis
  1st Provisional Battalion (drafts for the Kut garrison)
  23rd Mountain Battery (less one section), four guns
  One 15-pounder post gun (of Volunteer Artillery Battery)
  One Brigade section of a signal company
  Four wireless stations (one wagon and three packs)
  Medical units comprising:
    No. 18 Cavalry Field Ambulance, one British and one Indian
      section
    No. 131 Indian Cavalry Field Ambulance, of three Indian
      Sections
    No. 1 Field Ambulance of two sections
    Nos 5 and 6 Field Ambulances, improvised, consisting of two
      sections each

Transport comprising:
  1,353 pack mules
  865 carts with draught animals.

Royal Flying Corps with two aircraft

Reinforcements joining above force between the 4th and later in January 1916

6th Jats (21 Infantry Brigade)
9th Bhopal Infantry (7 Infantry Brigade)
41st Dogras (19 Infantry Brigade)
7th Division Ammunition Column
Divisional Staff (7th Division)
Staffs of 9 and 21 Infantry Brigades
2nd Black Watch (21 Infantry Brigade)
62nd Punjabis (36 Infantry Brigade)
2nd Rajputs (21 Infantry Brigade)
61st Howitzer Battery (7th Division), six 4.5-inch
howitzers

Naval Flotilla comprising:
    HM Gunboats *Butterfly*, *Dragonfly*, *Cranefly* and *Gadfly*
    Two minesweeping launches

Chapter Seven

Attempts at Relief

(Maps 9, 10, 11 and 12)

In front of the British on the road to Kut along the left bank of the Tigris was a long and narrow passage between the river on the left and the Suwacha Marsh on the right. This was the Hanna Defile, a passage that General Aylmer knew was going to be very difficult to negotiate. It was while he was preparing for this next advance that he was heartened by news that the Turks had set up a new position at the Wadi, not within the defile but 3½ miles in front of it. This meant that, although their right flank rested on the river, their left flank simply ended in the desert. In military parlance, this represented a flank that could be turned – in other words, a detachment could get round it and attack the enemy line from the rear.

It was an opportunity that he would not have if the Turks were established within the Hanna defile, with both flanks securely protected by the marsh and the river. He decided to take advantage of the opportunity. To give the impression that he meant to remain where he was for the time being, he ordered General Kemball to send two of his battalions up the right bank to a position about 5 miles upstream while his own force began to dig in.

According to a report from one of the aircraft, the main Turkish force was on the left bank with their troops entrenched in a line along the far side of the Wadi stream that flowed into the Tigris at this point. This stream was said to be easily fordable.

Aylmer decided on a night advance along with the gunboats that

98

would co-operate in the attack. He himself would sail with the Navy in the *Medjidieh*.

The night of 12/13 January proved to be cold and clear with bright moonlight; in the morning there was mist that soon cleared. A forward Turkish position was driven back by the naval guns and the Corps Artillery, but that was the only opposition encountered until they reached the Wadi that was indeed easily fordable by troops, although the steep banks were an obstacle for the guns and the transport which did not manage to get across until after dark the next night.

At noon, the infantry were in contact with the Turks who, realizing that they were about to be outflanked by the 7th Division and the Cavalry Brigade, moved to their left and entrenched behind an irrigation channel that ran back from the Wadi. Here they put up a stout resistance to the outflanking movement.

Meanwhile 28 Brigade was advancing directly towards the Wadi and came under fierce fire when they got to within 500 yards of it. The Turks had set up sticks in the ground in front of them at hundred yard intervals thus providing a convenient aid to their riflemen who took full advantage of them. Despite a courageous rush by the 56th Rifles and the 53rd Sikhs they were unable to get closer to the Turkish line than two or three hundred yards.

The attack was abandoned for the night, which turned out to be another wet and bitterly cold one. When the frozen troops were roused in the morning they found that the Turks had gone during the hours of darkness to take up a position within the Hanna Defile. The British had lost over 2,700 killed and wounded, the latter suffering very much in the terrible conditions of high winds, cold rain and exposure. Both the medical personnel and the transport for bringing the wounded back to the river and for carrying them down to hospitals were, as usual, totally inadequate.

The attack might well have succeeded if there had been a better means of communicating between the various elements of the British force, and if there had been better maps and methods of pinpointing the positions of the units in the featureless desert, which by now was turning into a mass of clogging, clinging mud in the continuous rain.

This fact helps to answer the question as to why the British did not go round the Suwacha Marsh. To do so would have meant a march of 50 miles in those horrendous conditions, coping not only

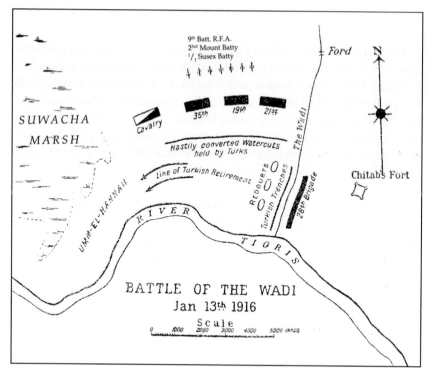

Map 9.   Battle of the Wadi

with the mud but with the irrigation ditches that were everywhere, many of them hundreds of years old, but still presenting very awkward obstacles to wheeled vehicles. If it had been possible to get round, one practicable passage running due south to Kut would probably have been open.

On 15 January, the day after the battle, General Aylmer decided to push forward towards the enemy's new positions that night, but even this movement became impossible as heavy rain continued to pour down and the river began to rise in flood. The troops found that they were completely bogged after a few yards and any movement covered both them and their weapons in clinging slime.

General Townshend now made a third estimate of his food supplies and ability to hold out and announced that he could survive no longer than 3 February. In view of this pronouncement, General Aylmer decided that, because he could not anticipate what hold-ups might occur, particularly in the prevailing weather conditions, he ought to push forward as soon as possible and cover some ground at least.

Consequently, at 1830 hrs on 20 January he issued orders for a dawn attack the next day by the 7th Division on the left bank, aided by a preliminary bombardment from the guns of the *Cranefly* and the *Dragonfly*, and fire from guns, howitzers and riflemen ferried across to the right bank of the Tigris. From there they could enfilade the Turkish trenches at Hanna, which offered a good target, consisting, as they did, of two lines with barbed wire in front and a series of communication trenches behind that stretched down to the river.

Morning mist caused a delay in starting the bombardment but when it lifted on to the Turkish second line, the troops on the other bank dashed to the assault despite a withering rifle fire. The Black Watch and the Jats overran the Turks' front-line trench, taking over some 150 yards of it and building barriers at each end to block attempts at recapture. It was a promising start.

The rest of the attackers were not so successful, suffering severe casualties from the accurate rifle fire. Attempts to reinforce the troops in the captured trench gradually came to nothing and in the face of furious attacks from the enemy who had broken through the barriers, what was left of the Black Watch and the Jats were forced to evacuate.

By 1115 hrs the attack had definitely stalled, so General Younghusband gave orders for a fresh attack to be pressed home after another ten-minute artillery bombardment. At this point the weather broke once more. The wind got up and the rain again turned the whole area into glutinous mud. Telephonic communication, never very effective at the best of times from brigades back to divisional HQ, broke down completely. When the infantry started their attack after the inadequate bombardment, the men got up from the ground soaked and numbed by the biting gale and attempted to stumble forward through the mud that was now knee-deep in some places.

A discussion now took place between General Younghusband and General Aylmer's senior staff officer who had come up to assess the situation, telephonic communication now being out of the question. Younghusband told him that in view of the conditions he intended to order a withdrawal. As he announced this decision, he was under the misapprehension that the staff officer had authority to approve

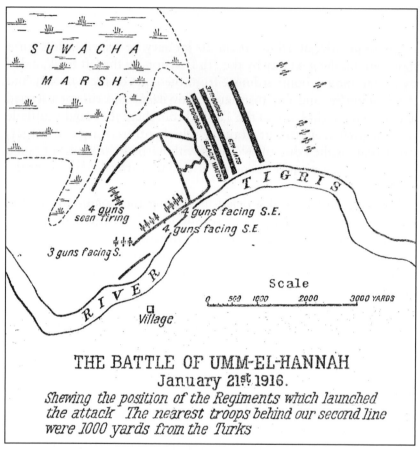

THE BATTLE OF UMM-EL-HANNAH
January 21st 1916.
Shewing the position of the Regiments which launched
the attack The nearest troops behind our second line
were 1000 yards from the Turks

Map 10.   Battle of Umm-el-Hanna

of the proposed action. However, this was not the case and when General Aylmer heard the news he was dumbfounded since Younghusband still had four battalions in reserve and, in his opinion, need not give up ground that he had won. But it was too late to rescind the order and the retirement had taken place.

That night the men, drenched and exhausted, passed a miserable night in the waterlogged trenches they had returned to. Rifles had become clogged with mud and, in the conditions and without the necessary materials, were very difficult to clean. There was little food and no hot drinks. When the wind dropped, the marsh froze. The wounded could not be moved and lay all night in the pitiless,

102

icy rain, crying out and dying of exposure. In the morning, many were dead and those wounded who were lucky to have been picked up in time were slowly jolted, petrified and sodden with freezing mud, in the springless AT carts to dressing stations already in a state of chaos. Some men arrived at Amarna with untended wounds that were putrefying, gangrenous and full of maggots. Arrangements were made with the Turks for a six-hour armistice to collect wounded lying close to their trenches and bury the dead. The British casualties were 2,741. In those battalions in the front line of the advance the casualty rate amounted to between 50 and 90 per cent.

The wounded were taken to the British camp at Orah where two sections of one of the five divisional ambulances had arrived, the rain having settled into a steady downpour. Tents had been put alongside the ships on ground that was ankle-deep in mire and the wounded were carried into the pools of gluey mud that had accumulated inside them. All who could help carried tea and rum to the wounded from the ships where injured soldiers lay on every inch of the decks.

Those who could stand crawled out of the tents and stood around the lascars' cooking stove, a brazier that was the only warm place. They made a swaying ring, their teeth chattering, the cigarettes in their mouths jerking with ague, faces bespattered by blood and mud, with the red glare on their faces, but still joking, like a group of the damned trying to make merry in hell. (Candler)

Nearly every boat on the river took cartloads of wounded downstream to the hospital at Amarna, huddled on the bare decks without cover from the rain. The ships' companies could do little for them, splints and dressings and doctors were non-existent and they arrived with their field dressings still unchanged after eight days on the boats.

On 21 January the floods arrived in Kut – it had started raining on the 17th and did not stop. Trenches were flooded up to the occupants' necks at the first onrush of water. The Turks were also in trouble, retreating over the top with British gunners taking advantage of the situation to fire pot-shots at them. In the north-west sector a mile of silver water surrounded the town. Inside the enceinte it was difficult to stay upright in the mud, while the dugouts were squelchy underfoot and tiny rivulets of water percolated through every gap in the sandbags.

103

Townshend had reported on 28 January that the strength of the Kut garrison was 8,356 effective troops, 2,157 non-effective troops and 2,908 Indian military followers. The Arab population was 6,300, making a total of 19,721 mouths that had to be fed.

He also postulated three possible courses of action he could take if General Aylmer was unable to relieve him:

(1) To attempt to break out of Kut by crossing the Tigris to the right bank and then make straight for Shaikh Saad, being met halfway if possible by a column sent by General Aylmer.
(2) To hold Kut to the last.
(3) To open negotiations with the enemy for surrender.

On 4 February the British Intelligence staff estimated the Turkish numbers and their dispositions as follows:

(1) In the Hanna Defile, in front of Aylmer's force on the left bank, were the 35th, 51st and 52nd Divisions – approximately 12,000 riflemen and over 26 guns.
(2) In the Es Sinn position on the right bank, 1,500 to 2,000 regular cavalry and two battalions of infantry, which were being reinforced by part of the recently arrived 2nd Division.
(3) Around Kut, the 45th Division – 4–5,000 rifles.

General Lake, on his arrival to take over from Nixon, saw the end of the first phase of the attempt to relieve Kut. It had been a serious defeat for the Tigris Corps, strategically as well as tactically, and part of the reason for it was obvious to the General as soon as he stepped off the boat at Basra. Administratively, the campaign was in a state of chaos. Nixon, never a man for organization or 'babu's work', had let what system there was run itself. This inattention had been compounded by his lack of sufficient experienced staff.

While the Tigris Corps was being shot down at Hanna, 10,000 men and twelve guns were lying idle at Basra because they could not be got to the front. In midstream of the Tigris, off Ashur, a long line of ships lay waiting for offloading, while on shore the congestion and confusion was indescribable, with troops and stores crowding every foot of dry ground.

They were simply waiting for transport upstream which was not possible because of the lack of suitable craft to transport them. What craft had been sent to Mesopotamia were, like the paddle steamers, unwieldy in the conditions on the Tigris, or, like the square-ended barges, a complete failure. This was because the specifications originally set out by Messrs Lynch Bros, the Basra-based river transport firm, who knew what they were about since they had been trading up the Tigris for years, had been altered by those experts in London who thought they knew better.

General Cowper, Assistant Quartermaster-General to the expedition, took the opportunity of Lake's arrival to draft a strong complaint to India about the transport situation on the Tigris, describing it as 'so frightfully serious' that Lake would have to abandon the idea of relieving Kut. Sir Percy considered the telegram but made little change to the wording and sent it off. He had a swift reply from Sir Beauchamp Duff who had decided that the wording of the telegram was intemperate and that the demand for improvement was unnecessary. He added: 'Please warn General Cowper that if anything of this sort again occurs or if I receive any more querulous or petulant demands for shipping, I shall at once remove him from the force and will refuse him further employment of any kind.'

Lake's first task was to sort out this situation, to build wharves, extend the area of the base and see whether it would be possible to build railways and roads. For this task he appointed Sir George Buchanan, a distinguished but pugnacious engineer who, with the help of the War Office who had now taken control, radically reorganized the system for the better.

Lake also had to deal with the repercussions of the defeat at Hanna that had caused alarm in London and at Army HQ in India. The Viceroy tried to play down the situation by writing to the Secretary of State to say he felt no anxiety about Kut and suggested that using words like 'besieged' and 'relief' was only arousing unnecessary alarm. However, the War Committee in London was alarmed and called for a full appreciation of the situation in Mesopotamia and for a full enquiry into the control of the campaign (the Mesopotamia Commission); they also ordered the General Officer Commanding in Egypt to prepare the 13th British Division for despatch to Basra.

Sir Percy Lake was in an unfortunate position from another point of view. As Chief of the General Staff in India he had been responsible for the despatch of Sir John Nixon to relieve Sir Arthur Barrett, and for every subsequent decision of importance regarding the size and equipment of the Force – as a result he was rightly regarded as having been constitutionally responsible for at least some its deficiencies and for past errors of strategy.

However, his first task was to consult with General Aylmer, whom he knew well as his erstwhile colleague as Adjutant-General in India. On the way upriver a message from General Townshend informed him that he could hold out at Kut for a further two months (the end of March) rather than until 3 February, his previous estimate. Almost immediately afterwards he telegraphed to say that he had now discovered that he had could hold out for eighty-four days, until 17 April. This was the result of a house-to-house search of the more prosperous Arab houses which turned up a good number of very large food hoards.

In the middle of February, General Aylmer decided to attack the Turkish force that was blocking the Hanna defile, hoping to destroy their main camp and perhaps disrupt them sufficiently to make it possible to clear them out of the defile. The weather was running true to form and the project was postponed for a day because of rain, but then a brigade made a pretence crossing of the Tigris in the Turkish rear. At daybreak on 22 February, General Gorringe led a force up the right bank of the river and bombarded the Turkish camps north of the Fallahiya bend across the river causing a good deal of surprise and some confusion. Part of his column pushed on further as far as Sannaiyat where the right bank of the river was higher than the left. Despite the rain the river was low and the current slack; Gorringe said that if he had had a pontoon train with him he could have crossed the river and shut the Turks up in the Hanna Defile. As it was, he could do nothing more than return to base. Townshend had seen the gunfire from his roof in Kut some 20 miles away and noted in his diary: 'We could clearly see the shells bursting over Hanna and the smoke . . . Apparently much confusion was caused in the enemy's main camp behind the Hanna position; but they did not retreat. As is the Turkish custom when defending, they held like grim death, their officers, revolvers in hand, behind them, shooting if any man tried to get up and go.'

On 16 February the campaign in Mesopotamia had become the responsibility of the Imperial General Staff in London who were to co-ordinate the military efforts as part of the whole British war plan. India was to remain the base for the force, and questions of policy likely to affect her internal and foreign relations were to be referred to the Indian Government.

The Chief of the General Staff summed up the situation as follows:

(a) that security was to be the main consideration;
(b) that the force would not be reinforced, but would be adequately supplied;
(c) that no importance was attached to Baghdad or Kut after its relief;
(d) that the force would be ordered to withdraw on Amara or Qurna, but for the fact that such course of action might cause tribal risings and might add to the difficulties in Persia or Afghanistan.

On the other hand it might have been argued that if a forward policy was maintained the Russians could be assisted in their advance from Erzerum to Kermanshah, which was reached on 25 February.

The general situation was complicated by the state of the Tigris which was now in full, turbulent, yellow flood. It menaced the safety of storage grounds at the base and hindered communication both on the river and alongside it. Although Lake was soon to have his force augmented by the 13th Division, it did not necessarily mean an increase in his offensive power unless his transport could be developed to carry and supply extra troops at the front. The equation was between numbers of troops at the front and efficient river transport. However, he decided that he must attack as soon as Aylmer's force was in a fit state to do so – a conclusion with which Townshend heartily agreed.

Around Kut the river was rising fast, three feet in two days, while the rain poured down. Apart from a large increase in cases of scurvy due to the lack of fresh vegetables, anthrax had broken out in the town and all offal was ordered to be buried. On 1 March the Turks launched the biggest artillery bombardment that they had yet delivered. About ten batteries opened up and the firestorm lasted for two and a half hours. The Turkish shells were old and burst, if they did burst, on contact with a baked mud wall. The building usually stood undamaged but the shell fragments were the danger, some of them as big as half a loaf. At the height of the action two aircraft appeared overhead dropping 100-pound bombs to add to the noise and the confusion. Townshend was appalled when the airmen targeted the hospital despite the large red-cross flag draped across the roof.

He often visited the hospital and in his biography of Townshend, his cousin records that he received a letter from a private in the 7th Hussars telling him that on one occasion when he was in the hospital Townshend sent him his last bottle of wine. He added: 'So I can also testify to his goodness of heart: I think that bottle of wine saved my life and my gratitude is still felt.'

During the night following bombing raid or shelling the Arabs buried their dead alongside the river, and the wails of the mourners would last until morning. Jewish funerals also took place at night to avoid drawing Turkish fire and the participants would mourn in the same high-pitched way as they walked in procession to the river bank, carrying tiny candles in little tins.

Meanwhile, Lake telegraphed to Aylmer: 'I fully realise the difficulty of your task. Deeply regret your losses and suffering which wounded must necessarily undergo under present climatic condition. Hope you will continue to press attack when circumstances admit and I am confident of successful result.'

Aylmer's force was entrenched on the left bank of the river at distances varying from 900 to 1,500 yards from the enemy, and were sending out reconnaissance parties to try to find a way through Suwacha Marsh. On the right bank considerable areas had become flooded but the soldiers there managed to find positions that enfiladed the Turkish trenches on the left bank.

As an alternative to another assault upon the narrow Hanna Defile, General Aylmer decided to mount an advance on the right bank while leaving a small holding detachment on the left bank. No way had been found across the Suwacha Marsh and the distance around its perimeter was too great for an army equipped as it was at the time.

If he were successful in defeating the Turks on the right bank he would then be able to advance up the Tigris, across the Hai to the Shumran Bend, and either cross to the left bank of the Tigris in the rear of the enemy, or cover the withdrawal of the garrison from Kut to the right bank, after which the whole force would be able to fall back.

However, setting aside the difficulties of execution, although the idea might seem to be a simple one, the plan decided upon turned out to be rather more complicated. The force used was to be made up of 4 regiments, 28 battalions and 68 guns. In order to obtain surprise, the force was to move to its battle positions by night and to march in three separate groups, the first being organized in two separate columns. The object was to attack the right of the enemy's position between Sinn Aftar and the Dujailah Redoubt with one group, while another marched round the right flank and the third was held in reserve.

The Turkish entrenchments on the right bank of the Tigris ran from the Tigris southwards past the Sinn Banks for about 8 miles to groups of mounds about 20 feet high, crowned by the Sinn Abtar and Dujaila Redoubts. From there the Turks dug a series of short trenches at 500-yard intervals back towards the Hai.

The country was the usual Mesopotamian plain dotted with small sandhills, mounds, banks and dry water-channels, the remains, as in other parts of the land between the two rivers, of ancient irrigation systems dating back thousands of years. These features were imperceptible a couple of hundred yards away and so were no use as landmarks.

Distances were not great. From the Pools of Siloam (Ruined Hut), where the force was to assemble, to the point at which the groups were to make their first divergence was 9 miles. From there the first two groups were to continue the march for another 4½ miles to where one column was to form up for the assault, its left covered by the other column, and with the outer flanks of both columns protected by the cavalry.

A difficulty that arose straightaway was the problem of navigating in the desert, where landmarks were extremely scarce and there were no practicable maps. This was complicated by the need to preserve secrecy by restricting reconnaissance in advance of the march. Perhaps if the subordinate commanders were given some leeway in the orders, problems might have been lessened, but the plan laid down was a very rigid one allowing no scope for initiative.

While the enterprise was being put in train, General Townshend reported on the morning of 4 March that he had overestimated the amount of barley by 200 tons and that he could not hold out longer than the end of the month, so General Aylmer decided to attack on the right bank at once. A conference was held on 7 March at which subordinate officers were put in the picture as Gorringe explained the plans. If things went very well they might be able to burst through the enemy lines and arrive on the river bank opposite Kut,

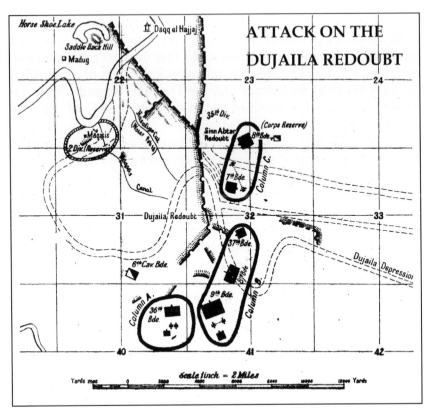

Map 11. Attack on Dujaila Redoubt

so it was essential that the capture of the Dujaila Redoubt should be carried through with the utmost vigour. General Aylmer reinforced this point, stressing the need for 'dash' in the operation – which was not quite how things turned out.

The heavy rain prevented any start being made earlier than the night of 7 March. In Kut, *mahailas*, a launch and the *Sumana* were standing by to carry a brigade across the Tigris to cut off the Turkish retreat after they had been defeated.

The *Sumana* was still usable despite being regularly used for making nightly deliveries of food across the river to Liquorice Village and was just as regularly greeted by a fusillade of Turkish rifle fire.

The assembly was without incident apart from taking longer than estimated because of hold-ups in one column in which the infantry

110

was delayed by having to keep pace with the slower transport animals and the field artillery batteries. For some reason they were included amongst the fighting troops in the column instead of marching in the rear. Coloured lights were used to guide the troops to their respective places in the columns. So the force started off on its first leg of 6 miles two and a half hours late and did not start deploying until after dawn. Hold-ups on the march resulted in transport drivers being overcome by sleep so deeply that they were difficult to wake up when it was time to move on. In some cases, transport was actually left behind on the line of march.

It was the custom of the Turks to stay out of sight until an attack was launched against them and as the British approached the Dujaila Redoubt there was no sign of the enemy. General Kemball, in charge of the column, thought this was par for the course and the Turks were playing their usual hide-and-seek with him, so instead of advancing unopposed under cover of darkness across the open plain and seizing the position, which would have been a death trap in daylight, he ordered the column to take cover in a depression while he awaited the arrival of the other columns. But he was being fooled – the Turks had actually evacuated the position.

He reported his supposition to General Aylmer by telephone who, also thinking that enemy could not be ignorant of the arrival of the British, and were simply waiting until they advanced closer before spraying them with bullets, ordered the Corps Artillery to open fire to cover the forming up of the infantry columns.

This took some time and it was getting lighter by the minute; two of General Kemball's brigadiers, seeing the enemy hurrying back into the Redoubt, realized that the chance of an unopposed attack was slipping away and asked him to let them advance on the Dujaila Redoubt at once. But General Kemball, mindful of the rigidity of the orders that General Aylmer had laid down, did not feel justified in ignoring them and the chance of a cheap victory was lost.

It was not until the whole column was ready at 0935 hrs that the attack started, but by that time the Turks had reoccupied their defences and brought down heavy rifle, machine-gun and artillery fire on the men advancing across the open plain. As a result the attack failed and a death trap the Redoubt proved to be. The one successful action was that of 8 Infantry Brigade who almost succeeded in retrieving the blunder of the attack. Despite the great distance they had to cover and having the sun in their eyes, they reached the Redoubt, stormed it and actually seized the crest of the hill – but they were unsupported and turned out by an immediate Turkish counter-attack.

In Kut the besieged garrison from their rooftops could see hordes of Turks rushing by into the Shatt-el-Hai support trenches to take part in the counter-attack.

Three and a half thousand British and Indian soldiers fell in the advance. 8 Infantry Brigade had gone forward across 3,000 yards of open plain with 2,300 men – they came back with 1,127, a loss made even sadder by the fact that the best chance the force would have of relieving Kut had almost certainly been thrown away.

By the evening, it was clear that there was nothing else to do but order a retreat as there was not enough transport to keep the widely dispersed force supplied with food and water. They withdrew to the Wadi with the Turks following up.

After the battle the cavalry were heavily criticized for not playing any useful part in the attack. 'They hovered about in an ineffective way on the left, usually somewhat in the rear of the infantry'. (*Critical Study of the Campaign in Mesopotamia*) Had they been capably led or used to some effect like harrying the enemy's re-inforcements who were hurrying to the Redoubt, they might have helped to turn the attack into a success. During this and previous engagements it was judged that they had not played a part commensurate with the heavy drain their presence entailed on the transport that had to carry up the necessary fodder. It was also said, perhaps rather brutally, that 'the despised Arabs on their ponies made rings round them every time.' (*Critical Study*)

Like earlier battles, instructions were issued that wounded were to be collected and taken forward to the objective of the advance, in this case, the Dujaila Redoubt, which of course was impossible and a good deal of suffering took place, not least from the lack of water, even though a few pits dug a few feet down would have provided a good supply.

The wounded were taken back to the Wadi in springless AT carts as there were still no motorized vehicles in Mesopotamia. Stretcher-bearers had to be accompanied by an armed escort to drive away Arab marauders who pillaged the dead by stripping and even killing wounded men. No object seemed to be too trifling for them – blankets and clothes in which the dead had been buried, sometimes months before, were dug up and eagerly seized upon.

Townshend issued another of his regular communiqués to the besieged garrison in which he repeated the telegrams he had received from General Aylmer on the failure of the attack. He continued in his typically comradely but still egotistical style:

I am speaking to you as I did before, straight from the heart, and as I may ask your sympathy for my feelings having promised you relief on certain dates on the promise of those ordered to relieve us . . . I have had to further reduce your ration. It is necessary to do this in order to keep our flag flying. I am determined to hold out and I know you are with me in this heart and soul.

In the officers' messes in Kut, Aylmer was being referred to as Faylmer. 'Alphonse', as Townshend was known amongst his officers, a reference to his penchant for everything French, let it be known that there was one ray of hope and the rumour got round the garrison that the Russian general, Baratoff, was almost through the Persian mountains and into Mesopotamia. Some budding poet produced the doggerel verse:

> The mountains looked on Baratoff
> And Baratoff looked on me
> And in my evening dream I dreamed
> That Kut might still be free.

The Turks considered that Aylmer's attack had been an extremely dangerous one for them. In the rear of their XIII Corps was the besieged army of General Townshend ready to attack; on their left was the Tigris which could only be crossed at the Maqasis crossing and on the right was the Shatt al Hai. There was no ready means of retreat and they believed that defeat would have meant the relief of Kut. The result of the battle had been on a knife-edge in the first hour of the attack: if the Redoubt had been stormed in the first hour of the approach, as it could and should have been, they were convinced that they would have had to abandon the siege.

Immediately after Dujaila, operations were suspended as both sides were confined to their trenches by fresh floods. Recriminations after Dujaila also resulted in the dismissal of General Aylmer. His rigid orders and the disparate forces he used for the operation were considered to have contributed largely to its failure. Military opinion in London shared the opinion that the operation was probably the best chance that the relieving force was to have of reaching Kut. The Dujaila Redoubt was only a matter of 9 miles as the crow flies from Kut. Difficult miles, it must be admitted, but the demoralized Turks might well have been driven back and the village of Woolpress seized.

General Gorringe was selected to take Aylmer's place and his appointment as GOC Tigris Corps provided him with the chance to make the final effort to relieve Townshend's force.

Although the floods prevented any immediate movement, Gorringe had at his disposal an additional division, the 13th, commanded by Major General Maude, fresh from the Dardanelles. His own troops could now be rested for a time but there was little relaxation – no pleasant billets, no amusements or leave in civilized parts. Falling sick in Mesopotamia was not a comforting experience either – in most cases the conditions were quite the opposite.

The only operation during this period was a push to take over some positions on the right bank some 3 to 4 miles south of the Tigris. Although successful the attack cost a further 300 British casualties.

On 11 March the Chief of the Imperial General Staff, General Sir William Robertson, telegraphed to the Commander-in-Chief in India describing the military advantages which would flow from the relief of Kut. He made a number of points, not all seemingly valid, describing the Turks' fighting value as being lower than our own, although events in Gallipoli and Mesopotamia certainly did not bear this out. He also said that experience had shown that, given adequate artillery bombardment, trenches could be taken – ignoring the fact that this was by no means always the case on the Western Front, let alone the Somme. He recommended that every effort should be made to accumulate at the front a lavish stock of artillery ammunition, especially high-explosive and howitzer, and questioned why howitzer batteries were at Basra and not at the front. It was clear that General Robertson had little understanding of the shortage of river craft in Mesopotamia and the difficulties they had in navigating the Tigris and bringing up more than the bare minimum of supplies and necessities.

The telegram went on to say that in Mesopotamia we had attacked two or even three times just before additional reinforcements could arrive, and questioned the advisability of General Lake establishing his HQ at Basra instead of at the front. Premature advances were certainly true of the attempt to rescue Townshend but, of course, there had been a sense of urgency behind these.

Although badly misdirected, it was an extensive catalogue of criticism and must have fallen like a douche of cold water in India, especially as it came from Robertson who himself had spent many years of service in that country.

The guns at General Lake's disposal included 150 light guns, ranging from 10- to 18-pdrs, eight 60-pdrs, two 4-inch guns and thirty-six 4.5- and 5-inch howitzers. Ammunition included 18,800 rounds of high explosive and 4,000 rounds of shrapnel.

On 11 March the total available steamers and tugs was thirty-seven, plus sixty-eight barges. They were a heterogeneous collection, each requiring different spare parts, and were difficult to service and maintain. When they were all in operation, which was seldom, they could deliver 300 tons of stores at the front every day against the requirement of 400 tons – and this was without carrying troops who could not march up the Tigris, there being no adequate roads.

Despite the efforts made at Basra by Buchanan to increase the wharfage, the continuous line of vessels some miles in length were still waiting in midstream to be unloaded, a situation that was very unlikely to be speedily remedied.

On 18 March, Townshend telegraphed that his supplies would only last until 15 April, which provided Lake with a clear deadline. Life within the town was becoming unbearable. Mousley records in his diary that he used to creep out on the waterfront unseen by the Turks across the river in the village of Woolpress and sit in a disused trench where he could enjoy a cool breeze from the river. Enteritis was increasing in the town. Symptoms included violent intestinal pains and an overwhelming desire to vomit, brought on, he suggests, by bad and insufficient food.

The floods were proving a definite hindrance to preparations for a further advance, not only on both banks of the river in the fighting zone but downriver where they hindered the journey upstream. In several places the river was threatening to burst its banks and troops had to be diverted to become water engineers. Floods were not usually expected on the right bank but areas opposite Sannaiyat were under inundation and made reconnaissance difficult. By far the best way to reconnoitre was from the air. Gorringe had seaplanes that could take off from the river when the wind was from the right direction but three new land aircraft were on the way up from Basra and the General decided that he would wait until they arrived before starting any fresh initiative.

What he had in mind was another attack on Hanna. When the aircraft arrived, he used them to take photographs of the Turkish trenches and these allowed him to give the 13th Division a briefing on what they were going to come up against – probably the first time in British Army history that soldiers were given a briefing using air photographs especially taken for the purpose.

Early in the morning of 5 April, the 13th Division, which had taken over from the 7th Division four days earlier, assaulted Hanna at dawn and found the position empty. The Turks had gone back to Fallahiyeh. The same evening the 13th Division moved forward and attacked the Fallahiyeh position which they captured after a short struggle with the loss of 1,885 casualties inflicted by the three Turkish battalions that formed the garrison, the rest having retreated to the Sannaiyat position On the right bank, progress was also being made as the 3rd Division went forward to take the Abu Rumman trenches opposite Fallahiyeh.

At dawn on 6 April the 7th Division launched an attack on the Sannaiyat trenches, but the Turks knew it was coming and were fully prepared. The two leading brigades, 28 and 19, were lashed by gunfire from both banks of the river and by rifle and machine-gun fire described by the Official Eyewitness, Edmund Candler, as a 'torrent of death'. The Ox and Bucks lost all their officers and 220 other ranks out of 266. The 51st Sikhs and the Leicestershires lost nearly 50 per cent of their effective strengths. They were now some 500 yards from the Turkish trenches but to advance further over an open plain without artillery support was out of the question.

The artillery was slow in coming up, having been delayed by the obstacle presented by the Turkish trenches at Fallahiyeh. When they were in position they opened fire and kept the Turks' heads down sufficiently for the British front line to consolidate and try to dig in. Younghusband sent word back to Corps HQ that he hoped to move forward again after dark.

At 2200 hrs 40 Brigade was sent forward to join in the coming attack but the weather now took a hand. Under the influence of the north-west wind, the water of the Suwacha Marsh flooded into the trenches on the right of the 7th Division and despite strenuous efforts to hold it back made under hostile fire, by 0100 hrs the forward trenches of 28 Brigade and the northern trenches to the north of them had to be evacuated.

Many of the guns were surrounded by water which was kept back by frantically throwing up earthen banks around them. The Tigris, too, was rising rapidly and threatened to combine with the marsh and inundate the whole of the area. Orders for the night attack had to be cancelled.

Townshend, who had been anxiously observing the scene from his rooftop in Kut, turned his 5-inch guns on the Turkish ferry at Maqasis and the Turks gave up ferrying until 0900 hrs when the mirage came down and the target became invisible. After it lifted in the afternoon, his guns opened up again.

During the early afternoon, the hostile gunfire decreased and some of the 51st Sikhs and the Leicestershires managed to withdraw from their precarious advanced positions and join their brigade entrenchments further back. At the same time numbers of the wounded were brought in, the Turks refraining from firing when this was happening. For the first time on the Tigris front there had been a few motor ambulances in operation.

At 1940 hrs some of the British artillery on both banks began to bombard the Sannaiyet position as a feint to cover the 3rd Division's advance along the right bank. By 2300hrs 8 Brigade with the 1/1st Gurkhas were dug in with their machine-guns facing northward along the river where they could enfilade the Sannaiyat entrenchments. Later that night the Tigris overflowed behind the 3rd Division, spreading southwards and threatening to join up with the marsh at Umm-al-Baram.

General Gorringe was determined that he must capture the Sannaiyet position by 8 April if he was to relieve Kut in time. The advanced trenches of the 7th Division were still too far from the Turkish position for an assault from them to offer any chance of success, but floods on the right bank made a move there impracticable so he decided that the Division should advance as far as possible without committing itself to an engagement.

Next morning the order to push forward in earnest was given and by 1940 hrs the 53rd Sikhs and 56th Punjabi Rifles of 28 Brigade, and the 92nd Punjabis and 125th Rifles of 19 Brigade had covered 300 yards but this was as far as they got as enemy fire forced them to dig in a thousand yards or so from the enemy trenches. No reinforcements could reach them for the rest of the day.

After dark on 8 April, 19 and 21 Brigades moved up into line and the British artillery carried out a five minutes' bombardment of the Turkish trenches followed by a discharge of rockets. This resulted in the Turks sending up flares which identified the line of their trenches and allowed a second more accurate British bombardment to take place.

Two hours later when the moon had set, the three brigades of the 7th Division crept silently forward two to three hundred yards and dug in. The rest of the night was spent in unobtrusive patrolling which revealed the fact that there were gaps in the breast-high wire entanglement in front of the Turkish trenches.

On the right two officers ventured into the Suwacha Marsh and found that they could wade through it, splashing through some 4,000 yards of thigh-deep inundation and coming out about 2 miles north-west of the Sannaiyat defence lines. The return journey took an hour and a half on a bottom that was hard enough for both troops and guns and nowhere more than three feet deep. But this promising route was rejected by General Gorringe as he thought the marsh floor would be cut up by the artillery mules and the laden troops. Nowadays a commander might have pushed some lightly laden men through in a commando raid behind the Turkish lines and timed it to coincide with the next frontal assault.

This was carried out by the wholly British 13th Division in a carefully planned assault on a frontage of 600 yards with two brigades, 36 and 40, advancing in four lines with 39 Brigade in support. The troops lay out on the cold ground for some time before the order to advance was given when they staggered to their feet and moved forward at 0300 hrs. Chilled by the long wait they were unable to move at the pace required in their orders. At some point in the advance the second line faltered as the Turks opened fire and finally fell back, causing uncertainty in the lines behind that soon turned to panic.

Meanwhile the leading troops continued in the face of intense enemy fire and those that survived reached and occupied part of the Turkish front line where they hung on, throwing bombs until they ran out. Behind them confusion was so widespread that it became impossible to reorganise the mass of infantry into an ordered advance to reinforce those in the Turkish lines. Eventually the survivors of that gallant band were forced out and dug in about 400

. The Right Hon Baron Hardinge. (*Loyalties*)

2. Sir Beauchamp Duff in 1898.
   (*Acknowledgments to the British Library*)

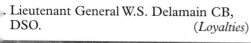

. Lieutenant General W.S. Delamain CB,
 DSO.   (*Loyalties*)

4. Field Marshal Sir A. Barratt GCB, KCSI,
   KCVO.   (*Loyalties*)

5. Lieutenant General G.F. Gorringe KCB, KCVO.   (*Loyalties*)

6. Major General Sir Percy Cox KCIE, CS. (*Loyaltie*

7. General Sir John Nixon KCB
   (*Acknowledgments to the National Army Museum*)

8. William Wassmuss.
   (*Unable to trace owner of photo*)

. Major General Sir Charles V.F.
Townshend CB, DSO. *(Sherson)*

10. Major General Sir C.J. Melliss VC, CB.
(Loyalties)

1. Lieutenant General Sir Percy Lake
KCB, KCMG (CGS India) *(Loyalties)*

12. Lieutenant General Sir F.J. Aylmer VC,
KCB. *(Royal Engineers Library, Chatham)*

13. Lieutenant General Sir Stanley Maude
    CB, CMG, DSO.   (*Tennant*)

14. Major General L.G. Dunsterville CB,
    CSI.   (*Dunstervill*

16. Lieutenant General Sir William Marsha
    KCB, CB, KCSI, GCMG.   (*Marsha*

15. General N.N. Baratoff.   (*Dunsterville*)

17. The Mesopotamian Railway. *(Highland)*

18. Arthur Creek, Basra. *(Highland)*

19. The tree of knowledge at
    Qurna.   (*Highland*)

20. A creek in southern
    Mesopotamia. (*Highland*)

21. River craft at Basra. (*Candler*)

22. Paddle steamer 32 on the Tigris. (*Dr Gerard Bulger*)

23. A BE2 being serviced in the desert at Sheikh Saad. (*Dr Gerard Bulger*)

24. British troops re-entering Kut in February 1917. (*Dr Gerard Bulger*)

yards back. They had sustained 1,807 casualties.

Conditions were now becoming almost impossible for campaigning. On the left bank the waters of both the Suwacha Marsh and the Tigris began to approach each other, further narrowing the Hanna passage. Flies abounded. In his book *Mons, Anzac and Kut*, Aubrey Herbert describes the situation:

> Nothing that I have ever seen or dreamed of came up to the flies. They hatched out until they were almost the air. They were in myriads. The horses were half mad. The flies were mostly tiny. They rolled up in little balls when one passed one's hand across one's sweating face. They were on your eyelids and lashes and in your lips and nostrils. We could not speak for them and could hardly see.

Reinforcements to the Relieving Force by 27 February 1916

The 7th Division had its 35 Infantry Brigade replaced by 21 Brigade
    comprising:
  Composite English Battalion of 2nd Norfolks and 2nd Dorsets
  6th Jats
  9th Bhopal Infantry
  Composite Mahratta Battalion (drafts for garrison in Kut)
3rd Division was added to the force comprising:
  7 Infantry Brigade comprising;
    1st Connaught Rangers (including drafts for 2nd Queen's Own
      Royal West Kent Regiment
    27th Punjabis
    89th Punjabis
    128th Pioneers
  8 Infantry Brigade comprising:
    1st Manchester Regiment
    2nd Rajputs
    47th Sikhs
    59th Rifles
  9 Infantry Brigade comprising:
    1st Highland Light Infantry
    1/1st Gurkhas
    1/9th Gurkhas
    93rd Infantry

4 Brigade RFA (7th, 14th and 66th Batteries = 18 guns)

20th Field Company, Sappers and Miners
21st Field Company, (Sappers and Miners
34th Sikh Pioneers
One squadron, 16th Cavalry
No. 3 Divisional Signal Company
Mobile Veterinary Section.

The Corps Troops were reinforced by 35 Infantry Brigade less 102nd
Grenadiers from the 7th Division, and the addition of the
36th Division comprising:
1/6th Devons
26th Punjabis
62nd Punjabis
82nd Punjabis
Together with more units comprising:
12th Company Sappers and Miners (less one section)
13th Company Sappers and Miners
Field Troop, Sappers and Miners
Artillery comprising:
13 Brigade RFA (2nd, 8th and 44th Batteries = 18 guns)
60th Howitzer Battery R.G.A. (4 x 5-inch guns)
61st Howitzer Battery R.G.A. (4 x 5-inch guns)
23rd Mountain Battery (less one section) = 4 x 10-pdrs
Home Counties Brigade RFA (1/1st and 1/3rd Sussex Batteries
= 8 x 15-pdrs)
72nd Heavy Battery RGA (4 x 5-inch howitzers)
77th Heavy Battery RGA (4 x 5-inch howitzers)
One Section 104th Heavy Battery RGA = 2 x 4-inch guns
7th Divisional Ammunition Column
Signal units comprising:
Wireless – one wagon and two pack stations
No. 1 Army Corps Signal Company
No. 12 Divisional Signal Company (less two Brigade sections)
No. 33 Divisional Signal Company (less two Brigade sections)
Medical Units reinforcements were:
No. 3 Combined Field Ambulance (two sections)
No. 20 Combined Field Ambulance
No. 7 British Field Ambulance

No. 8 British Field Ambulance
No. 19 British Field Ambulance
No. 20 British Field Ambulance
No. 21 Combined Field Ambulance
No. 111 Indian Field Ambulance
No. 112 Indian Field Ambulance
No. 113 Indian Field Ambulance
No. 128 Indian Field Ambulance
No. 129 Indian Field Ambulance
No. 130 Indian Field Ambulance
No. 19 Combined Clearing Hospital
No. 4 Sanitary Unit
Air Service comprising:
    One flight RNAS (only one serviceable aircraft)
    'B' Flight No. 30 Squadron RFC (three serviceable aircraft)

En route to join Tigris Corps:
    27 Infantry Brigade comprising:
        1/4th Somerset Light Infantry
        1/2nd Gurkhas

Chapter Eight

The Surrender of Kut

(Maps 12 and 13)

Both General Gorringe and General Lake were now beginning to feel greatly concerned about the relief of Kut. They knew that the situation had become critical and were extremely doubtful about relieving Townshend by 15 April. Townshend announced that he would cut the already scanty rations again and be able to hold out until the 21st. When General Lake arranged to have the aircraft drop food into the besieged town Townshend decided that he could hold out until 29 April, but that for the last week all the food would have to be supplied from the air.

They also agreed that the right bank should be the place for the next attack. The main problem was the floods that the Turks could actually manipulate by virtue of their position upstream of the British, where they could breach the banks of the river whenever they thought an inundation would discomfort the enemy. Another problem was that Gorringe had only five days' supply of food in reserve and could not get more as the track further south between Sheikh Saad and Amara was under water.

Opposite Fallahiya where the General was hoping to build a boat bridge, a sheet of water extended almost as far as Umm al Baram. Attempts were made to build embankments to control these waters but they were at the mercy of the wind which could move them around very quickly. In front of the British the Turks were widening a break in the Tigris embankment to increase the floods which were acting as a kind of moat to their position.

On the day designated for the attack, rain began to fall by 0830 hrs and within a short time there were two inches of water on the ground over which the advance was to be made. On the night of the 11th there was a fierce thunderstorm and next day a waterspout, a hailstorm and a hurricane. The spray on the Tigris was 4 feet high and the yellow waves beyond the bund were above the level of the tents. Despite this the attack went in on the 12th and progress was made in pushing forward the British line at a cost of over 400 British and Indian casualties.

A north-easterly gale blew up in the late afternoon and flooded the trenches of the 7th Division so that the next day much time had to be spent in repairing the damage and rebuilding the bund; the right bank also had to be repaired.

It was clear that the plan to fly sufficient food into Kut was impracticable – amounts were so small that it was clearly a waste of time. As a result a plan that had been mooted some time before by General Lake was revived which he discussed with Vice Admiral Wemyss, the C-in-C East Indies Squadron, who was visiting the front. The idea was that a ship should be used to run the gauntlet of the Turkish guns along the river bank to provision Kut. It would be extremely dangerous but it was agreed that it would have to be tried if all else had failed.

It was decided that before any further movement could be made towards the Dujaila Redoubt which might open the way to Kut, the Turkish position at Beit Aieesa on the right bank just below Nukhailat must be captured, for it was here that the Turks were breaking down the embankment and persuading the waters to flood the British positions. As a preliminary to this attack, a Turkish position to the south, known as Twin Pimples, would be captured to protect the left flank of the British advance.

The forward movement was done at night in pouring rain and the fighting began before daylight. It was completely successful, both parts of the Turkish position being overrun by the Connaught Rangers and parties from the 27th Punjabs.

On 16 April preparations were made for an attack on Beit Aieesa, a defensive line that stretched from the River Tigris in a long curve towards the west and joined up with the Turkish dispositions around Kut. The section that was to be attacked was not immediately adjacent to the river which was protected by the floodwaters of the Turks' own making, but the next stretch south where the trench line began to curve towards the west. Parallel canals 700 yards apart were to be utilized as markers to the flanks of the attacking force.

The attacking force had about a thousand yards to cover and their rush was preceded by an artillery bombardment that started at 0645 hrs on 17 April. This bombardment was to lift at 0710 hrs, but the attacking force reached the Turkish lines before the bombardment had finished. Notwithstanding this, the infantry, consisting of the 27th and 89th Punjabis and the Connaughts dashed on and captured the trench, killing 900 Turks and capturing 180.

That evening there were indications that the Turks intended to counter-attack. Townshend reported that a column of 1,400 reinforcements had marched past Kut and shortly afterwards the Turks opened a bombardment along the whole British line. The Gurkhas received the first shock and the Turks pushed past them to attack the rest of the British positions, reaching the units in the line south of Twin Pimples where 8 Brigade, in the words of the Official History, 'covered themselves in glory' and by 0530 hrs had turned the Turks advance into full retreat with machine-gun and rifle fire, and shells from the heavy British guns.

The Turks probably lost between four and five thousand men, whose bodies could be seen massed along the British line. Within 500 yards of 8 Brigade there were twelve or fifteen hundred bodies, while the trenches in front of 7 and 9 Brigades were blocked with corpses. But to the Turks the sacrifice might have seemed worthwhile since it stopped the British drive to relieve Kut on the right bank.

On the left bank the last hope to get through to Kut was to capture the Sannaiyat positions between the Suwacha Marsh and the Tigris, but any immediate progress was made impossible by the wind veering round to the north, driving the waters of the marsh south into the 7th Division trenches.

While the British waited for the waters to go down, they bombarded the Turkish trenches and transferred thirty-six machine-guns and an 18-pdr battery to the left bank. General Gorringe and General Lake had decided to assault on the driest part of the 7th Division's front. Even though it was covered with water it was thought to be only ankle deep and passable by the two brigades that were to make the attack, each on a frontage of 300 yards.

The Turkish position consisted of three main lines of trenches, whilst in the rear was another short line, the whole linked by communication trenches; it was probable that some of the trenches

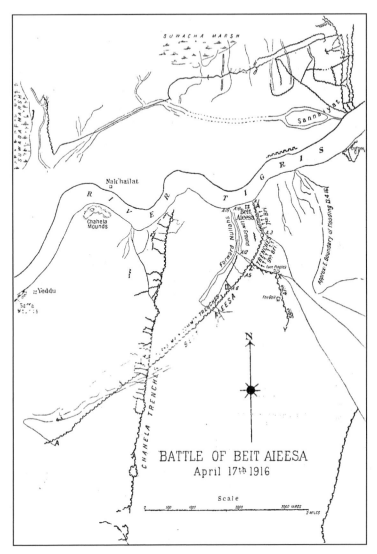

Map 12. Battle of Beit Aieesa

in the north of the position were flooded by the waters of the
Suwacha Marsh. In normal circumstances the approach to
the Turkish trenches would not have been thought suitable for an
attack, but this was ignored in view of the desperate urgency to
relieve Kut.

At the last moment, one of the attacking units, 21 Brigade,

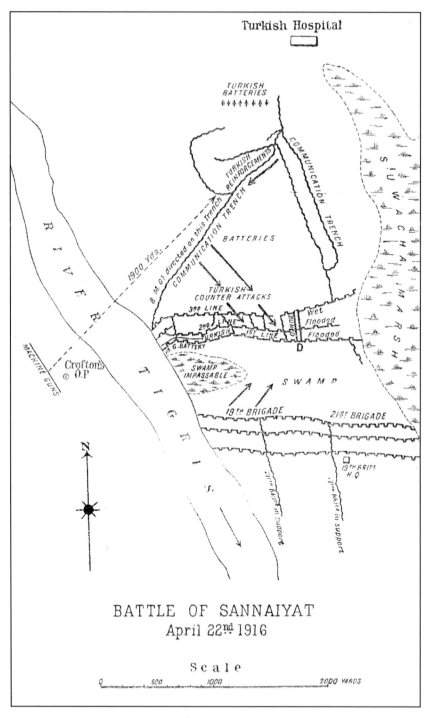

Turkish Hospital

TURKISH
BATTERIES

TURKISH
REINFORCEMENTS

COMMUNICATION TRENCH

COMMUNICATION TRENCH

S I W A C H A M A R S H

1900 Yds.

8. M.Gs directed on this Trench

BATTERIES

TURKISH
COUNTER ATTACKS

3RD LINE

2ND LINE

TURKISH 1ST LINE

Wet
Flooded

Flooded

D

M.G. BATTERY

MACHINE GUNS

Crofton's
Ⓞ O.P.

SWAMP
IMPASSABLE

S W A M P

R I V E R   T I G R I S

19TH BRIGADE

21ST BRIGADE

2ND BN. IN SUPPORT

1ST BN. IN SUPPORT

19TH BRIGE
H.Q.

N

BATTLE OF SANNAIYAT
April 22nd 1916

Scale

0   500   1000   2000 YARDS

Map 13.   Battle of Sannaiyat

126

telegraphed to say that the water was too deep for them to go forward, although this seems inexplicable, for the water level was actually falling. So 19 Brigade had to attack on its own at 0700 hrs. The level of the water had fallen a couple of feet and they were able to make good progress, keeping up with the artillery barrage before it ceased. They were met with heavy fire, and deeper water closer to the Turkish trenches meant that some were wading up to their armpits in mud and water. The Turkish first line was full of water and the Highland Battalion, a composite one from the Black Watch and Seaforths, together with the 92nd Punjabs, reached the second line, likewise water filled, the ground around it pitted with shell-holes. Some of these claimed victims, both wounded and unwounded men, who drowned in the deep water; others suffocated by sinking in the soft mud with which they were filled.

Khalil, the Turkish commander, realized the battle had reached a critical stage and determined to make a supreme effort to defend Beit Aieesa, which would otherwise give the British full freedom to manoeuvre on the right bank. He collected all available men in the area between Maqasis and the north end of Sinn Banks and with these 10,000 men organized a counter-attack. This was supported by every gun he could muster and elements of the famous 2nd Ottoman Division.

This well-timed blow fell on 19 Brigade and it was during this unearthly struggle in which rifles were choked in mud, and water threatened to overwhelm all the combatants, that an unauthorized order to retire was given by an unknown British officer on the flank of the battle. As a result, the 92nd and 125th Battalions went back, the 125th being almost obliterated in a morass of mud and barbed wire. During the night the brunt of the fighting fell on 9 Brigade, eight attacks being beaten off. Next day, hundreds of Turks were found lying in front of their trench line but it was a sacrifice that foiled further efforts on the part of the British to relieve Kut on the right bank of the Tigris and effectively ended the attempts to rescue Townshend.

Before midday, the Turks suddenly raised flags of truce and their medical officers and stretcher-bearers came forward. Firing ceased and for the rest of the day both sides rescued the thousands of disabled men who lay in the mud.

On the 24th the attempt to revictual Kut by using the *Julnar* was put into operation. Lieutenant Firman RN was in command with

Lieutenant Commander Cowley RNVR as 2i/c, Sub Lieutenant Reid RNR as chief engineer and a crew of twelve unmarried ratings selected from the gunboats on the river.

The *Julnar* started upstream from Fallahiya at 1900 hrs carrying 270 tons of supplies. Despite efforts to hide the noise of her engines by gunfire she soon came under machine-gun and rifle attack at Sannaiyat but she carried on, battling to make 6 knots against the strong current, and at Sinn Banks was fired upon by artillery. At Maqasis a shell struck the bridge killing Firman and a seaman, and wounding Cowley. A few hundred yards further on, the ship struck a cable, swung round in the current and grounded on the right bank. Here, despite frantic efforts to get her off, she was forced to surrender.

There were persistent reports later on that Cowley was shot by the Turks as a traitor – they claimed he was an Ottoman subject since he had spent so long in their dominions, but there is incontrovertible evidence that he was British,

It was the last British throw of the dice. The garrison's capitulation was now inevitable.

General Lake suggested that negotiations for the surrender of the town would have a better chance of success if carried out by Townshend himself. But there was no quid pro quo to be offered, except possibly money, for the Turks held all the cards.

On the 26th Townshend wrote to the Turks to say that he was authorized to open negotiations, and in reply was told that the Turks demanded unconditional surrender and added that General Townshend and *all his soldiers* would be treated with all honour due to them for their heroic defence. Townshend thereupon blew up his guns, destroyed his ammunition, cut up all harness and saddlery and threw all rifle bolts into the river.

General Lake advised Townshend that he was allowed to offer a million pounds if necessary in the negotiations in an attempt to ransom the garrison; this was later increased to two million. General Townshend suggested that General Lake, as GOC, should ask Khalil Pasha, the Turkish C-in-C, to permit the garrison to leave by ship on parole, the town itself being surrendered. These, he said, were honourable terms, for the Turks could not afford to feed or pay the garrison, or take them to Baghdad in any other way than on foot, in which case the men would die from weakness or at the hands of the marauding Arabs. But Halil Pasha, the Turkish commander who conferred with Townshend on a launch in the river, insisted on unconditional surrender.

Three Britons undertook the task of talking to the Turks: Aubrey Herbert MP, Captain T.E. Lawrence (of Arabia) and Colonel Beach, Head of the Expeditionary Force Intelligence Branch. Herbert, the Turkish speaker, led the delegation but from the beginning thought that Townshend, after his defence of Kut, could have got better terms off his own bat.

After a desperately hot and sweaty blindfolded journey on horses through the Turkish lines, Beach and Herbert arrived at Khalil's encampment. Lawrence had hurt his leg at the start of the journey and was following behind since he could not ride. Herbert had met Khalil previously at a British Embassy dance in Constantinople before the war and they discussed the exchange of civilian prisoners, the gallant last journey of the *Julnar*, the Arab population in Kut whom Khalil emphasized were Turkish subjects, the sending of British ships to transport the English prisoners up-river to Baghdad and ships for the sick and wounded.

Khalil was angry that Townshend had destroyed his guns. He wrote later: 'I could have prevented it by bombarding, but I did not want to.' Herbert was authorized to offer the £2m in exchange for the garrison but the Turks refused it and, since they were in the driving seat, practically dictated the terms. There is some mystery about who originally suggested the idea of offering money to the Turks. The attempt to bribe the Turks was apparently suggested originally by General Townshend (on 23 April, an unfortunate date), and seized upon by Headquarters in Simla and Lord Kitchener at the War Office. It did Britain's reputation little good in the Middle East. However, there is some doubt about this suggestion since Townshend was a Turcophile and considered them to be honourable opponents. The idea that Khalil would be willing to pocket £2m in exchange for the garrison seems much more likely to have emanated from a source ignorant of the conduct of the fighting in the campaign, such as Whitehall, or even India. Later, some of the points of the surrender terms were clarified. Sick and wounded prisoners would be exchanged, the British sending ships to Kut for the purpose, but they were not allowed to supply vessels to transport the other prisoners to Baghdad – they would have to march.

Herbert found the whole situation upsetting – the flies, the blazing heat and the sight of bodies lying on the river bank or racing downstream in the swift current combined to make it seem unreal. Sir Percy Cox refused to have anything to do with the haggling because he was strongly against the offer of money. As Chief Political Officer he thought his advice should have been sought regarding the inhabitants of Kut about whom he was best suited to negotiate.

On surrender of Kut on 29 April the garrison consisted of 13,309, of whom 3,248 were non-combatant followers. During the siege the total casualties were 3,776, either killed, wounded or died of wounds or disease. Amongst the civil population, 247 had been killed or died of wounds, and 663 had been wounded. Halil Bey announced that he had lost 300 officers and 10,000 men during the operation.

When the Turks entered the town some of the Arab population waved crescent flags and danced and chanted in the streets. Crowds of unkempt bearded men armed with rifles and bayonets flooded through the buildings and hospital in search of loot.

Mousley was in hospital suffering from malaria and mild enteritis. He records:

> In the early dawn some Turkish troops entered past the sentry whom they ignored. I had slept in my boots and hidden all my loose kit, but they commenced to seize what they wanted from the others. One took General Mellis' boots from under his bed and another his shoes and made off, notwithstanding the General's loud protests. Sir Charles jumped out of bed and followed them. A scuffle ensued in the street. The General reappeared and put on his cap and jacket showing his rank and decorations and then returned to the fray. The soldier, however, seized him by the throat, and the General, in a highly in-dignant frame of mind and looking very dishevelled, returned and got leave to go to General Townshend which he did in his socks. While he was gone, more Turks swarmed in and robbed patients who were too ill to move, taking shoes, razors, mirrors, knives and anything they fancied.

In a short time British and Indian soldiers were cleared out of the town, those who were anywhere fit being sent upstream into captivity and the sick and wounded sent downstream to freedom.

Khalil Pasha had already been warned by General Townshend that the men of the garrison were too emaciated to march any distance and in a written reply was told that every care would be taken of them, and they would be transported by steamer to Baghdad and thence by carts. In another message to Townshend, Enver Pasha said that the prisoners would become the honoured guests of the Turkish nation. The rank and file would be sent to Asia Minor to be interned in places in a good climate near the sea. He offered Townshend the chance to go to India on parole which Townshend decided to refuse.

The reality turned out to be very different Those of the garrison who could walk were marched upriver 8 miles to Shamran where they were left without shelter and fed on a few poor quality Turkish ration biscuits. Three hundred died of gastro-enteritis during the next few days. While they were there Townshend had a last sight of them when he passed upstream in a launch on his way to captivity. They gave him a cheer and waved 'Our Charlie', as he was known amongst them, out of sight.

After a few days at Shamran the Turks realized that few of their captives would reach Baghdad unless further food was sent and General Gorringe was permitted to send up supplies. Many of those who died at Shamran were carelessly disposed of by the Turks, their bodies being thrown into a ravine where some of their remains were found in July 1917. General Melliss, who, as we have seen, had been in hospital at the time of the surrender, left his sick bed and, together with Colonel Chitty, marched with the troops and spent a few days at Shamran. But he fell ill again and with Colonel Chitty was taken to Baghdad by boat along with the other officers.

Chapter Nine

A Nightmare Journey

(Map 14)

On 6 May the rank and file departed from Shumran carrying their kits on their backs under an escort of Arab cavalry. The British soldiers left camp singing, laden with cooking pots, water bottles, blankets and spare clothes, but the singing didn't last nor did the goods they were carrying. They were next seen at Bughaila, 20 miles further upriver where Captain Mousley, on board a boat that was taking officers up to Baghdad, describes the scene:

We tingled with anger and shame at seeing on the other bank a sad little column of British troops who had marched up from Kut driven by a wild crowd of Kurdish horsemen who brandished sticks and what looked like whips. The eyes of our men stared from white faces, drawn long with the suffering of a too tardy death, and they held out their hands towards our boat. As they dragged one foot after another some fell and those with the rearguard came in from blows from cudgels and sticks. I saw one Kurd strike a British soldier who was limping along. He reeled under the blows. We shouted out and if ever men felt like murdering their guards, we did. But that procedure was useless. We prevailed on the Turk who was in charge of our boat to stop and take some of the men. It seemed that half their number were a few miles ahead and the rest strewed the road back to Kut. Some have been thrashed to death, some killed, and some robbed of their kit and left to be tortured by Arabs. I have been told by a sergeant that he saw one of the Sumana crew killed instantly by a blow on the head from a stirrup iron swung by a Turkish horseman for stopping by a road for a few seconds. Men were dying from cholera and dysentery and often fell out from sheer weakness.

He describes conditions on the boat he was travelling on:

Every now and then we stopped to bury our dead. The awful disease, enteritis, a form of cholera, attacked the whole garrison with greater vigour after Kut fell and the change of food no doubt helped this. It showed also that before surrender the garrison had drawn on its last ounce of strength. A man turned green and foamed at the mouth. His eyes became sightless and the most terrible moans conceivable came from his inner being, a wild terrible retching sort of vomiting moan. They died, one and all, with terrible suddenness. One night several Indian soldiers were missing. Others reported that these had fallen overboard or jumped overboard to end their wretchedness.

Those who survived this ordeal – which for the troops involved a march of over 100 miles in eight and a half days at the hottest time of the year – were paraded through the crowded streets of Baghdad for some hours.

On their first arrival in Baghdad all but the worst of the sick and the wounded had been placed in an unsheltered enclosure on the right bank of the Tigris at some distance from the river. Then those who could walk were rapidly sent northwards. Of the rest who remained, many died, although after repeated protests from British medical officers the camp was eventually shifted to the river bank a mile below the city where the trees offered a little shade from the scorching rays of the sun. Those in another enclosure in a bare field near the railway station were less fortunate. No water was brought to them. For some days, mad with thirst, they struggled round a tiny, foul pool into which the sick crawled and collapsed.

On 8 August, twenty-two officers and 323 sick men were sent downstream from Baghdad in exchange for an equal number of Turks. They reached Basra a few days later and were hastily moved on to India. Whilst in Basra they were forbidden to speak of what they had suffered and seen. Censorship enveloped them, presumably because the force had been repeatedly told what all in authority knew to be false, that the prisoners were being well treated by the Turks, although, of course, there were certain unavoidable hardships! There seemed to be a belief in Indian military circles that it was bad policy to speak ill of the Turks or the Turkish Government which was always represented as the misguided victim of German intrigues.

The mass of the prisoners had left Baghdad in June and July in groups, following the route already taken by their officers and some of the men. As far as Samarra, 70 miles north of Baghdad, they travelled by rail in open cattle trucks; from there it was footslogging for 500 miles.

Details about this ordeal are scanty apart from what was seen by a party of officers who followed the same route. These officers had been delayed by illness at Baghdad and followed after the first batches of men had left Samarra. One sent an urgent message back to Baghdad to the Turkish Commander-in-Chief demanding a hospital establishment and an English doctor to be sent up. This was done and the establishment at Samarra picked up the hundreds of sick who had fallen out of the march in its early stages, collecting them from the roadside where they had dropped in every stage of dysentery. Many were beyond saving and so were those in the main body who had passed on and out of reach.

The same party of officers found them by the road, parties of men lying exhausted under any shelter they could find, dying of both dysentery and starvation, half clothed and without boots, having sold them to buy a little milk. There was little that the officers could do for them apart to give them what food they could spare, or to attempt to persuade local Arabs to give them a little care. From the soldiers they heard stories of their treatment, some of them difficult to believe – young soldiers of the Hampshires and Norfolks being repeatedly buggered by Turkish soldiers, and sick men being buried by the roadside while they were still breathing.

Here and there some attendant had been left to look after parties of the sick but without drugs or any other medical treatment. Some Arab villagers were kind, but many more mercilessly robbed them of anything they had left. The officers of the local police posts ignored them and protested that they had no orders to help. Many dead lay unburied beside the roadside, stripped of their clothes.

At Tikrit, Captain Shakeshaft, of the 2nd Norfolks, amongst the same party of officers as Mousley, wrote in his diary:

We met a number of unfortunate British and Indian soldiers who were standing together at the door of a miserable yard, where they

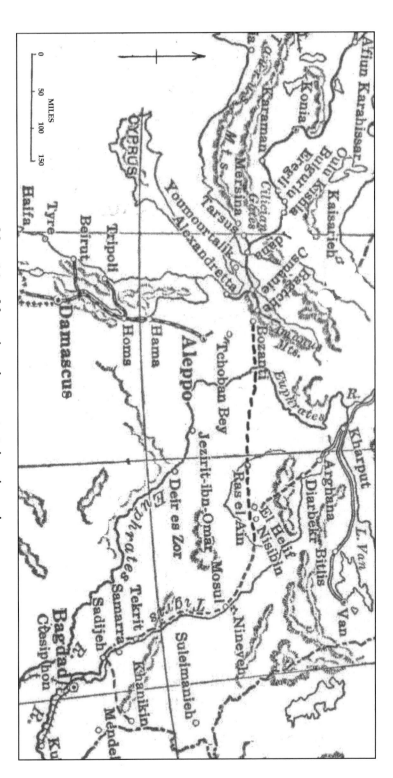

Map 14.　Map showing route taken by prisoners

were herded together. They looked ghastly. The Arabs used to bring milk and eggs to sell and asked exorbitant prices, consequently they would soon have no money and would die of starvation and neglect. There were no guards over them and they were completely abandoned. Sometimes, when a sick man would crawl out of the hovel they lived in, Arabs would throw stones at him and chase him back into the yard.

Of Ash Sharqat he wrote on 13 June: 'We found a large number of men lying in some outhouses in a most pitiful condition. Most of them were slowly dying of dysentery and neglect.'

Of Ali Mawsil (Mosul) he wrote on 17 June: 'Most of the men looked half-starved and very ill. The place was in a filthy condition and words would fail to describe the sanitary arrangements.'

In his book, *Lives of a Bengal Lancer*, Captain Yeats-Brown wrote:

I saw a party of twenty English soldiers who had marched from Kirkuk across the mountains, arriving moribund on the barrack square at Mosul. They were literally skeletons alive, and they brought with them three skeletons dead. One of the living kept making piteous signs to his mouth with a stump of an arm in which maggots crawled. Presently he died in a fit.

Then there was the saddest tea-party at which I have ever assisted. We had bribed a sentry to allow to give two of these men a meal of bread and buffalo cream which we had prepared out of our slender resources. Our guests told that they were kept in a cellar with hardly enough room to lie down. Only drinking water and bread was supplied to them. They could not wash. Three times a day they were allowed to go to the latrines and sometimes not then, for if a prisoner possessed anything that the sentry wanted, he was not allowed to go until he had parted with it.

When our pay was given us and an opportunity occurred to bribe the guards, it was a heart-breaking business to decide which of the sufferers we should attempt to save. Some were too far gone to help, others might manage to live without our smuggled food. But it was little enough we could do before we were transferred to Aleppo.

The soldier survivors followed. Many were clubbed to death by the sentries and stripped naked. Others, more fortunate, were found dead by their companions after the night's halt when they turned out to face another day of misery.

136

Captain Mousley visited the 'hospital' at Nusaybin and saw:

A bare strip of filthy ground ran down to the river some two hundred yards off. Along the wall, protected by only a few scanty leaves and loose grass flung over some tatti work of branches through which the fierce sun streamed with unabated violence, I saw some human forms which no eye but one acquainted with the phenomenon of the trek could possibly recognise as British soldiery. They were wasted to wreathes of skin hanging upon a bone frame. For the most part they were stark naked except for a rag around their loins, their garments having been sold to buy food, bread, milk and medicine. Their eyes were white with the death hue. Their cheeks were covered with the unshaven growth of weeks. One had just died and two or three of the corpses just been removed, the Turkish attendant no doubt having heard of the approach of an officers' column. But the corpses had been there for days. Some of the men were too weak to move. The result of the collection of filth and the insanitary state in the centre of which these men lay in a climate like this can be imagined. Water was not regularly supplied to them and those unable to walk had to crawl to the river for water. One could see their tracks through the dirt and grime. Three or four hard black biscuits lay near the dead man. Other forms near by I thought dead but they moved unconsciously again. One saw the bee-hive phenomenon of flies which swarmed by the million going in and out of living men's open mouths.

Of the march to Ras al 'Ayn he writes:

The padre was awfully good and diligent in assisting men but, nevertheless, from out of the night one heard the high Indian wail: 'Margaya, sahib, margaya' 'Dying, sahib, dying'. For the most part British soldiers stayed with their friends until they were dead. I saw some of the finest examples history could produce of the British soldier's self-sacrifice and fidelity to his friend. It was a grim reality for the sick of the column. I shall never forget one soldier who could go no further. He fell resignedly to the ground, the tiny stump of a cigarette in his mouth and, with a tiredness born of long suffering, buried his head in his arms to shut out the disappearing column and smoked on. Night was around us and Arab fires were near. We were half a mile behind the column. I was quite exhausted. One sick soldier was hanging on to a strap of my donkey, my orderly on another. His feet were all blood as his boots had been taken from him. A soldier went to a sick man behind but I did not see him again. Shortly after, on the same awful night, I saw another man crawling on all fours over the desert in the dark quite alone. He said he hoped to reach the next halt and get his promised ride for half an hour and by that time he might go on again to the next place. We picked him up and I gave him my strap. Another sick orderly held him up. He was all bone and could scarcely lurch along. We eventually got him to a halt and gave him a place in a cart.

At another place we came across a British soldier whose suffering had been so acute that he had gone out of his mind and lost his memory. He had been had been left in a cave and had evidently eaten nothing for days, but had crawled down to the water. He was delirious and jabbering and thought he was a dog. We carried him along in the cart to the next camp.

At Ras al 'Ayn on 20 June, Shakeshaft wrote: 'We found six British soldiers in a fearfully emaciated condition lying in a filthy stable. Of course, the Turks had done nothing for them. One of the men said 'We are like rats in a trap and they are just slowly killing us'.

At Islahiya, north of Aleppo, on June 23: 'A German warrant officer told me that there were a number of British troops suffering from dysentery in some Arab tents nearby . . . He said they were being starved to death. He had been to see them several times, but the Turks had warned him off.'

On 24 June: 'We came to a spring and lying around it were three British soldiers . . . all were horribly emaciated and in a dreadful state. They had been left behind by a column that had passed two days earlier as they could not march.'

Many weeks later, at a desert village some three days' journey from Aleppo, a group of six British soldiers and a dozen Indians had lain on the bare ground for three months in a mud-walled enclosure living off scraps of food thrown to them by Arabs or passing caravans. There had originally been fourteen. Of these, eight had died along with several Indians and of those who survived only one had the strength to crawl to a place where there was water.

In these circumstances one can understand why, of the men who surrendered at Kut and who marched into captivity, more than 3,000 were never heard of again.

After his recovery, General Melliss left Baghdad on 10 June and followed much the same route as the prisoners. He was shocked by the conditions of those who had simply been left behind by the Turks and were dying at various places by the roadside. He complained to every Turkish official he came across but was met with evasion and empty promises. What money he had he used to buy food for them. Melliss encountered a number of German and Austrian soldiers at several places and these were invariably helpful, doing what they could to provide food and in some cases offering some elementary medical help. After he got to the hotel at Bursa where the generals spent their captivity, Melliss described what he had seen in a letter to Enver Pasha, the Turkish War Minister, whom he asked to ensure that the prisoners were treated properly. Enver Pasha replied that, having given orders for the proper treatment of the prisoners, he could not believe that General Melliss' reports were true.

The survivors, when they eventually reached Turkey, were in a dreadful state but they were still considered to be a useful source of labour. Most of the Indians were left behind at Ras al 'Ayn where the Constantinople to Baghdad railway was being pushed over the flat plain to Mosul. The rest of the Indians and all the British went on to the south-eastern corner of Asia Minor where tunnels were being blasted through the Taurus and Amanus mountain ranges. The two or three thousand prisoners were assigned to a German construction company and after a few days' rest were set to work.

On the northern side of the Taurus mountains, the few hundred British prisoners taken at the Dardanelles the summer before were being employed on the railway and their conditions were apparently tolerable. But it was a different matter for the exhausted Kut survivors. Most broke down at once and the German hospitals were soon full. In September the construction company handed them back to the Turkish authorities as useless for work purposes.

They decided to send them to camps in the interior of Asia Minor travelling in railway trucks as far as the break in the line at the Taurus mountains, and then by foot over the mountains for several days to Bozanti where the railway line restarted. This journey was a rerun of the journey the prisoners had endured in Mesopotamia. Here no food was provided and no provision made for them at any point en route. They were forced onward by the rifle butts of the gendarmes until many simply dropped and died on the track. A few were taken in by German and Austrian military camps in the Taurus mountains but the main body was somehow beaten and driven across the mountain range.

Some of the exhausted and sick men were helped by charitable Americans including the United States Consul at Mersin who made appeals to the military authorities, and many sick were taken to hospitals in Adana and the American college at Tarsus.

Eventually the remainder reached Afyon where they were placed in camps, but the sufferings of those at one camp which was in the charge of a Turkish naval officer who habitually flogged prisoners with a cowhide whip continued until he was removed under pressure by the Turkish Government. The condition of these men after their journey appalled the British prisoners already in the camps. Many of the prisoners were suffering from dysentery and ended up in the camp hospital where there was a Turkish doctor with no medicines. Those who died were buried by their friends in the local Christian cemetery. All this time there were British officers at a nearby camp, amongst whom were two doctors who were forbidden to go near the sick men.

The officers were distributed in a number of different camps in Asia Minor where conditions varied a great deal, but theirs was a life of ease compared with that of the rank and file. Two them, a Welshman and an Australian, devised between them an extraordinary plot to deceive the Turks into believing they had gone mad and eventually they were repatriated to Britain as lunatics. Their story was told by one of them, E.H. Jones, in his book *The Road to En-Dor*.

Of the 2,592 British rank and file taken prisoner at Kut, more than 1,700 or nearly 70 per cent died in captivity. Of about 9,300 Indian rank and file, and followers, about 2,500 died, but figures are not exact. Some Indian ex-prisoners of war turned up years later in their villages in India having been left behind on the trek and survived as best they could, before eventually making their way home.

General Townshend has received a bad press on account of these horrendous sufferings. It is said that he was living in luxurious accommodation in Constantinople while his troops were enduring these extreme hardships but we do not know how much he knew about them. He certainly met some of the survivors of the *Julnar* on the road to captivity. They had set off in advance of the prisoners from Kut so were not among the groups who had been so badly maltreated. Sub Lieutenant Reid RNR, in charge of the party, told Townshend that they had been made to pay for the hire of the donkeys on which they were riding even though one of the party was ill, so Townshend made his Turkish escort give him fifteen liras to help in these payments and delivered a stern lecture to the Turkish officer in charge of the naval party.

His journey to Constantinople took twenty-two days so he was there before many of the prisoners had gone far on their journey, but it is probable that some rumours reached him after the prisoners had reached Turkey itself.

In the biography of his cousin, Erroll Sherson states that Townshend worked for the relief of the British prisoners of war who had been in Kut in co-operation with Mr Philip of the American Embassy. Apparently Philip was helping unofficially since the official Embassy line was one of neutrality, but the result was that bales of warm clothing were despatched from the USA to the various prison camps. Whether this means that Townshend was aware of the full details of the brutality suffered by the majority of the Kuttites at the time of the march is difficult to say. He says in his book that Enver Pasha's response to a complaint on the subject of ill-treatment was to allege that Turkish officer prisoners in Cairo were being treated badly by the British.

As far as the Indian authorities were concerned, they played down the scandal, an attitude that was shared by the British Government. A Parliamentary report published in 1918 is typical of this curious lack of clear condemnation of a scandalous episode. The following is the byzantine introductory passage:

The history of the British prisoners of war in Turkey has faithfully reflected the peculiarities of the Turkish character. Some of these, at any rate to the distant spectator, are sufficiently picturesque; others are due to the mere dead weight of Asiatic indifference and inertia; others again are actively and resolutely barbarous. It has thus happened that at the same moment there have been prisoners treated with almost theatrical politeness and consideration, prisoners left to starve and die through simple neglect and incompetence and prisoners driven and tormented like beasts. These violent inconsistencies make it very difficult to give a coherent and general account of the experience of our men. Almost any unqualified statement can be contradicted again and again by undoubted facts; and the whole subject seems often to be ruled by nothing but mere chance.

This was apparently an attempt to duck the issue and did little to pay to those who died on the infamous journey the respect that they were due. The rest of the report does tell the story of the sufferings of the prisoners briefly, and towards the end pays tribute to the American citizens in Turkey and to the American Ambassador, and, after America entered the war, to the Netherlands Legation at Constantinople who helped the prisoners with food and money.

As far as the Turkish side of the controversy is concerned, they would say that they could not have fed the prisoners in Iraq and had to move them into Turkey; and that they carried the prisoners by rail whenever possible but did not have the shipping to transport them by river. So the march was inevitable. The alternative – to let them go free after Kut – the course of action encouraged by the British with the £2m sweetener was probably impossible if the victors were to retain their enhanced reputation in the Arab world. What is unforgiveable is the lack of care of the prisoners on the march, especially of the Indians, their employment as virtual slaves on railway construction and the almost total absence of medical treatment. What the Turks would not admit to in relation to the last indictment is that Turkey at the time was virtually a third-world country with no developed medical system.

Chapter Ten

The Capture of Baghdad

(Maps 15, 16 and 17)

The Turkish Commander, Halil Bey, was resisting suggestions from higher command that he should transfer some of his troops to Persia. In his memoirs he says:

At that time we had won a magnificent victory in Iraq. But what we had won was just a battle. The war was still going on. Therefore we should have left the victory behind and plan what we should be doing next. It was obvious that the British would not let us get away with it. There surely would be a revenge, a bigger settlement . . . However, it was not the logic, which was working. It was dreams. Some German officers in Baghdad were playing weird games. It was all about Persia! . . . One day I received an order from the High Command in Istanbul. It was asking me to leave sufficient forces to defend the Tigris and to use the rest of my forces to reinforce the Persian front and capture the town of Kermanshah. Yes, it was only dreams . . . There would be nothing but an adventure. I immediately replied to the High Command. I said that the British, who didn't forget their defeat at Kut, have now gathered a force of 100,000 rifles only 110 kilometres south of Baghdad. When they are doing this, it would be only an ignorant and bloody adventure if we move our forces from the Tigris to some place in the middle of Persia. However, the Deputy Head Commander was insisting on operations in Persia. When they were insisting, I was refusing.

But his plea fell on deaf ears.

His opponents had a good deal more on their minds. After the fall of Kut the War Committee was forced to redraft its policy. The new policy was declared to be:

(1) To uphold British influence in the Basra Vilayet.
(2) To protect the oil wells in Arabistan.
(3) To minimise the effect of the fall of Kut by 'maintaining a bold front' on the Tigris and 'containing' the Turkish Army Corps about Kut and Sannaiyat.
(4) To co-operate in the Russian advance in Persia where General Baratov had 10,000 cavalry, 10,000 infantry and 38 guns.

British policy in Mesopotamia was strictly defensive and stated that no special importance was attached to the possession of either Kut or Baghdad.

In explanation of this policy, the War Committee pointed out that the Tigris Corps lay exhausted across the Tigris opposite the Turkish defences at Es Sinn and Sannaiya and that the river would soon be at its usual annual low summer level which would increase the difficulties of navigation, expose sandbanks and offer channels too narrow for many craft, so that supplying the force would become even more of a strain on the transport service. Withdrawal to a line further south seemed to be a good solution to this administrative problem. Such a line, for example Ahwaz-Amara-Nasiriyeh, would require fewer troops and shift the problems of the river on to the Turks if they decided to attack the new line. Stratigically then, the best solution was withdrawal.

But voices, perhaps siren voices, were raised to emphasize two points contained in the War Committee's policy: prestige, of course, always an important consideration in the Middle East; and aiding the Russia advance (a chimera rather than an actual event as it turned out) seemed especially to concern those not actually involved in coping with the difficulties of the situation in Mesopotamia.

General Sir William Robertson was in favour of withdrawal while the Indian Government was not: the mere idea of withdrawal threw the military top brass there into a state of extreme apprehension. In the event, Robertson left the argument with them and they gave instructions to General Lake to maintain his position as far forward as was tactically secure. India did however pass on the warning that no more reinforcements would be sent and an assurance that no blame would fall upon him if he decided to fall back at any time. This flameproofed their position and seems to have been a typically Indian Government resolution.

More important than anything else at this time was the growing concern in England over the medical situation that needed to be radically reorganized and had to cope immediately with the casualties and poor health of the Tigris Corps after their latest ordeals, but that consideration didn't figure largely in any of the arguments.

The Tigris Corps, therefore, remained where it was and settled down to the monotony of trench warfare: Western Front life, some might call it, but it was endured in a heat so scorching that men would climb out from between the furnace-like walls and risk a bullet; in a torture of flies that never left them; plagued also by sickness with few remedies; the usual dull fatigues; the impossibility of a rest tour behind the lines in a local town with estaminets and other amusements; and, of course, the sense of utter isolation in a flat, featureless desert.

On very sultry days the sandstorms came. A dense, khaki-coloured cloud arose on the horizon and then rolled towards the encampments. Troops rushed to strengthen tent pegs and guy ropes, and collect all loose kit, but often these precautions were a waste of energy for tents could be blown down like a pack of cards and their inhabitants had to hide their heads under anything they could manage to hold onto as it was impossible to face the blasts of cutting sand. In violent storms the sand made a black darkness that lasted for hours. When the storm passed, the troops emerged, shaking themselves like wet dogs, their eyes bloodshot, their mouths and nostrils coated thick and black with sand and mud, and their clothes impregnated with thousands of irritating grains that would take days to get rid of.

Only in the spring was there any variety in the monotony of the landscape. Then flowers and grass had their short hour: shepherd's purse, dwarf mallow, yellow trefoil and wild mustard appearing as streaks of yellow on a brown canvas alongside the green of the wild barley. Flights of mallard, teal, pochard and geese grazed on the marshes along with sandgrouse, bustard and black partridge, while occasional hares and wild boars could sometimes be seen. (Candler)

The Turkish Commander, Khalil Pasha, could not afford to relax

145

to any extent even though General Gorringe did not seem anxious to move forward. Despite his opposition to the policy, he had to comply with the order to send troops to the north where the Turkish XIII Corps was opposing General Baratov who was hoping to advance on Baghdad. However, as a result, early in June, the Turks defeated the Russians so decisively that Baratov fell back, reporting that the enemy's strength was five times his own.

India at once suggested that this was the moment for General Gorringe to move forward since the Turks had withdrawn troops from in front of him. But all he was in a position to do was advance on the right bank of the Tigris and take over as many of the abandoned Turkish positions as he could maintain in the current lamentable administrative situation.

His advance base was at Sheikh Saad and work was going on to construct a light railway to link it with Sinn Abtar further south as at that moment the amount of food reaching there by river was not enough to maintain the Tigris force on full rations. Not that the Tigris force was at full strength. At this time the 'effective strength' of a battalion was the number of men who were not ill enough to be entirely useless. Every available vehicle held by the Tigris Corps was in use carting water, food and stores across the 14 miles of broken desert between the riverhead and the front line. 'Luxuries' like sun-proof tents and sun helmets were out of the question.

During the month of June, 11,000 sick/casualties were evacuated to India, travelling down the Tigris and across the Persian Gulf in the scorching heat. Even then there remained in hospital in Mesopotamia 16,500 invalids. Reinforcements were arriving but of these a considerable percentage fell sick as soon as they entered the red-hot funnel that was Iraq, and had to be evacuated from the theatre of war without having done even an hour's service in it.

Motor vehicles were an answer to many of the Army's supply problems. Despite the lack of roads the large-diameter wheels of the period could cope with rough tracks, and even unsurfaced desert if it was hard enough, as it was in summer. They were invaluable both for transporting stores and as armoured cars, but there were still very few of them. In July, General Lake was short of motor-transport companies, 110 ambulances and passenger cars, squadrons of armoured cars and motorcycles. Later in the campaign many hundreds of Ford lorries would be brought into service, as well as squadrons of Rolls Royce armoured cars, which were able to carry out many of the duties of the cavalry quicker and with fewer supply requirements like fodder.

Aircraft were proving of immense use in the flat, open country that was Iraq where no camouflage could be really effective. Aerial reconnaissance became crucial and the use of the camera made it invaluable. Accurate maps could be produced and these became a major tool in the hands of successive commanders from 1916 onwards. In May of that year the force possessed five antiquated machines, but by December there were twenty-four up-to-date aircraft equipped with both bombing and photographic equipment, with twenty well-trained pilots.

Things improved slowly. Equipment and supplies were now coming from Britain as well as from India. Basra, the base port, was being reconstructed, while roads were appearing alongside the rivers and railway lines were being laid. A sort of administrative offensive had been initiated by General Lake and, although it would take months for these organizational improvements to be completed, they laid the foundations without which final success in Mesopotamia could not have happened.

Political officers in Basra were being worked off their feet since, as the War Office was determined not to be involved in supply more than was necessary, goods had to be sourced wherever they could be found. A multitude of things were needed: straw and barley for the animals, wheat and dates for Indian troops, sheep and oxen, vegetables, milk, chickens and eggs for hospitals, reeds for making bricks, mats for temporary shelters, sand for building purposes and stone for roads. Stone was eventually quarried near Zubair in the Yemen and a railway line built to access it. Ready made bricks came from Ahwaz, gypsum for mortar from Shushtar, timber from Malabar, seashells for making lime from Khor Musa, sand and rough stone from Kuwait. Every part of the Persian Gulf was being utilized to supply the force.

General Lake did not stay in post long enough see his work come to fruition. He was over sixty and the War Committee decided at the end of August 1916 that it was time for him to be replaced by Lieutenant General Sir Stanley Maude, who had served in France and Gallipoli and was at that time in Mesopotamia commanding the 13th Division.

In October General Sir Charles Munro visited Mesopotamia on his way to India, where he was taking up the appointment of

Commander-in-Chief in place of Sir Beachamp Duff. He and General Maude discussed the situation which they agreed was now becoming more favourable for an advance.

By the beginning of December, the strength of the two armies on the Tigris was as follows: Turkish, on the left bank, about 17,500 infantry and 55 guns; on the right bank about 2,500 infantry and 15 guns. British: 3,500 cavalry, 45,000 infantry and 174 guns. General Maude had a distinct advantage in numbers and now his administrative and supply system was being improved.

In the south, communications were being brought up to scratch by the construction of railways. One was started from Sheikh Saad and reached Sinn Banks by the beginning of September. A line was also started from Basra to Nasiriya and 75 miles of 2ft 6in gauge was opened on 28 November from Qurna to Amara, saving 95 miles of river, the most tortuous and difficult of all stretches on the Tigris. These railways revolutionized the transportation of supplies into the interior of the country and created a system that supply officers of 1915 could only dream of. Then, round trips from Basra to Sheikh Saad, a distance of 240 miles, took fourteen days by river – after completion of the railway this was cut to nine days. Likewise, Sheikh Saad to Kut, a distance of 220 miles, would now be reduced to three days. Later, Kut to Baghdad, after its capture – some 220 miles – took twelve days, and the journey from Basra to Baghdad, using both rail and river, twenty-four days.

Maude decided that, in view of the problems that had plagued the transport system in the past, the only sensible strategic plan was to move forward in a series of limited phases, and to set as an objective the defeat of the enemy and not the capture of Baghdad. This plan he put to General Robertson who gave reluctant permission but laid down a limit of twenty-five per cent casualties.

So the offensive was begun on 12 December with an advance to the River Hai. The plan was to surprise the Turks by moving at night and pushing forward on the right bank to capture the line of the river. By the 18th, III Corps had reached it, six bridges had been built across the stream and the light railway extension to Atab on the Hai had been completed.

However, there was a setback on 26 December when the weather broke and rain fell heavily until 6 January. As the ground became saturated, the desert turned to mud. The problem that had to be solved was how to get within assaulting distance of the

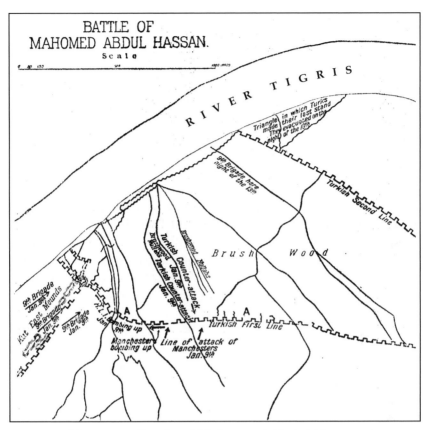

Map 15. Battle of Mahomed Abdul Hassan

enemy and Maude's solution involved a great deal of hard work. Strong standing patrols were sent out by night to establish positions hundreds of yards in advance of the British front line and these were joined up on succeeding nights by digging a continuous new front line. This exercise was repeated further forward on the night of 26/27 December and further again the next night. Even that was still not close enough so on the night of 30/31 December, advanced communication trenches were dug like saps and on subsequent nights the ends joined up to form a continuous front line some 200 yards from the enemy. All this work was done in the pouring rain.

Perhaps other commanders would not have attempted to fight a battle in the prevailing conditions, but for some reason Maude was

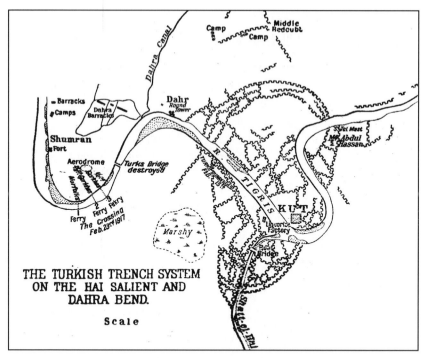

Map 16.   Turkish Trench system on the Hai Salient

in a hurry, so on 9 January, after a heavy bombardment, the attack was launched. The Turks resisted fiercely.

In the fighting, one company of the Manchesters was almost annihilated. Overwhelmed by the enemy, their Lewis guns jammed by mud, their advance was stopped in its tracks until an artillery bombardment and reinforcements from another company of the Manchesters allowed the attack to continue. Side by side with the Lancashire soldiers were Indian regiments who lost men just as heavily and whose bravery matched theirs. In the following days the Turks resisted doggedly and counter-attacked with spirit. Thereafter a raid on the Turkish positions opposite Khadairi on the night of 18/19 January succeeded in driving them back across the river after ten days of resistance that cost the 3rd Division 1,639 casualties.

The Turks looked upon this battle as a very serious defeat. Mohammed Amin, a staff officer in XVIII Corps, referred to it as the turning point of the whole campaign and a costly reverse. A special order was issued by the Turkish Corps Commander stating

150

that 'the steadfastness of the troops . . . in spite of bloody losses, is above praise. The Corps Commander kisses the eyes of all ranks and thanks them.'

The next step was to capture the Hai Salient, the area south of Kut on the right bank of the Tigris where the Hai entered the main river. This was the salient in which the Liquorice Factory village stood alongside the Tigris opposite Kut. After more sapping operations the attack was made simultaneously on both side of the Hai, the fighting lasting from 25 January until 4 February when the Turks evacuated their positions. It had cost the British 8,524 casualties and inflicted what Maude estimated were far heavier casualties on the enemy.

This battle was followed by an attack on the next bend of the Tigris, at Dahra, where the Turks occupied a strong position on the west bank of the river. Following some preliminary moves which evoked strong resistance from the enemy, on the 15th the British moved across open and flat ground in front of the Turks, who by this time were pinned into the bend. After an intense artillery bombardment, the 13th and 14th Divisions charged forward and by 1600 hrs had virtually completed the capture of the position which was finished off by III Corps during the night. Meanwhile, further west, the Cavalry Division, supported by a brigade of the 13th Division had captured the line of the Massaq Canal which ran south from the next bend of the river at Shumran.

On 17 February, an attack was planned on the Turkish positions at Sannaiyat, from which the Turks had been withdrawing troops, in which 21 Brigade was to deliver a surprise attack without a preliminary bombardment, but would be supported by all the Divisional and Corps artillery firing from the other side of the river. Delay was caused by the condition of the muddy and slippery trenches. Two assaulting battalions reached the Turkish front line and hung on there waiting for 19 Brigade to come up behind them, however accurate Turkish shellfire and a strong counter-attack unnerved them and they retreated in a panic, racing back to the trenches they had left. There was no hope of renewing the attack as the trenches were blocked with troops trying to distribute bombs and equipment which should have been done beforehand.

During this time significant events had been taking place elsewhere. In the Caucasus the Russians were planning an offensive against the Turkish Second Army and an advance to the south towards Mosul, Samarra and Baghdad. In Persia, General Baratov, who had been reinforced, was also contemplating an advance. So if the British attacked from the Tigris, the Turks would find themselves under pressure from three directions.

In these circumstances the Chief of the Imperial General Staff asked General Maude what force he would need to capture and hold Baghdad, whilst making it clear that this was only a theoretical enquiry and that the policy remained unchanged.

From the Turkish point of view it seems that the failure of the British attack at Sannaiyat must have confirmed Khalil, the Turkish Commander-in-Chief, in his opinion that the Tigris front was now stable. He had been working on a plan to bring XIII Corps back from Persia to cut Maude's communications between Sheikh Saad and Amara, and was so obsessed with the idea that he refused to reinforce XVIII Corps which was opposing Maude. The Commander of XVIII Corps was Kiazim Karabekir, a capable soldier who maintained the morale of his force despite their inferior numbers. He had been acutely aware of the danger posed to Baghdad by the possibility of a Maude offensive and had several times warned Khalil about it. However, Khalil failed to make any defensive plans for covering Baghdad and even neglected to maintain the five defensive posts between Aziziya and Baghdad established by his more far-seeing predecessor, Nureddin.

When Maude's offensive was fully underway, Khalil awoke from his dream and ordered XIII Corps back to Baghdad on 16 February. But it was too late to get the units together since their concentration was prevented by Baratoff's offensive and the snows in the mountains, so that only small detachments arrived, from which many had deserted. In one instance a Turkish report stated: 'the unit is coming but the Battalion Commander has deserted.'

After Dahra, the next bend in the river was the Shumran but the difficulties of moving large bodies of troops around in the flooded area on the right bank turned Maude's attention to the left bank. The Turkish force there had originally been blocking the Hai passage, but the British successes on the right bank that extended their occupation of it further towards Kut meant that the Turks had constantly to detach units to position themselves along the left bank in order to keep in confrontation across the river. By 15 February, their forces were strung out along 25 miles of river bank.

Maude decided that the best plan was to cross the river at Shumran and attack the Turks at opposite ends of this attenuated line. It would mean only the one crossing of the river since at Sannaiyat the British 7th Division was still in position fronting the Turkish trenches. But, as so often in Mesopotamia, the elements intervened and heavy rain fell on the 17th causing the attack to be abandoned; it continued to pour intermittently until the 21st. On the 22nd the 7th Division the attacked the Sannaiyat lines and broke through to the second line where they consolidated. It had cost 1,332 casualties.

The next task was to get a bridge across the river on the eastern side of the Shumran bend. On the other side of the river, a few hundred yards away, were the enemy trenches. At 0530 hrs three pontoons were silently launched into the Tigris when it was just light enough to see the opposite bank. The enemy was taken by surprise but recovered quickly and two out of the three pontoons were brought to a halt by rifle and gun fire. The third persisted despite the artillery bombardment and by 1500 hrs all three battalions of the covering force had forced themselves onto the left bank and were able to hold back the Turks while the bridge construction started. The fighting continued to be hot and the bridge builders were hindered by heavy baulks of timber that the Turks launched into the raging current which itself was proving a problem. But by midnight the thousand-foot-long bridge was completed and the whole of the 14th Division was across having suffered 350 casualties.

The naval force passed through the bridge and by the evening of the 24th, the largest gunboats, drawing 5 feet of water – the *Mantis* and its sister ships of the Insect Class, *Tarantula* and *Moth* – together with a swarm of 'Flies' – *Butterfly, Gadfly* and *Snakefly* – were anchored off Kut and the British flag was hoisted again over the deserted town next morning.

At the same time the 7th Division resumed its attack at Sannaiyat and seized the third and fourth lines of trenches. By the end of the day the cavalry had swept through the last lines at Sannaiyat and on to the Turkish positions at Nakhailat and Suwada to overrun them both, while on the other side of the river III Corps and the Cavalry Division were in the Shumran Peninsula and clearing it out.

The 13th Division of III Corps, advancing along the left bank the following morning, met with very stubborn resistance at a canal running north from the north end of the Husaini bend. Fierce fighting went on all day until the Turks fell back in the evening. In the village of Imam Mahdi the Cavalry Division was also held up but, instead of using its mobility and making a detour, they got bogged down. At 1930 hrs they had to be withdrawn and brought back to the Tigris to water the horses.

Armoured cars had been used since Ctesiphon and were now as useful for scouting and skirmishing as the cavalry, and were certainly capable of inflicting equally substantial damage on retreating troops or on artillery batteries, two of the cavalty's main functions. They also had the advantage of not having to be withdrawn from a position to be watered.

During the night the Turks withdrew so that in the morning III Corps was able to make good progress on the left bank, with the Naval Flotilla pressing forward in typical naval style. Some way beyond Baghaila they came under fire from the 4-inch gun on the *Firefly*, captured by the Turks in December 1916, and from the armed launch *Pioneer* positioned in a bend of the river some distance ahead.

The *Tarantula* with its 6-inch guns and Captain Nunn on board was in the lead. At Nahr al Kalak they came up to the Turkish rear-guard entrenched at the apex of a hairpin turn in the river. The channel was narrow and every ship would be under continuous fire from artillery, machine-guns and rifle fire at ranges varying from 100 to 500 yards from three directions and for 5 miles as they navigated through the horseshoe. Captain Nunn did not hesitate but drove ahead followed by the rest of the flotilla, coming under heavy fire to which each ship responded with all her available armament.

As a naval engagement it must have been unique. Many of the crews were hit, the *Moth*, last in line, was holed beneath the water-line and hit eight times by shells, one of which pierced her boilers, but she was kept going despite losing four out of her five officers and half her complement.

Having passed the rearguard, the flotilla overtook the main body of the enemy and opened rapid fire with every available weapon. The armed tug *Sumana*, captured by the Turks after the fall of Kut, was retaken and the *Firefly*, on fire and run ashore by its crew, was boarded, the flames put out and a prize crew detached to hoist the white ensign and get her under way again. The sight of the approaching ships had now converted the Turkish retreat into a rout and they streamed away towards Baghdad.

Shortly afterwards, the steamer *Basra* fell into the Navy's hands. She was packed with wounded Turks who could be smelt half a mile away for almost to a man their wounds had turned to gangrene. As darkness fell, Captain Nunn anchored far ahead of the British main body.

The airmen, too, had done their bit to harry the retreating Turks, flying low and mowing down lines of men with their machine-guns. Captain (later Colonel) Tennant, the Commanding Officer, in his book *In the Clouds above Baghdad*, describes the scene: 'a spectacle amazing and horrible; dead bodies and mules, abandoned guns. Wagons, and stores littered the road, many of the wagons had hoisted white flags, men and animals, exhausted and starving, lay prone on the ground. Few of these, if any, survived the attentions of the Arab tribesmen, hanging round like wolves on their trail . . . I turned home sickened.'

On the 27th the Cavalry reached Aziziya where the pursuit drew rein and where Townshend's dash had come to a halt the year before. General Maude decided to pause for a couple of weeks and re-organize. The cavalry camped east of Aziziya, III Corps between Aziziya and Bughhaila, and I Corps closed up to Qala Shadi.

During this respite Maude telegraphed to London for instructions. The opinion of the General Staff had been that the occupation of Baghdad would have no effect on the war, but nothing succeeds like success and in the reply he was told to press on to Baghdad if he himself thought it 'useful and feasible', and providing he thought he could maintain a force of four divisions of infantry and one of cavalry there. Again, as so often in this campaign, the higher author-ities passed the buck down to the man on the spot and divested themselves of the responsibility of changing their own policy.

On 5 March, General Maude therefore advanced from Aziziya and ran into a Turkish force of infantry and artillery at Lajj, 20 miles upstream, which held him up all day. During the night they decamped and the advance resumed. The next opposition was met at the River Diyala. Thinking this was the rearguard of a larger force, Maude ordered III Corps to force a crossing under cover of darkness on the night 7/8 March while he had a bridge built across the Tigris at Bawi so that he could get troops onto the right bank and advance directly on Baghdad.

Khalil, the Turkish commander, seems to have lost his head as the British approached the city. Three days after Maude crossed the Tigris, he withdrew his HQ to Baghdad informing XVIII Corps Commander that he did not intend to make a stand south of

Samarra. Next day he changed his mind and ordered Karabekir to halt at Aziziya and fight it out. But this order was impossible to obey since the British were already there, so Karabekir Bey disregarded it and continued his retirement to Lajj where, as we have already seen, the British ran into him, and to Ctesiphon where he halted for several days preparing a defensive position while the Army Commander decided what to do next.

Khalil had no plan and it was only as an afterthought, due probably to his belief that the British were unable to continue the pursuit, that he decided to defend Baghdad. His indecision had wasted several valuable days.

According to the Turks, if Khalil had made use of the two-week respite the British had given him and co-ordinated a system of defence on the line of the River Diyala, with organized inundation of the surrounding countryside, there was no reason why he should not have been able to hold up the British advance for some time with the force he had at his disposal. His total strength during the fighting for the city must have been between 11,000 and 15,000 on the Diyala alone. As it was, he failed to flood the countryside and his force was unable to hold a sufficient frontage to avoid having its flanks being turned.

The River Diyala and the Kharr (or Mahsudiya) Canal were the only two obstacles of any importance guarding Baghdad from the south and south-west. Except for numerous irrigation canals and some small mounds, the surrounding countryside was absolutely flat and would require a large force to prepare extensive field works that could be defended adequately.

On the right bank of the Tigris, by opening up the irrigation channels from the Kharr Canal, a large tract on the west and south-west would be made impassible, thus reducing the frontage that must be defended to a narrow strip west of the river. On the left bank during flood season from March to May, the whole country between the city and Diyala could have been flooded by cutting the embankments north of the town. By sinking boats and damming the Diyala about 20 miles upstream, a great deal of the desert east of the Diyala and the Tigris could have been inundated and thus a turning movement of an approaching force from the east or north-east could have been prevented.

Khalil would then only have to watch the line of the Diyala for some 14 miles, while on the right bank he could have held a line from Tel Aswad (a halt on the railway south-westward out of Baghdad) to the Tigris, a distance of about 10 miles, with a main position in the rear which, with the help of the Kharr Canal, could have watched the line from Umm ut Tubul (north of Tel Aswad) to Tel Atab (9 miles further north) right up to Lake Aqarqui (even further north), thus effectively guarding the right flank. The Kharr Canal was a good obstacle, 25 yards wide, 30 feet deep and with steep banks.

But no concerted plan was adopted. When Karabekir Bey withdrew to Aziziya against orders, he was told to prepare a defensive position at Ctesiphon, while the 14th Division, that had now arrived on the scene, prepared the line of the Diyala with a supporting position in the rear from Tel Mahommed, 10 miles south-east of Baghdad, to Qarara, on the Tigris, a distance of 8 miles. A short defensive position was begun closer in to the city from the Tigris to Umm ut Tubul. Khalil neglected the northern flank in favour of the south because he wished to keep open communications with XIII Corps on its way back from Persia.

He then changed his mind and decided to hold the Diyala and a much longer line from the Tigris to Tel Aswad, 8 miles away. Accordingly the Umm ut Tubul fortifications were abandoned and 3 miles of trench were started near Tel Aswad.

When Karabekir was shown what he was to hold with a 52nd Division numbering only 23,000 men, he told the Army Commander that his forces were insufficient to hold such a long line. He pointed out the British could easily pin him down on the Diyala, transfer the bulk of their forces to the right bank of the Tigris and occupy Baghdad from the west. Therefore the right bank was the dangerous one and it would be better to hold the shorter Umm ut Tubul line. Accordingly, work on the Tel Aswad position was abandoned and recommenced at Umm ut Tubul. But by this time it was too late as the British were already at the River Diyala and neither position was complete.

In Persia the Russians started to follow up the rearguard of XIII Corps west of Kirmanshah on 3 March. The CIGS told General Maude that Baratoff, the Russian commander, had been instructed to push on to Khaniquin on the upper Diyala. The CIGS thought the 6th Turkish Division might escape but that General Maude should be able to cut off the 2nd Turkish Division and join up with the Russians. The 6th Division did get away but only reached Baquba

157

and apart from its 44th Regiment XIII Corps did not participate in the defence of Baghdad.

Thus on 7 March, when the Tigris Force arrived on the Diyala the Turkish forces were: XIII Corps withdrawing on Khaniquin, their 6th Division in the lead; 64th and 156th Regiments arriving from Fallujeh on the Euphrates to the west; 37th Regiment arriving from Baquba, on the Diyala, 30 miles north of Baghdad; XVIII Corps and the 14th Division on the Diyala and the Tigris right bank.

A pontoon bridge over the Diyala had been dismantled and towed upstream by the Turks while an old wooden bridge had been destroyed and stringent orders were issued that all bridging material was to be shifted to the right bank of the Diyala. However, a few pontoons had been forgotten by the 44th Regiment and the Turks blamed them for the initial British crossing of the river, but this was actually unfair since the British used their own pontoons.

While two battalions of the 3rd and 44th Regiments were holding some 10 miles of the Diyala river front with posts on the left bank, the remainder of the 51st and 14th Divisions were preparing the Tel Mahommed line. On the right bank, the 52nd Division, assisted by local labour, was improving the main line of resistance from the Tigris to the Decauville railway at Umm ut Tubul and thence northwards towards Tel Atab.

The 43rd Regiment, with part of the 37th Regiment, was holding the Tel Aswad–Tigris line as a forward line to give the other defenders time to complete the main positions in the rear while the bulk of the Turkish artillery was on the Karrada Peninsula (inside the big river loop south of Baghdad) or between the Kharr railway bridge, south-west of Baghdad and Tel Atab to the north.

Turkish resistance was fierce and they disputed the Diyala crossing with ferocity – it was not until 0400 hrs on the 10th that they were pushed back and the 13th Division were able to cross the river. On the right bank the cavalry found the going difficult over drainage ditches and canals that were not shown on the inadequate maps they had. They came up with the Turks at the Umm ut Tubul sandhills south-west of Baghdad. Instead of galloping on to the surprised Turks, the Cavalry Commander decided to outflank them and leave the charge to the infantry. Surprise was thrown away and when the 7th Division went in they were able to make little progress, losing 700 casualties. Meanwhile the cavalry failed to outflank the Turkish right.

Aerial photography of all parts of the front was now becoming a priority. The photographic section developed and printed the film throughout the night and the mapping section turned out accurate maps that were distributed by air to units in the front line in the morning. Often the latest editions of these, showing enemy earthworks photographed a few hours previously, would be dropped to units just about to attack. They were used with advantage in the Baghdad operation and, in this respect, were matched by the aerial reconnaissance of the Turks who had several new aircraft and a complement of German mechanics in Baghdad. They always knew accurately the movements of the British forces.

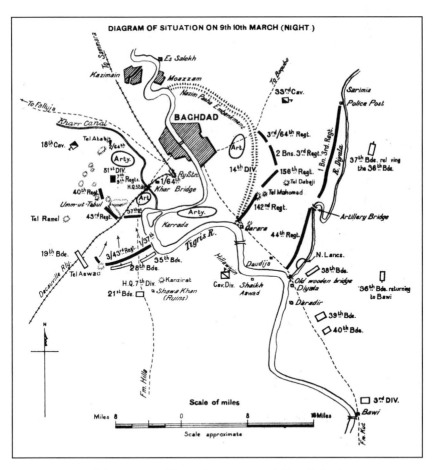

Map 17.   Situation around Baghdad

159

During the night of 9/10 March, while the 13th Division was forcing the crossing of the Diyala, the Turks withdrew from their advanced position and at daybreak on the 19th the 7th Division was able to advance and attack the main position at Umm ut Tubul. Here again, the enemy put up a strong resistance and throughout the day held off the attackers, who suffered very much from being swept by strong winds and dust storms, enduring agonies of thirst. But by nightfall the Turks were beginning to lose heart. On both sides of the Tigris, the British, in greatly superior numbers, were pressing back the defence, their columns steadily converging upon Baghdad. To continue to stand outside the city would mean the annihilation of XVIII Corps. On the night of the 10th, after having put up a valiant struggle, it withdrew from the positions surrounding Baghdad that it had defended and retreated northwards up the river.

Next afternoon, 11 March, General Maude entered Baghdad but this triumph provided his troops little rest. He spent the rest of the month consolidating the position which meant advancing against strong resistance in the increasing heat to a defensible line covering the city, some 20 miles north, from Sharabin–Mushaidi–Fallujeh.

Littered behind him on the left bank of the Tigris was the debris of a routed Turkish army. Since 22 February the Turks had lost 63 of their 91 guns, of which 33 had been captured and the rest thrown into the river; 4,300 men had been taken prisoner; and all their bridging train, three supply steamers, the *Sumana* – the erstwhile HMS *Firefly* – and a quantity of rifles, machine-guns and other miscellaneous equipment had been captured.

Many of the population of Baghdad welcomed the arrival of the British Army, but not all. Like most eastern towns, the place smelt abominably and was littered with dead animals and filth, but a feature of the town that delighted the British Tommies was the great abundance of oranges. Neither fresh fruit nor vegetables had been available for months and they could now bury their faces in large, cool, fresh fruit.

The Turkish XVIII Corps was thought to be boarding trains at Mushaida Station on the line to Samarra, north of Baghdad, and Maude was determined to stop them. He sent three brigades in pursuit, with 21 Brigade with the Gurkhas and the Black Watch in the lead on the left. As they approached the railway station, they were faced with an entrenched position which the Black Watch charged and overran, losing 40 per cent of their men, and the

Gurkhas all but one of their British officers. They borrowed another from the Black Watch and the remnants of the two battalions, reinforced by two companies of the Seaforth Hughlanders, reached the railway station. But the platform was empty of Turks – the last train had already left.

Order of Battle of Force under General Maude

Cavalry Division comprising:
   6th Cavalry Brigade comprising:
      14th King's Hussars
      21st Cavalry
      'S' Battery Royal Horse Artillery (six 13-pdrs)
      6th Squadron, Machine Gun Corps
      2nd Field Troop, Royal Engineers
      131st Cavalry Field Ambulance
      Mobile Vetinerary Section
   7th Cavalry Brigade comprising:
      13th Hussars
      13th Duke of Cornwall's Own Lancers
      14th Murray's Jat Lancers
      'V' Battery, Royal Horse Artillery (six 13-pdrs)
      7th Squadron, Machine Gun Corps
      Field Troop, Royal Engineers
      119th Cavalry Field Ambulance
      Mobile Vetinerary Section

I Indian Army Corps comprising:
   3rd Lahore Division comprising:
      7 Brigade comprising:
         1st Connaught Rangers
         27th Punjabis
         91st Punjabis
         2/7th Gurkhas
         131st Company, Machine Gun Corps
         7 Brigade, Supply and Transport Company
      8 Brigade comprising:
         1st Manchester Regiment
         2/124th Baluchi Infantry
         47th Duke of Cornwall's Own Sikhs

59th Royal Scind Rifles
132nd Company, Machine Gun Corps
8 Brigade, Supply and Transport Company
9 Brigade comprising:
1st Highland Light Infantry
1/1st Gurkhas
93rd Burma Infantry
105th Mahrattas
133rd Company, Machine Gun Corps
9 Brigade, Supply and Transport Company
Divisional Artillery comprising:
4 Brigade, RFA (three 18-pdr batteries, each of three guns)
215th Brigade, RFA (three 18-pdr batteries, each of four guns)
Two 4.5-in howitzer batteries, each of four howitzers

34th Sikh Pioneers
18th, 20th and 21st Companies of the 3rd Sappers and Miners
Small Arm Ammunition Column:
3rd Divisional Signal Company
Two British and three Indian Field Ambulances
3rd Divisional Supply and Transport Company
Sanitary Section
Mobile Veterinary Section

7th Meerut Division comprising:
19 Brigade comprising:
1st Seaforth Highlanders (Ross-shire Buffs)
28th Punjabis
92nd Punjabis
125th Rifles
134th Company, Machine Gun Corps
19 Brigade, Supply and Transport Company
21 Brigade comprising:
2nd Royal Highland Fusiliers
9th Bhopal Regiment
20th Duke of Cornwalls's Own Infantry (Brownlow's Punjabis)
1/8th Gurkha Rifles

135th Company, Machine Gun Corps
21st Brigade, Supply and Transport Company
28 Brigade comprising:
2nd Leicestershire Regiment
31st Sikhs
53rd Sikhs
56th Punjabi Rifles
136th Company, Machine Gun Corps
28 Brigade, Supply and Transport Company

Divisional Artillery comprising:
9 Brigade, RFA (three 18-pdr batteries, each of six guns)
56 Brigade, RFA (four 18-pdr batteries, each of four guns)
121st Pioneers
1st, 3rd and 4th companies of 1st Sappers and Miners.

Small Arms Ammunition Column comprising:
7th Divisional Signals Company
Two British and three Indian Field Ambulances
7th Divisional Supply and Transport Company
Sanitary Section
Mobile Veterinerary Section

Corps Troops:
32nd Lancers (less two squadrons)
No. 1 Printing and Lithographic Section
No. 1 Corps Signal Company

111 Indian Army Corps comprising:
13th British Division comprising:
38 Brigade comprising:
6th King's Own Royal Lancaster Regiment
6th East Lancashire Regiment
6th Prince of Wales Volunteers, South Lancashires
6th Loyal North Lancashire Regiment
38th Company, Machine Gun Corps
38 Brigade, Supply and Transport Company
39 Brigade comprising:
9th Royal Warwickshire Regiment
9th Worcestershire Regiment

7th North Staffordshire Regiment
7th Gloucestershire Regiment
39th Company, Machine Gun Corps
39 Brigade, Supply and Transport Company
40 Brigade comprising:
    8th Royal Welch Fusiliers
    8th Cheshire Regiment
    4th South Wales Borderers
    5th Wiltshire Regiment
    40th Company, Machine Gun Corps
    40 Brigade, Supply and Transport Company
Divisional Artillery comprising:
    55 Brigade, RFA (four 18-pdr batteries, each of four guns)
    66 Brigade, RFA (four 18-pdr batteries, each of four guns)
    One howitzer battery of four 4.5-in howitzers

8th Pioneer Battalion, Welch Regiment
71, 72 and 88 Companies, Royal Engineers

Small Arms Ammunition Column comprising:
    13th Divisional Cyclist Company
    13th Divisional Signals Company
    13 Division, Supply and Transport Company
    Three Field Ambulances
    Sanitary Section
    Mobile Veterinary Section

14th Indian Division comprising:
    35 Brigade comprising:
        1/5th East Kent Regiment (the Buffs)
        37th Dogras
        2/4th Gurkha Rifle
        3rd Brahmans (replaced 19 Dec by 102nd Grenadiers)
        185th Company Machine Gun Corps
        35 Brigade, Supply and Transport Company
    36 Brigade comprising:
        1/4th Hampshire Regiment
        28th Punjabis
        62nd Punjabias
        82nd Punjabis

186th Company, Machine Gun Corps
36 Brigade, Supply and Transport Company
37 Brigade comprising:
1/4th Devonshire Regiment
36th Sikhs
45th Sikhs
1/2nd Gurkhas
187th Company, Machine Gun Corps
37th Brigade, Supply and Transport Company
Divisional Artillery comprising:
13 Brigade, RFA (three 18-pdr batteries, each of six guns)
One howitzer battery of four 4.5-in howitzers
128th Pioneers

12, 13 and 15 Companies, 2nd Sappers and Miners

Small Arms Ammunition Column comprising:
14th Divisional Signal Company
14th Divisional Supply and Transport Company
Five Field Ambulances
Sanitary Section.
Mobile Veterinary Section

Corps Troops:
Two Squadrons 32nd Lancers
No. 2 Printing and Lithographic Section
3rd Corps Signals Company
General HQ

Army Troops comprising:
Royal Naval Air Service :
No. 14 Kite Balloon Section

Artillery:
134 (Howitzer) Brigade RFA (two batteries each of six 4.5-in howitzers
74th Heavy Artillery Group, RGA (three batteries each of four 60-pdrs)
159th Siege Battery, RGA (four 6-in howitzers),

Anti-Aircraft Battery (four 13-pdrs)
Anti-Aircraft Section (two 12-pdrs)

Engineers:
Nos 1, 2 and 3 Bridging Trains, Bengal Sappers and Miners
No. 5 Printing and Lithographic Section
No. 6 Printing Section

Royal Flying Corps:
No. 30 Squadron

Supply and Transport:
Army Troops, Supply and Transport Company
Army Supply Column

Chapter Eleven

Advances in the North

(Maps 18, 19, 20, 21, 22 and 23)

The Russian army under General Baratoff was still approaching Baghdad from the north-east with the residue of Ali Ihsan's Turkish XIII Corps withdrawing in front of it. Despite the fact that the Russian Revolution had started the day before General Maude entered Baghdad, Baratoff was sticking to the order to pursue the Turks vigorously and co-operate with the British in destroying them; he had two Cossack divisions for the purpose. The Turkish line of retreat, if it continued, would take them obliquely across the front of the British, north-east of Baghdad, crossing a range of hills called the Jabal (meaning mountain in Arabic) Hamrin, a higgledy-piggledy attenuated mass of high ground through which the River Diyala forced a passage in a narrow gorge on its way south-west. These hills were hardly mapped but nowhere rose higher than 600 feet.

General Keary was ordered by Maude to advance towards them in the direction of the town of Shahraban, with 7 Cavalry Brigade, 8 and 9 Brigades of the 3rd Division and five gun batteries. However, air reconnaissance reported that at least 2,000 Turks were already through the high land, crossing the Diyala river and entrenching to the east of Shahraban. During the night a force was detached from Keary's main body and moved forward to attack the enemy but was delayed by having to cross two canals.

The Turks had built their entrenchments in the entrance to the gap in the Jabal Hamrin through which the road passed. As the light

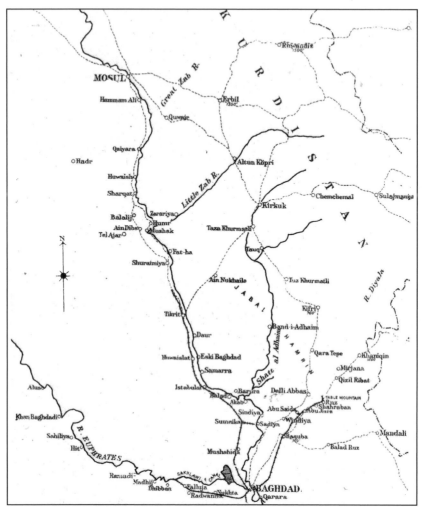

Map 18.   Northern Mesopotamia

strengthened, 9 Brigade, in the lead, came under heavy fire when they approached the Turkish positions. There was little cover and the fire was so fierce that they suffered nearly 1,000 casualties without getting close enough to launch an attack. The order to retire was given and the troops withdrew with difficulty with the help of covering fire from 8 Brigade.

News came on the night of 26/27 March that the Turks were aiming at joining up XIII Corps, who were continuing to cross the

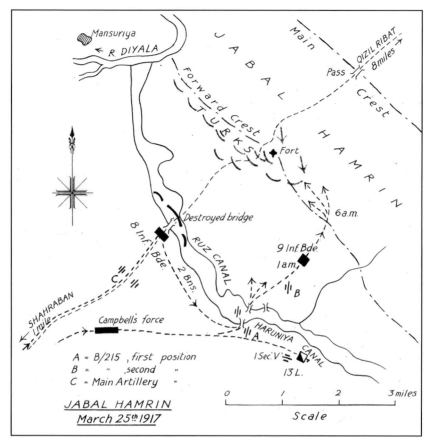

Map 19.   Battle of Jabal Hamrin

Diyala river unopposed, with XVIII Corps, at the moment about 25 miles to their west, close to the junction of the Tigris and Shatt al Adhaim rivers. Maude determined to prevent this. Keary was ordered to stay where he was while III British Corps would take care of the Turkish XVIII Corps.

XVIII Corps crossed the Shatt al Adhaim and advanced down the Tigris to Mara some 40 miles north of Baghdad, were they were met by General Cayley and the 13th Division. He divided his force into two groups to attack the Turks at a place where they were using some ancient ruins as a focus for their entrenchments. Then, on 29 March, the Warwicks and the Gloucesters of 39 Brigade began to advance under cover of artillery fire over 3,000 yards of perfectly open ground, but the heat and the mirage were both increasing and a halt of three hours was made to allow stragglers to catch up.

The artillery came up to close range at about 1400 hrs and the advance continued, all battalions moving forward in line. As they did so, marauding bands of Arabs got up behind them and started cutting their telephone cables. Brigade HQ was nearby and, immediately seizing their rifles, all members from the Brigade Major to the lowliest private drove them off while the front-line troops completed the advance with great dash and gallantry. But the enemy, as usual, took to their heels as the British troops got close.

The Turkish commander of XIII Corps, Ali Ihsan, had skilfully extricated his force from his dangerous position between the British and the Russians, having displayed a quick grasp of the situation. In this, he was helped by the Russians who were not behaving very vigorously and by the problems the British had in operating in difficult country where they were lacking a good deal of the bridging material necessary for crossing wide canals. Although there were no good maps of the country, British aircraft should have been able to report the presence and location of these obstacles and the force should therefore have been better informed and better equipped to prepare for the advance.

On 1 April, 8 Brigade met an advance party of Baratov's Russian Cossacks, who came in at a walk on their thin little ponies, their sheepskin caps, jackboots, rifles, knives and curved Caucasian scimitars making an exotic spectacle. The country they had covered had been an uninhabited waste through which seven separate armies had passed in the previous ten months. Villages had been abandoned and food both for the men and the horses was almost unobtainable. The Cossacks filled themselves and their animals with bully beef, ration biscuits, jam and dates and in the evening they disappeared never to be seen again.

This was all the British troops ever saw of the Russians with whom they were supposed to link up. The 10,000 troops Baratoff said that he had, turned out to be only 3,000 since a good number had decided that the war was over for them and had made off. In any event, Baratoff refused to cross the border into Mesopotamia, declaring that his orders were to clear Persia, which he had done, and he was going no further. It seems that the Russian Revolution was beginning to have its effect.

Further south, at Mara, close to the Tigris, battle was joined on 5

April by 40 Brigade when the Wiltshires advanced and captured some rifle pits in front of the enemy's front line, although the mirage was interfering with the artillery and they had to cease fire. Later in the day it was decided to postpone the attack until the next morning, by which time the Turks had decamped.

On 8 April the Turks had begun to move westward from positions in the Jabal Hamrin, their XIII Corps advancing on both sides of the Khalis Canal while being kept under observation both by the cavalry division and by aircraft. During the period 11–14 April there was much manoeuvring of the British units, but despite two distinct attempts they did not actually succeed in bringing the Turks to battle. Much of the problem arose from the fact that both Maude and Marshall were trying to control the actions and the senior officer on the ground, General Cayley, was not being allowed a free hand. The Turks retired to their positions in the mountains.

The Shatt al Adhaim winds down from the northern end of the Jabal Hamrin, the river itself is some 80 yards across and its valley about a mile wide with steep cliff-like banks. On the west side the Turks had dug themselves in on the edge of the western cliffs, strung out over a distance of about 3½ miles, their line varying from between a few yards to a mile from the winding river. 38 Brigade was ordered to cross the stream and chose a spot where it hugged the eastern bank. Before it was light on 18 April, the East Lancashires waded across and were followed by the 6th King's Own in boats; between them they captured the main Turkish position by shortly after noon. By noon too a bridge had been thrown across the river so that 35 Brigade and the cavalry were able to dash over and pursue the retreating enemy, capturing 1,250 prisoners.

At this juncture the Turkish XIII Corps once more appeared on the scene, sending their advanced troops down from the hills along the west bank of the Adhaim. Maude decided to ignore them for the moment and continued with his plan to capture Istabulat, a station north of Muahahida on the Baghdad railway. Turkish positions were distributed parallel to the River Tigris along the railway and between it and the Dujail Canal. The Black Watch and the Gurkhas, forming 21 Brigade, working together again, advanced and captured the positions between the Canal and the river, whilst 19 Brigade attacked positions between the Canal and the railway.

But 21 Brigade's advance ground to a stop in the face of fierce

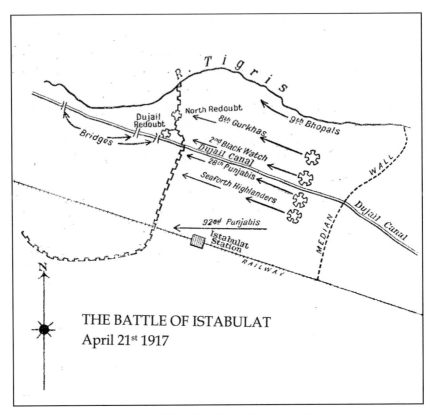

Map 20. Battle of Istabulat

counter-attacks and it was decided to halt both brigades until the next day, the 22nd. As it got light it was seen that the Turks had vanished and so at 0500 hrs the pursuit began with 28 Brigade in the lead, closely followed by 19 Brigade. Eight miles further north they came up against the Turks in a prepared position, which was assaulted and captured by the Leicesters, who pushed on beyond it, seizing seven guns. But the Turks suddenly counter-attacked and the Leicesters were halted for a time before the attack died away at nightfall. Next day the Turks had done their usual disappearing trick and on the 24th the British force marched a few miles north to Samarra, the ancient town and the terminus of the railway. The Turkish XVIII Corps retired to Tikrit.

It was now time to deal again with XIII Corps who had despatched their 14th and 2nd Divisions to advance down the Adhaim. With the

Turkish 14th Division halted near Dahuba waiting for the 2nd Division to catch up, Marshall decided to engage the left flank of the 14th Division before the 2nd arrived. It was to be attacked by half of 38 Brigade, while 7 Cavalry Brigade was to outflank the enemy to his rear and prevent the 2nd Division joining it.

Thinking it was cut off, the 14th Division forded the Adhaim, which ended the action. Both Turkish divisions drew off to the north up the valley of the Adhaim and eventually linked up at the village of Adhaim, before taking up positions astride the river. The main British attack fell on the Turkish 14th Division on the left bank of the river, while its right flank was attacked by 40 Brigade and its left by 38 Brigade.

40 Brigade approached the Turkish entrenchments with the Cheshires on their left and the South Wales Borderers on the right. By pushing ahead of their fellows, led by their ebullient colonel, the Cheshires captured both Turkish lines and the village but lost their Commanding Officer in the process.

A dust storm then blew up and lasted for two hours. In the gloom both the Cheshires and half of the South Wales Borderers in the village were cut off and were captured by reserves who had been sent up from the main Turkish camp further north. The remaining battalions of 40 Brigade were sent to the rescue but only succeeded in recapturing the village. XIII Corps retreated again taking their prisoners with them in the direction of Tikrit.

It was the hottest summer in living memory and both sides went into summer quarters, the British forward headquarters being in Samarrah, the burial place of the Roman emperor Julian and the terminus of the railway line. The temperature was higher than in the two previous years and the heat had begun earlier. Most things in camp were too hot to touch – even inside a tent the rim of a tumbler burnt a man's mouth; dust and sand scorched the soles of men's feet through thick-soled boots. Various methods of keeping cool were tried by the troops, the majority of whom were under canvas. The one that seemed to work best was to sink the floor of the tent three or four feet into the ground, erect a canopy of rushes over the top and fill up the opening on the windward side with a framework of wet camel-thorn.

During the past few months relations had become strained between General Maude and the Civil Administration represented by Sir Percy Cox, who was anxious to bring all the country behind

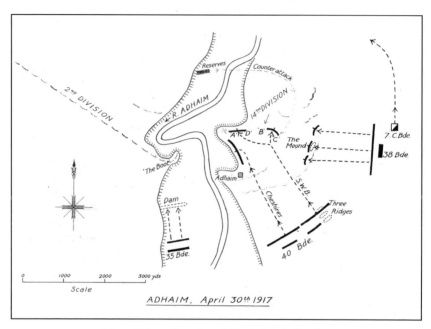

Map 21. Battle of Band-I-Adhaim

the British army under political control, and who wanted General Maude to garrison the line of the Euphrates from Felujah to Nasiriyeh. This was a sensible precaution but General Maude refused to do it on the grounds that it was militarily unwise to scatter the force more widely than it already was. The Civil Administration also complained that the Army Commander tended to ignore the Arabs who, because of this, were becoming so resentful of the British that the Civil Administration was having trouble in finding any who were willing to co-operate with them, although this was also partly because the Arabs still retained the fear that the Turks would return and punish them. Many Arab leaders, particularly the Sunnis, remained pro-Turkish until after the war.

There was also some dispute between Sir Percy Cox and General Maude as to their responsibilities. Maude tended to be rather high-handed and to centralize under his control matters that should have been the responsibility of the Civil Administration. After the capture of Baghdad, the General had issued a proclamation to the people of the Baghdad wilayat (region), drafted by Sir Mark Sykes, a confirmed orientalist, that managed to ignore the different minori-

174

ties in the area and envisaged a united Arabia that would include Mesopotamia. This upset both the Political Service and a good many national groups – the Kurds, for example – since it seemed to suggest that they would be placed under the control of the hated and despised Sunnis.

As at Basra, a military officer was appointed as Governor of Baghdad but General Maude, despite his military duties, attempted to control in detail the work of the Military Governor. The job was complicated enough without additional interference for when the Turks left they had destroyed practically every administrative record so that the British government of the city had to start practically from scratch.

Leading Arab families were not anti-Turk; on the contrary the landed gentry and the subordinate clerical staff who remained in Baghdad were on the whole hostile to the Arab regime that was outlined in General Maude's proclamation. In their hearts they preferred the Turk with all his failings, in preference to an untried Anglo-Arab combination. Many of the leading Arabs had been educated in Constantinople, Turkish rather than Arabic was the language of polite society and they regarded the Turkish capital as their cultural centre. The majority, too, both in the town and in the desert, were Sunnis, with definite Turkish sympathies. They nursed a number of grievances. On the waterfront, 200 fair-sized houses were requisitioned as billets for the garrison. Pre-war rates plus 10 per cent was paid as rent which was but a fraction of what could be made in the period of wartime inflation that had developed. House-to-house searches for arms, the enforcement of vigorous and not very welcome sanitary precautions and almost daily promulgations by the Military Governor on a bewildering variety of subjects were sources of irritation. Little or no attempt was made to apply the experience gained by the more liberal and easy-going regime that had developed in Basra. As with other aspects of the campaign this perhaps could be said to have a modern resonance.

There were, of course, ongoing problems outside Baghdad. On the Tigris, the British were in possession of Samarra but the proximity of the Turks prevented much being done to improve matters there. Supplies of seed were short and the Arab farmers, from bitter experience of the Turkish habit of seizing whatever they needed, refused to sow their usual cash crops in the desert and were in any case very short of plough animals. The presence in the area of large British forces involved a vast amount of necessary but somewhat thankless work for the Political Service – inquiring into complaints on both sides and acting as intermediaries between the inhabitants and the army. Many military roads that had been hastily constructed had blocked innumerable small canals; the simple farmers proceeded to cut ditches through the roads at their leisure, especially at night, to irrigate their fields. To construct all the necessary culverts was not an easy task, nor was it at first the complete solution for the Arab, finding a culvert a little smaller than he might wish, thought nothing of grubbing it up and blocking the road.

To the west on the Upper Euphrates, the problems were not very different. Until the fall of Ramadi (50 miles west of Baghdad) in September 1917 the British position was, in Arab eyes, not very secure – the powerful Anaiza tribe under Sheikh Fahad ibn Hadhdal stayed aloof, while the Dulaim tribe were for the most part under Turkish influence. Demands by the army for sheep and cattle tended to deplete their flocks seriously and restrictions on their movements irked them.

It was on the Middle Euphrates that the problem of restoring peace seemed most difficult amongst a population that was partly tribal and partly settled, although the authority of the tribal sheikhs was mostly still effective. An Arab Government Agent had been appointed by the Turks and he sat astride the whirlwind of local intrigue. He had taken up his quarters at Daghara, on the Shat Hilla river, 60 miles west of Kut, but his life was anything but peaceful. Tribes demanded money for keeping the peace even though inter-tribal wars were in progress, besieging him in his house and keeping him awake at night by dancing on his roof until the money was forthcoming.

Below Hilla there were no British soldiers before December 1917. Until October the Arab Agent was Hamid Khan, a cousin of the Aga Khan at Najaf, but he resigned and became the deputy to a British officer who experienced the same difficulties. When his attempts at mediation between the townsfolk and the tribes led to a riot in which the Najaf office was destroyed, he turned to the Mujtahid (an authority on Moslem law) for help and peace was restored. In the desert, the leading sheikhs, using money borrowed from the British, began cleaning out their canals before sowing grain which the British provided in exchange for a pledge to keep the peace. Later, small garrisons were placed at Hilla, Kifi, Kufa and Abu Sukhair, but not in Najaf since with a population of over 40,000 a large garrison would have been needed.

It was clear that further military action against the Turks and the occupation of the towns on the Middle Euphrates by British troops was required if British influence was to be spread further, but it was some months before anything could be undertaken. However, it was thought necessary to repair the Sakhlawiya Dam since it was feared that floods would threaten the Samarra Railway, so a force was sent at the hottest time of the year to occupy Dhibban and protect the working parties on the dam. General Maude also wanted to make a sortie against Ramadi further up the Euphrates where there were a thousand Turkish soldiers and six guns. The attack on Ramadi took place on 11 July and was a failure. The troops were struck down by the sun, some died of thirst, some lost their reason, so we are told, and out of the 566 casualties, 321 were due to heat. As a result, the force retired to Dhibban, being attacked by Arabs all the way.

During the summer, General Maude was in constant communication with Sir William Robertson and the British Government over the strategic situation in the east. Sir William was still of the opinion that a defensive posture was the best policy in Mesopotamia so that troops would be available for the Western Front. Conscription had been introduced and Britain was feeling the strain of raising as many troops as were necessary.

Lloyd George's government, on the other hand, thought that there was little chance of a victory in France in 1917, and looked for successes in Syria, Palestine and Mesopotamia. It also maintained that one of the main guiding reasons for supporting Mesopotamia was the security of India, a claim that rang rather hollow in the ears of the Indian Government, who complained that it was the Mesopotamian demands for men and munitions that were bleeding India dry and making her vulnerable.

Clearly, the pleas of India were not heard for it was decided to reinforce General Maude with two Indian cavalry regiments, a regiment of cavalry and a horse artillery battery from France, another RFC squadron, the 63rd, and replace his mules with more Ford vans since plenty of petrol was available from Abadan. In addition, more artillery, the 18th Division, more Light Armoured Motor Batteries and more machine-gun companies were scheduled to reach Mesopotamia early in 1918.

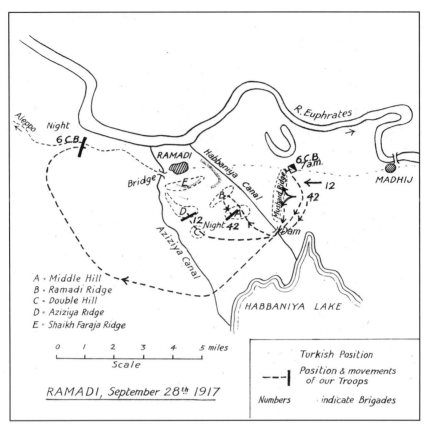

Map 22.   Battle of Ramadi

What was Maude to do with his extra troops? It was decided to
secure the eastern flank of the Baghdad vilayet by having another go
at capturing Ramadi on the Euphrates. Major General Brooking was
in command of the 15th Division and he started by building a
dummy bridge and road leading from it along the north bank of the
river, which made the Turks think that he intended to attack along
the line of the Euphrates. Having completed these constructions on
the night of 27/28 September, he sent 6 Cavalry Brigade by a wide
detour round the town to the west while he approached it from the
east with 12 and 42 Brigades, taking up positions on the Mushaid
Ridge behind the Habbaniya Canal.

During the night of 28/29 the Turks made repeated attempts to
break through the cavalry cordon to their west, while the two

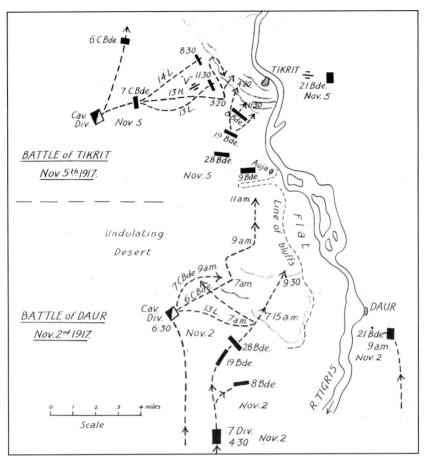

Map 23. Battles of Daur and Tikrit

brigades crossed the canal and were pushing into the town from the south. There was some hard fighting in bright moonlight but by 1100 hrs next day the Turks were ready to surrender. The booty included 13 guns, 12 machine-guns, 2 armoured launches, 2 barges and quantities of ammunition, while 3,500 men were taken prisoner. Most of the 1,000 British casualties were lightly wounded.

It was also necessary to secure the British position on the right flank so the town of Mandali, close to the Persian frontier, was taken over without any difficulty and the pass through the Jabal Hamrin was occupied.

This had scarely been completed when the area to the north,

179

further up the Tigris, required attention and the 7th Division began an attack on Turkish infantry near Huwaislat. They hastily retreated to Daur, up the river to the north, and after waiting a few days Maude directed General Cobbe to attack them there on 28 October. The attack was carried out by the Cavalry Division and the 7th Division on the right bank of the river, with 21 Brigade on the other side. By 0930 hrs on 1 November, after a dawn attack, the Turks retreated, moving further upriver to Tikrit, birthplace of both Saladin and Saddam Hussain, and were attacked there on 5 November. They resisted strongly but eventually retreated, leaving behind 137 prisoners and 300 dead. The British had 1,800 casualties, of whom 161 were killed. Attempts to follow up were thwarted by the dust and gathering darkness.

General Maude died on 18 November from cholera having refused inoculation earlier in the year, and was buried in the British cemetery just north of Baghdad. He had become increasingly concerned with the rift that had developed between him and Sir Percy Cox over the summer months. While General Maude was concerned solely with the military problems of the moment and was content to act on instructions from the Imperial General Staff, it was the responsibility of Sir Percy to formulate and give effect on the spot to a political policy which should be consistent with the spirit, rather than the letter, of the sometimes contradictory utterances of the authorized exponents in London of British policy in the country. As far as Baghdad was concerned, Maude was mainly responsible for the decision to take and hold the city, but he was unwilling to help to develop a civil machine that would make his military success a worthwhile, long-term decision.

After his death wild rumours were current in the bazaars that he had been poisoned by a cup of coffee he had drunk at a theatrical performance organized by the Alliance Israélite of Baghdad. These were given full publicity by an American reporter and eventually an enquiry was ordered by GHQ, to be carried out by the CID. Two ex-employees of a German trading firm in Baghdad were deported as prisoners of war by Maude's successor, William Marshall, quite unjustly as he later admitted, and this may well have been done to shift the focus of the rumours from the Jews in the city who, as usual in Arab countries, were the obvious suspects. The CID's conclusion was that no evidence of foul play existed.

Maude was a generally regarded as a charming individual who

achieved some notable victories as a commander, and had done as much to make the soldiers' existence in Mesopotamia as comfortable as could be in the circumstances, which made him popular with the men. Lieutenant Colonel Tennant, who commanded the RFC in Mesopotamia, got to know him well. He says in his book, *In the Clouds above Baghdad*:

> He led the troops himself; G.H.Q had never moved beyond Basra, three hundred miles behind the army; but when Maude had finished with his work at the Base he left it for good. He was often too far to the front; at Sinn his advanced G.H.Q. was in front of the 1st Corps at Sannayet, during the pursuit his river-boat was generally close up behind the cavalry; cavalry commanders, annoyed to see the G.H.Q. ship passing them, pressed on . . . With a quaint regard for weather conditions, the tall figure of the G.O.C. would be seen in home-service khaki and Norwegian boots, when all others were as sparsely clad as possible.

The inhabitants of Baghdad must have liked him too for they contributed to setting up a hospital at Baghdad which bore his name. An equestrian statue of him was erected in front of the British Residency but was torn down by the mob in 1958. However, the plaque fixed to it was rescued and attached to an inner wall of the Embassy by Sir Terence Clark, the then Ambassador, in 1986.

Although successful as a soldier he was inclined to centralize control to himself, not allowing, for example, the cavalry full rein or allowing his subordinate commanders to exercise their initiatives as they should have been allowed to. But he had a harder and bolder enemy to face than did Nixon and was almost always successful in defeating it.

General Sir William Marshall moved up from commanding III Corps to take Maude's place. A plain-speaking and rather pugnacious little man, he had his own very definite ideas. For example, he abolished the Cavalry Division as being too cumbersome a formation, while the 13-pdr guns of the Royal Horse Artillery were relegated to Line of Communication duties and their places taken by 18-pdrs. However, he continued what he assumed was his predecessor's policy. A force under his successor in command of III Corps, General Egerton, was sent to clear the Turks away from around Qara Tepe, a place beyond the Jabal

Hamrin on a tributary that flowed southward into the Diyala.

In December the CIGS decided that the time had come to cut down the size of the army in Mesopotamia and the 7th Division was sent to Egypt. The main problem that now faced the British in Mesopotamia was that, as Russia had gone out of the war entirely, there was a danger of the Turks seizing the southern Caucasus, an area they had long wanted to get their hands on. Tiflis, the capital of the region, was the most important city, being close to the railway between Batoum on the Black Sea and Baku on the Caspian, the valuable oilfields of Baku, the minerals in the Caucasus Mountains and the grain and cotton grown on the shores of the Caspian Sea. If the Turks could seize Tiflis and its hinterland, then, with the Russian Army disintegrated after the Russian Revolution, the way was open for an advance further east to India, thus making concrete a fear that had long haunted the British Government.

Order of Battle – Tigris Front after Winter of 1917/18

During this period, the 7th Division was sent to Egypt and the 3rd Division to Palestine, being replaced in I Corps by the 17th and 18th Divisions fresh from India, while the 15th Division was raised in III Corps. Ford vans had already appeared in the country and more were being supplied. Another squadron of aircraft also made its appearance.

The new Divisions comprised:

> 15th Division comprising:
> > 12 Infantry Brigade comprised of:
> > > 1/5th Queen's Royal Regiment
> > > 2/39th Garwhal Rifles
> > > 1/43rd Erinpura Regiment
> > > 90th Punjabis
> > > No. 128 Machine Gun Company
> > > 12th Brigade Supply and Transport Company
> > 42 Infantry Brigade comprised of:
> > > 1/4th Dorsetshire Regiment
> > > 1/5th Gurkhas
> > > 2/5th Gurkhas
> > > No. 130 Machine Gun Company

42nd Brigade Supply and Transport Company
50 Infantry Brigade comprised of:
  1st Oxfordshire and Bucks Light Infantry
  6th Jats
  24th Punjabis
  1/97th Infantry
  No. 256 Machine Gun Company
  50th Brigade Supply and Transport Company
  'D' Squadron, 1/1st Hertfordshire Yeomanry
Artillery comprising:
  215 Brigade, RFA (1086th, 1088th, 2/1st Notts, 524th
    Batteries totalling 22 guns)
  22 Brigade, RFA (375th, 1070th, 1072nd, 77th Batteries
    totalling 22 guns)
  Three small arms ammunition sections
Engineers and Pioneers comprising:
  448th, 450th and 451st Field Companies, Royal Engineers
  48th Pioneers
  15th Divisional Signal Company
  No. 275 Machine Gun Company
  15th Divisional Troops Supply and Transport Company
  Nos 23, 34, 105 and 108 Combined Field Ambulances
  Sanitary Section
  Mobile Veterinary Section
Attached:
  One squadron, 10th Lancers
  No. 118 Anti-Aircraft Section
  Detachment No. 1 Mobile Bridging Train
  Half Section, Field Searchlight Company
  Two pack stations, 1st Wireless Signal Station
  'M', 'N', 'O' Light Trench Mortar Batteries

17th Division comprising:
  34 Infantry Brigade comprising:
    2nd Queen's Own Royal West Kent Regiment
    31st Punjabis
    1/112th Infantry
    114th Mahrattas
    No. 129 Machine Gun Company
    34 Brigade Supply and Transport Company

51 Infantry Brigade comprising:
  1st Highland Light Infantry
  1/2nd Rajputs
  14th Sikhs
  1/10th Gurkhas
  No. 257 Machine Gun Company
  51 Brigade Supply and Transport Company
52 Infantry Brigade comprising:
  1/6th Hampshire Regiment
  45th Sikhs
  84th Punjabis
  1/113th Machine Gun Company
  No. 258 Machine Gun Company
  52nd Brigade Supply and Transport Company
  One squadron, 10th Lancers
Artillery comprising:
  220 Brigade, RFA (1064th, 1066th Batteries totalling 12 guns)
  221 Brigade, RFA (1067th, 1068th Batteries totalling 12 guns)
  Three small arms ammunition sections
Engineers and Pioneers:
  Sirmur Sappers and Miners Company
  Malerkotla Sappers and Miners Company
  Tehri-Garhwal Sappers and Miners Company
  1/32nd Sikh Pioneers
  17th Divisional Signal Company
  No. 276 Machine Gun Company
  Divisional Troops Supply and Transport Company
  Nos 3, 19, 35 and 36 Combined Field Ambulances
  No. 1 Sanitary Section
  No. 7 Mobile Veterinary Section

18th Division comprising:
  53 Infantry Brigade comprising:
    1/9th Middlesex Regiment
    1/89th Punjabis
    1/3rd Gurkhas
    1/7th Gurkhas (temporarily att. to 15th Division)
    No. 207 Machine Gun Company

53rd Light Trench Mortar Battery
53rd Small Arm Ammunition Section
53rd Brigade Supply and Transport Company
Attached:
    Two sections, Field Searchlight Company
    One squadron, Patiala Lancers
    Two squadrons, 10th Lancers
    One section, 14th Light Armoured Motor Battery
    5th and 6th Companies, Sappers and Miners
    No. 37 Combined Field Ambulance
54 Infantry Brigade comprising:
    1/5th Queen's Own Royal West Kent Regiment
    25th Punjabis
    1/39th Garhwalis
    52nd Sikhs
    No. 238 Machine Gun Company
    54th Light Trench Mortar Battery
    54th Small Arm Ammunition Section
    54 Brigade Supply and Transport Company
55 Infantry Brigade
    1/5th East Surrey Regiment
    1/10th Jats
    1/94th Infantry
    116th Mahrattas
    No. 239 Machine Gun Company
    55th Light Trench Mortar Batgtery
    55th Small Arm Ammunition Section
    55 Brigade Supply and Transport Company
Artillery:
    336 Brigade, RFA ('A', 'B', 'C' and 'D' Batteries totalling 22 guns)
    337 Brigade, RFA ('A', 'B', 'C' and 'D' Batteries totalling 22 guns)
Engineers and Pioneers:
    2nd Field Company, Sappers and Miners
    106th Pioneers (less two companies)
    18th Divisional Signal Company
    No. 249 Machine Gun Company
    18th Divisional Troops Supply and Transport Company
    Nos 38, 39 and 40 Combined Field Ambulances

No. 22 Sanitary Section
No. 12 Mobile Veterinary Section

Royal Flying Corps:
  63 Squadron

Chapter Twelve

Dunsterville

(Map 24)

To counter any moves by the Turks on the southern Caucasus, three special military missions were assembled to go to the most dangerous of the possible invasion routes to India. The first was led by Colonel Bailey, a political officer, whose orders were to travel to Tashkent, the chief Russian town in Turkestan in the grip of the Revolution, and find out what the new Russian Bolshevik Government's intentions were in regard to India. The situation at Tashkent was complicated by large numbers of German and Austrian ex-prisoners of war who had no way of getting back home. It was feared that they might join up with a combined Turkish-German force that was advancing into the region.

The second Mission was led by Major General Malleson, an intelligence officer, who with a group of officers and NCOs, and an escort of Indian soldiers, was ordered to Meshed (now Mashad), a town close to the north-eastern Persian frontier, to gather intelligence about a possible Turkish advance. If such an advance took place, Malleson was instructed to destroy the Trans-Caspian Railway that led eastwards from that town, skirting the Karakum Desert, towards Samarkand and Central Asia.

The Mission that concerns this narrative is the one mounted from Baghdad and known as Dunsterforce. It was prepared to go to Tiflis (Tbilisi) under the command of Major General Dunsterville, whose early claim to fame was that he was the model for 'Stalky' in the Kipling school stories. Its purpose was remarkably ambitious – to re-organize the scattered remnants of the Russian, Caucasian and Armenian troops, cast adrift after the Russian Revolution, into a cohesive force which could oppose a Turkish advance into the region.

Tiflis is now the capital of Georgia and lies south of the Caucasian Mountains. After the Russian Revolution in November 1917, the Russian armies in the region faded away, leaving a vacuum through which the Turks could advance into the area south of the Caucasian Mountains, to the port of Baku and so across the Caspian to Krasnovodsk and the Trans-Caspian Railway, and so on to Afghanistan and even to India.

Dunsterforce was a unit composed almost entirely of officers and NCOs who were thought capable of creating a military force from the miscellaneous troops of various nationalities who were be found in southern Georgia. Their route was to take them to Tiflis via the Russian port of Baku on the western coast of the Caspian Sea. The force was drawn from various theatres of the war and from various white nationalities. As time was of the essence, Dunsterville had to 'push off' as he put it with a few officers as advance party, while the rest of the force was put together and joined him in various groups. General Dunsterville was chosen for his knowledge and sympathy with Russia and Russians. Some of his officers were Russian, others were Russian or French speaking, the rest only spoke English.

Five Rolls Royce cars and thirty-six Ford vans formed the transport for the advance party of fourteen officers (two acting as a recce party with an armoured car escort) and two clerks. Petrol had to be carried as well as a considerable amount of stores and several chests of Persian and English coins to pay the army they intended to raise.

Dunsterville aimed to make a rapid journey to Bandar-e-Anzali, a port on the Persian coast of the southern Caspian Sea in an area that was a Russian concession (Persian territory that was leased to Russia just as southern Persia was to Britain) and then sail north along the coast to Baku across the border in Russia. From there a road led westwards to the city of Tiflis.

Forty-one vehicles with forty-one drivers armed with rifles and one Lewis gun set off at 0700 hrs on 27 January 1918 from Baghdad, and covered the first 94 miles to Khäniqin in ten and a half hours. The next stage was to Pai-Taq, 61 miles further on, where they arrived in a violent gale and sleet, having taken ten hours over the journey. Then on to Eslamabad, 41 miles away, which was not

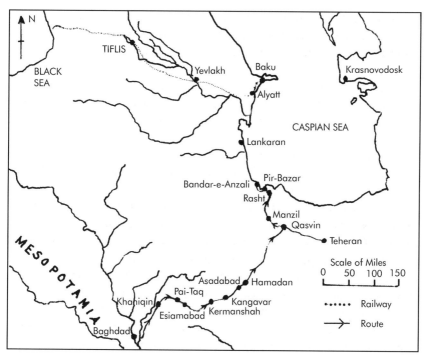

Map 24.   Dunsterville's map of his Area of Operations

reached until 2 February. During the first few miles of the journey
the vehicles had to be pushed up steep slopes and then coaxed
through the snowdrifts in the passes. Eslamabad turned out to be a
typical Kurdish village, ruined, but offering sufficient shelter for the
night.

Next day they arrived at Kermanshah after seven hours and were
met on the outskirts of the town by two Kuban Cossacks on shaggy
horses, members of Colonel Bicherakov's 'partisans'. Bicherakov
came from a tribe in the Caucasus Mountains, and commanded an
irregular mixed Cossack force that fought against the Turks with
such success that it earned its leader a CB and a DSO. Dunsterville
had dinner that night in the British consulate and next morning set
off with his convoy for Hamadan, a distance of 103 miles. At
Kangavar after 56 miles, a small Russian detachment welcomed the
party with a square meal before they set off again in the early
evening, reaching Asadabad where they stopped for the night in a
fairly clean roadhouse.

189

Next morning, when he stepped outside, Dunsterville found to his horror a foot of snow and it was still snowing hard. Despite employing gangs of villagers to clear the snow in the pass it was not until 11 February that the convoy reached Hamadan. Meanwhile, Dunsterville had gone on ahead where he met General Baratov who had been in command of the victorious Russian army in northern Persia. Now he was in command of a revolutionary army that would not obey orders.

Two days later the convoy reached Qasvin, a town of 50,000 inhabitants and one of the many earlier capitals of Persia. The people were not very friendly but contented themselves with scowls and passing anti-British resolutions in fierce meetings in the mosques. There was also some unwelcome news about the next stage of the journey. The tribal leader of the Gilanis, whose district they were going to cross, had vowed not to let the British through and he was hand in glove with the Bolshevik Committee at Bandar-e-Anzali, which was equally determined to bar the way.

Dunsterville, unfazed, was equally determined to carry on, even though he was heading for a hornets' nest. The Gilanis were also known as 'Jangali' (jungle folk) and this name was used as the title of a movement led by Mirza Kuchik Khan, a revolutionary with ideals who was being pushed from behind by a committee of German and Turkish interests. His troops were led by a German officer, von Passchen, drilled by Austrian instructors and equipped with Turkish machine-guns. Their attitude to Baratov's (now Bolshevik) Russian troops was not friendly but they were ready to facilitate their journey northwards back home from Persia because it allowed them to buy from them huge stocks of rifles and ammunition at very low prices.

As far as the British were concerned, the Jangalis were afraid that they were out to take the Russians' place as an occupying power, while the Bolsheviks imagined that the British were determined to keep Russia in the war.

The road from Qasvin was thronged with Baratov's evacuating Russian troops riding enormous Persian country carts with four horses harnessed abreast that were not easy to pass on the narrow mountain roads. At a roadhouse, where the convoy stopped to fill up with petrol from the inevitable gallon cans, they were surrounded by Russian soldiers who were friendly enough, but to any suggestion that they were still allies the invariable response was: 'We are not your allies; we have made peace with Germany, and you only want to prolong the war.'

The 70 miles from Manzil to the coast passes through a narrow gorge with towering cliffs on the left and a sheer drop to a roaring torrent on the other. After that there was dense forest with mossy banks, primroses and cyclamen. The armoured car led the column for fear of ambush. At Rasht the column passed fierce-looking and heavily-armed warriors with successive bandoliers of cartridges wound round them like waistcoats. In the town the British Consul met them and after a short conversation, the 20 miles to Bandar-e-Anzali was covered without incident.

They drew up beside the Customs House where they were welcomed by the Customs Officers. Despite the place being in the hands of the Bolsheviks, the Customs Service, as in the rest of Persia, was run by Belgians and they were very hospitable, inviting Dunsterville to dinner and locking his vehicles inside the Customs yard.

At dinner the Bolshevik Revolutionary Committee arrived to interview the English General, a conversation that Dunsterville was able to postpone until eleven o'clock the next morning. Then he and Captain Saunders presented themselves at the Committee HQ where they were given seats at a long table and subjected to a volley of questions from all sides about their presence in the town. After the President of the Committee managed to make himself heard, he announced that he, at least, knew all about the plans to go to Tiflis and help the Georgians and Armenians to continue the fight against the Turks – and he had orders, which came from German sources, to stop this happening. He finished his harangue with much arm waving and the statement that the Russians were no longer Britain's ally, Russia had made peace with the Germans, Turks and Austrians and, of all nations, the only one they mistrusted was Great Britain – perfidious Albion.

It was clear they held all the cards since they possessed the telegraph and telephone lines, the radio station, the petrol supply, all shipping and a gunboat lying off the town. They forbade any attempt to reach Baku which was under Bolshevik government. For them the war was over and they objected to a mission that was intent on prolonging it.

Dunsterville protested that his only object was to help Russia and he would carry on, if necessary, using his machine-gun to overcome any resistance since he did not recognize the right of the Bolshevik Government to impede his movements. With this, he and Saunders got up and left and, remarkably, got out of the room without being arrested.

After a night of discussion Dunsterville's party decided that all they could do was to retrace their footsteps and, on meeting the Committee again next morning, persuaded the umbrageous Chairman, Comrade Cheliapin, to issue a permit for the petrol they needed. Early next morning they set off and got back to Hamadan five days later. Here Dunsterville meant to stay.

Hamadan was built on the site of the ancient Ecbatana, the favourite summer residence of the Persian and Parthian kings, although nothing remained of its former glory. Half of the inhabitants were of Turkish origin and spoke the language, while the rest were Persian and a few Russians. It was from these inhabitants that Dunsterville recruited agents, some Russian, some Persian, who were able to find out what was going on in Persia, investigate the local situation in Hamadan and learn details of the nearest Turkish detachments.

General Baratov, the erstwhile commander of the Russian army in Persia, was in the town, engaged in repatriating his troops back to Russia. For this he was supposed to receive money from the Bolshevik Government in Tiflis which so far had failed to materialize. In addition, and rather strangely in the circumstances, the British Government had agreed to make fixed payments at regular intervals to defray some of the expense on condition that the repatriation was actually seen to be in progress. Baratov was continually in difficulties on account of the shortfall and spent time persuading Dunsterville to make representations on his behalf to the British Government to increase his allotment.

After a heavy fall of snow on 16 March, the weather cleared and this allowed the last of the Russian troops to get on the move, leaving only Colonel Bicherakov's detachment at Sheverin, 3 miles out of town. The Colonel told Dunsterville that he and his men were determined to leave for their homes in the North Caucasus as well, and would go as soon as transport could be arranged. This alarmed Dunsterville who would then be left without any support in northern Persia apart from the few White Russian officers who had joined him. He tried to tempt Bicherakov to throw in his lot with the British and eventually hammered out an agreement in which the Russian agreed to stay until sufficient British troops could be found to replace his force, but only on condition that the British paid his troops. As part of the deal he also agreed to co-operate with plans for later operations further north in the Caucasus.

The first operation in which they were both engaged was to save the town of Qasvin from a Jangali advance, which they did. During this operation, however, the Jangalis looted the bank at Rasht and captured two Britons, one, a Captain Noel, on his way from Tiflis with despatches for General Dunsterville.

At the end of March, famine set in. Bodies of the famished lay around in the streets of Hamadan, the dead unburied, others waiting to die and destined for a further lengthy wait thereafter until their burial became unavoidable. At the same time a detachment of thirty riflemen of the 1/4th Hants joined and the first aircraft arrived from Baghdad.

The General called on the Persian Governor of the city and other important individuals, each call being returned a few days later. At first formal, the meetings gradually became less frigid and Dunsterville began to institute tea parties to which all and sundry were invited; these friendly contacts became useful when his supplies were interrupted on direct orders from Teheran.

Famine was beginning to take a firm hand. War conditions, bad weather, the poor harvest of 1917 and profiteering all contributed to the dreadful conditions in the town, so General Dunsterville persuaded the British Government to fund the construction of new roads and so provide work and wages for the indigent. But there were all sorts of problems with the scheme which were never really solved. The best results were obtained by giving part of the wages in the form of food from a soup kitchen. Any attempt to give out food directly to the starving in the towns always resulted in a riot in which the strongest got the food and the weakest lost out.

On 24 April a squadron of the 14th Hussars under Captain Pope arrived from Baghdad. At about the same time an Armenian doctor came from Baku suggesting that the British might be able to help in subduing riots there that had broken out between the Tartars and the Armenians. With very few troops, the General could make no promises until he received reinforcements but he could do something in Qasvin, so he sent a small party of officers and NCOs there with instructions to spy out the land, start famine relief and reconnoitre for billets and supplies. The squadron of Hussars were sent into camp at Sultanabad about 5 miles from the town and Dunsterville set out for the place himself on 12 May.

Efforts were being made to raise levies of local men to act as volunteer soldiers. Three groups were recruited: two at Hamadan and one at Qasvin. Each group consisted of two companies of dismounted men, each 200 strong and one of mounted men of the same strength, making a total of 600 men. The companies were commanded by Persian officers, with the British acting as instructors. These men were to help in policing and other minor duties. One mistake in the early days was the enlistment of a complete gang of robbers!

After a visit to Teheran, the General decided to move his HQ forward to Qasvin where he would be better able to deal with the Jangalis and perhaps rescue from them the English captives in their hands. At about this time a fourth party arrived from Baghdad consisting of fifty officers and 150 NCOs who had walked all the way but were still cheerful.

Every day's delay in getting to Baku brought the Turks nearer to it and to its oil wealth. In Baku, Dunsterville would be in a position to control the shipping on the Caspian Sea. But if the mission was to move north it could endanger the fairly solid position they had built up in northern Persia, since pulling the British officers out of their present jobs would be like pulling the foundations stones from under a building. However, as a compromise, a move to Qasvin between Bandar-e-Anzali and Tehran would be a step in the right direction.

Compared to Hamadan, Qasvin tried hard to look like a city with European shops and inns with names of grand European hotels. Colonel Bicherakov's troops were in the town, keeping order in a rough-and-ready way. The methods of his lieutenant, Sovlaiev, were especially direct.

In early June, more British reinforcements arrived, including the remainder of the 14th Hussars, a thousand infantry, mountain guns and 500 Ford vans. Dunsterville was now in command of a considerable detachment and decided it was now time to make a forward move. An attempt to negotiate a passage through to Bandar-e-Anzali with Kuchik Khan came to nothing while he was still holding an English officer captive. It was time for fight rather than talk and a force was put together to march to attack the Jangalis at Manjil on the road to Bandar-e-Anzali and secure the bridge there. It included Colonel Bicherakov's force, consisting of a thousand Cossacks, one squadron of the 14th Hussars and two armoured cars. Two aircraft from the airfield at Qasvin would also take part.

The Battle of Manjil Bridge began by the Jangalis opening a furious but futile fusillade on the two aircraft with a number of machine-guns. Meanwhile Colonel Bicherakov advanced along the road at the head of his troops, a most unusual position for a modern commander. On both sides of the bridge and in the surrounding hills, the enemy had about 2,500 men in trenches. Battle was opened by Bicherakov coming round the corner by the tea shop where a small body of the enemy's troops were acting as advanced guard. Bicherakov, who had been badly wounded in the legs earlier in the war, and walked with a stick, strode up to them gesticulating with his stick and demanding to know what they were doing there.

'We are here to hold this post with the last drop of our blood!' was the proud answer.

'Get out of it at once!' shouted Bicherakov, waving his cane so threateningly that they turned and fled as one man down the road.

The next event was the arrival of a German officer, von Passchen, who commanded Kuchik Khan's forces in the field, with a white flag and a demand for a parley. Without waiting for an answer he launched into a hectoring speech asserting that Kuchik Khan regarded Russians as friends and as soon as Bicherakov disassociated himself from the British, he could send his men down the road to Bandar-e-Anzali. No British would be allowed to pass.

But the Colonel was not in the mood to parley. 'I do not recognise a German officer as a representative of Kuchik Khan and I consider your appearing before me in German uniform as a piece of insolence. I want no terms from the Jangalis and intend to open fire as soon as you get out of the way.'

The Cossack mountain artillery opened fire, the Hussars and the Cossack cavalry and infantry went forward and the armoured cars came into action. The Jangalis began evacuating their trenches, the cavalry crossed the bridge and beyond it the column reformed and marched 10 miles down the road through the rocky defile without firing a further shot. If one of the enemy machine-guns had stayed in action covering the bridge instead of taking to their heels, not one soldier would have survived.

The squadron of the 14th Hussars stayed at Manjil to hold the bridge as the first stage of the advance along the road to Bandar-e-Anzali. Bicherakov, still impatient to go home, pushed on to

Bandar-e-Anzali with his main body, leaving small detachments in towns along the road which would be relieved by British troops within the next week.

The Jangalis were emboldened enough by the departure of the Russians to attack a detachment of the 1/4th Hants on the road a few days afterwards; Captain Durnford was killed and six men wounded, but the enemy were driven off leaving a number dead. At Rasht the detachment was stationed beside the Russian consulate on the outskirts of the town and consisted of 450 infantry and two armoured cars. With the small number of troops at his disposal it was impossible for Dunsterville to put a substantial number of troops into the centre of the town. During this time the aircraft were busy bombing any concentration of the enemy close to the town, a difficult job in the circumstances, since the country surrounding Resht was dense forest.

The road to Bandar-e-Anzali was kept open by Lieutenant Colonel Matthews with the 1/4th Hants and some Gurkhas comprising a mobile column of 800 riflemen and two mountain guns, using the Ford vans. Bandar-e-Anzali was 50 miles away from Qazvin, through mountains and forest, and there were several hard-fought skirmishes with the Jangali along this route. Dunsterville travelled along this road on 26 June when he visited Bandar-e-Anzali, where he discussed plans with Bicherakov and interviewed the fractious Comrade Cheliapin. Bicherakov had decided to turn Bolshevik as he saw no other way of getting home and obtaining a footing in the Caucasus. This news caused a stir amongst the good people of Baku and he was offered the command of the Bolshevik troops, now known as the 'Red Army'. He was ready to set off at once and Dunsterville sent a British officer with him who had already accompanied him from Qazvin. Bicherakov decided to disembark, not at Baku, which would put his force too much into the hands of the Bolsheviks, but at Alyatt, a small port 50 miles to the south.

The situation in the area was becoming interesting. A Turkish Caucasus-Islam army, about 12,000 strong, composed of about half regular Turkish troops and half levies from local Moslems in the southern Caucasus, was advancing from Tiflis along the railway line with the object of capturing Baku. The Germans in Tiflis, however, were doing their best to hold back this force for they had a private agreement with Lenin, and through him with the Baku government, that the town should be handed over to them. To the Russians, the sight of Turks in Baku would be almost as bad as seeing the British there.

On 1 July the Turkish Army had not yet crossed the Kura river at the only bridge, at Yevlakh, a hundred miles from Alyatt; Bicherakov hoped to make a dash and seize it before they got there.

The British detachment at Bandar-e-Anzali was objected to both by Cheliapin and Lieutenant Alkhavi, military governor of the town and representative of the Baku Soviets, but Dunsterville pointed out that he was having a landing strip prepared there and he needed guards to look after the aircraft. Their kind offer to do the guarding for him was politely declined. With Cheliapin, the most important matter of dispute was the supply of petrol. Fortunately, he wanted motor cars so an exchange was arranged – £300 of petrol for every £100-worth of cars.

Back at Hamadan, Dunsterville tried the experiments of introducing a two-hour daylight saving scheme that was not very successful, renaming all the streets in the town with English names like Piccadilly and Bond Street to make it easier for the British drivers, and instituting a 'keep to the right' rule on the local roads, a recipe for chaos. Currency was becoming a problem with the bank finding it difficult to attract through its doors sufficient to meet the cheques presented by the Mission.

The Mission had more reinforcement in the shape of a party of the Royal Navy with several 4-inch guns sent up from Baghdad on the chance that Dunsterville would be able to arm some merchantmen and rule the waves on the Caspian.

Colonel Battine had also arrived to take command of a detachment to Krasnovodsk on the east coast of the Caspian opposite to Baku, a port only second in importance to it in the sea. Authorities in Krasnovodsk were anti-Bolshevik and pro-British. From Krasnovodsk the railway ran to Ashkhabad and Merv further east, where a mission under General Malleson had been sent to operate against a strong Bolshevik force there.

Dunsterville decided that he ought to make a trip back for discussions at HQ and set off on 14 July by road and air, arriving at Baghdad at daybreak on the 18th. After his return he heard that Bicherakov had landed at Alyatt on 5 July and marched east to take over the command of the Baku army that was positioned on the Tiflis railway near the bridge at Yevlakh. His own irregular troops were hurried up to stiffen the Red Army which was already being driven back by the Turks. All hope of securing the bridge over the Kura was gone and Bicherakov was forced to fall back on Baku with a very poor opinion of the Red Army troops.

This was reinforced by another incident when he ordered a reconnaissance by one of his Cossack squadrons supported by a British armoured car. As the party crossed a bridge held by a strong detachment of the Red Army, they impressed on its commander the importance of his post as the bridge he was guarding carried the road over an impassable nullah on their only line of withdrawal. Having carried out their mission, the reconnaissance party started back, only to find that the bridge was in the hands of the Turks – the Red Army Red had disappeared. Cossack cavalry put up a very good fight to retake the bridge and cover the retreat of the armoured car, but they suffered heavy losses and the armoured car was captured by the Turks. Later it transpired that the Red Army soldiers had left their post to attend a political meeting.

In the last days of July, the Red Army and Bicherakov's force were driven back into Baku by the Caucasus-Islam army which at the moment when it was expected to enter the town, was inexplicably seized by panic and turned on its heels, hotly pursued by Armenian troops. By this time the Red Army was beginning to suspect Bicherakov's conversion to their cause and this prompted him to separate his force from their troops and move away north towards Derbend.

In the middle of July the first detachments of 39 Brigade began to arrive in Qasvin, but reinforcements for Dunsterforce were meagre and would continue to be during the lifetime of the Force. This was down to the attitude of General Marshall in Baghdad who was opposed to the maintenance of a large force in Persia. He states in his book, *Memories of Four Fronts*, 'I hated the whole business.' This opinion was shared by Sir Arnold Wilson who had replaced Sir Percy Cox in Baghdad as Civil Commissioner, with Gertrude Bell as his assistant. In his book, *Loyalties*, he describes Dunsterforce as 'individually gallant but collectively ineffective filibusters'.

About this time the Jangalis decided to make another attempt at defeating the British and at daybreak on 20 July they launched an attack on Resht under the command of their German adviser, von Passchen. It was mainly aimed at the British detachment under

Colonel Matthews which was billeted outside the southern outskirts of the town and at the town itself. The Jangalis were defeated outside the town but successful in the town, cordoning off the British consulate which was surrounded by a maze of old houses from the roofs of which snipers could fire down into its courtyard.

News of the encirclement of the consulate reached Colonel Matthews early in the morning and he sent Captain McCleverty of the Gurkhas at once through the narrow streets with an armoured car to rescue the Consul and his staff. This daring exploit disheartened the Jangalis who broke off the attack with the loss of over one hundred dead and fifty wounded.

The next two days were occupied with clearing all Jangalis out of the town and appointing a military governor in place of the Persian one who had made off. Bandar-e-Anzali itself was next on the list for clearance. Major Browne of the 44th Indian Infantry was already busy there removing the Red Army obstructions in the harbour. In order to get them out of Browne's hair, Dunsterville invited the Bandar-e-Anzali revolutionary committee to Quasvin for discussions about motor cars and petrol, delaying them for two days during which time Major Browne completed making the port usable. Dunsterville spent the time trying to get out of the committee the exact nature of their relations with Kuchik Khan, convinced that they were hand in glove with him and he needed the evidence in order to arrest them.

In Qasvin, General Baratov's position was an absurd one. He was a general without an army and was probably in disfavour with the Soviet Government. He was sent an invitation from the British authorities to visit India and disappeared from the scene to safety – it was later learnt that for some time a price had been put on his head by the Bolsheviks.

An agreement was made between the Mission and the Russian Road Company to take over temporarily all their property and interests in the roads from Hamadan to Bandar-e-Anzali, and from Teheran to Qasvin. This was a good deal for the Mission since the telephone rights were included and the monthly payments were less than what was spent in keeping the road in repair. The advantage from the Company's point of view was that it safeguarded the road from being nationalized by the revolutionaries.

On 26 July a coup d'etat took place in Baku, the Bolshevik Government was thrown out and replaced by a body calling itself the Central Caspian Dictatorship. Two leaders of the Bolsheviks determined to escape and, with their followers, seized thirteen ships in which they embarked the greater portion of the Red Army and the contents of the arsenal, and set sail. The new government, after initial hesitation, sent their gunboats after them and brought the convoy back. They also relayed a message to the Mission to ask for reinforcements. Dunsterville sent Colonel Stokes with a small party of 1/4th Hants. Although, the townspeople were disappointed at the size of the party, it must have inspired them, for when a Turkish attack took place next day, every man seized a rifle and, under the command of the Colonel, sent the Turks packing. Small parties from the Mission followed the first detachment to Baku as transport permitted.

On 4 August Dunsterville moved his HQ to Pir Bazar, a place on the other side of the harbour to the old Persian town of Bandar-e-Anzali, which had been built by the Russian Road Company and was an uncomfortable but convenient location.

On the way he met the three members of the Bandar-e-Anzali Committee in British custody who protested that they were being unjustly accused of complicity with Kuchil Khan. The officer in charge, however, said that there was a letter from one of the committee which proved their complicity in efforts to destroy the British detachment at Resht, urging renewed efforts and promising all support in future attempts.

The first thing to do at Pir Bazar was to get hold of enough shipping to allow Dunsterville to evacuate his force from Baku if the necessity arose. By hook or by crook he managed to acquire a modern vessel of over 1,000 tons, named *President Kruger*, while Colonel Stokes in Baku acquired the *Kursk* and the *Abo*. The larger ship was equipped with a pack wireless that enabled her to keep in touch with both Baku and Enzeli while at sea. At Pir Bazar the port authorities had been nationalized and were consequently without funds, so Dunsterville took advantage of the situation by offering to pay their salaries and port expenses in exchange for all sources of income. In effect the British were running a communist port, but the system seemed to work satisfactorily.

But this is not to say that the reception in Baku was entirely friendly. Periodically the Baku newspapers would come out with a broadside against the British which seemed to assuage their indignation until the next outburst.

Away with the English Imperialists!
Away with their paid agents!
Away with the Bourgeois Counter-revolutionaries!
Hurrah for the People's Committees!
Hurrah for Independent Russia!
Hurrah for Russian Social Revolution!
What can the English give you? Nothing!
What can they take from you? Everything!
Away with the English Imperialists!
All to the front! To arms! All to the saving of Baku!

When his headquarters were transferred to the *President Kruger* on 10 August, Dunsterville hauled down the Red flag and raised the Russian flag. Immediately, a deputation from the local Committee arrived on board to protest, wanting to know whether the British were counter-revolutionaries. After some discussion a compromise allowed the Russian flag to be flown upside down!

Clearly, the revolutionaries did not know that the Russian flag flown upside down was the Serbian flag, so the upshot was that a British general at sea on the Caspian was aboard a Bolshevik ship named after a South African President and previous enemy, sailing from a Persian port to rescue from the Turks a body of Armenians in a revolutionary Russian town, all under the Serbian flag!

The *President Kruger* was managed by a committee of which the captain was an ex-officio member and this seemed to work fairly well, except that the Committee sometimes carried out manoeuvres without the captain's orders.

The first undesirable on board who Dunstetville had to get rid of was a drunkard addicted to 'gee-gee', a form of arrack, which seemed to drive its devotees crazy for a time. This addict danced a hornpipe, drew a long knife, leapt onto the ship from the dock scattering the crew right and left, and finished up by plunging his knife into a water-melon in a fury of stabbing.

A deputation of White Russians arrived from Länkäran, a strip of coast on the south-west of the Caspian, where they were forced to operate the inevitable 'committee' system. They were a rich community, producing large quantities of grain which they wanted to exchange for cotton fabrics and ammunition. With them they brought a cargo of flour and other commodities as samples. Dunsterville responded by sending a small party of officers and

NCOs to spy out the land at Länkäran, together with two Russian officers. They found that it was safe to remain there and set up a small HQ.

A letter from Colonel Keyworth at Baku was delivered on 10 August describing the defences and general situation of the town – it was clear that the Turks were nearby but the place was still not invested. However, Dunsterville's arrival with his troops could not be long delayed. Accordingly the die was cast and the *President Kruger* arrived off Baku on 17 August. From the sea the town looked imposing, the buildings closest to the sea front florid in German style, whilst behind them loomed the dome of the Russian cathedral, surmounted with a golden ball and cross. Close by in Black Town were the oilfields with the usual derricks, while the sea-front buildings ran for 9 miles along the shore with 2 miles of wharves that could accommodate some sixty vessels. The town streets were cobbled and very Victorian looking, with their horse-trams and outdated costumes.

Every available officer and OR was manning the defences built to the west of the town to oppose the advancing Turkish army, apart from the staff in the hospital, the supply and transport men and a small guard detachment. Accommodation was luxurious in the biggest hotels but the luxury stopped at the bedrooms for the meagre food in the restaurant was poor and expensive.

Next day Dunsterville inspected the front line. For the most part it was satisfactory apart from a gap in the west where Bicherakov's troops had been. This gap had not been filled and 3,000 yards away from it the Turks had dug their entrenchments. When the Warwicks and the Worcesters arrived they were sent up to strengthen this part of the line, the rest of the garrison being Armenians who did not believe in digging trenches.

The town was run by five Revolutionary dictators. The C-in-C was General Dukuchaiev assisted by two colonels, one Armenian, the other Russian. In order to protect against a possible attack from the sea Dunsterville proposed to convert six ships into armed merchantmen. However, the Caspian sailors were much against this proposal so it was only after a long argument that two ships were eventually handed over to be armed with guns sent from Baghdad. In the front line the troops were not up to the standard of the navy and were mostly ill-fed factory workers into whose unwilling hands rifles had been thrust. They knew more or less what they were fighting for but were badly trained and worse led.

By this time, the Turks were shelling the town. In reply, British artillery, 8th Battery, RFA, was in action along with thirty Russian guns. The arsenal that the Bolsheviks had sailed off with was now back and piled in confusion on the quay, so Dunsterville ordered Colonel Rawlinson to match serviceable guns with the correct ammunition. Meanwhile more 4-inch and 12-pdr guns arrived from Baghdad at an opportune time, for the Turks were pressing their attacks on the outskirts of Baku and it would not be long before they mounted a major assault.

Peace was eventually made with Kuchik Khan who became the main contractor for the rice harvest of Gilgan that was an important part of the food supply for Baku, and Captain Noel was at last released. Command in Qasvin had now been taken over by another British officer of the Indian Army and so Dunsterville was no longer responsible for anything in Persia.

If the British received reinforcement of infantry as well as the Turks then it would be possible to withstand their attacks – if they did not, it was a matter of postponing the final fall of the town and making the best arrangements for getting the British troops away. But the Turks were clever enough to foresee that a column might be sent to the rescue, so to forestall this eventuality they advanced along the Qasvin road and set up a road block.

Turkish shelling was becoming more frequent and accurate, particularly in the area around the Hotel d'Europe, the British HQ. It was so marked that Dunsterville was convinced that the Turkish gunners had someone in the town spotting for them. When the HQ was transferred from the Europe to the Metropole, the Turkish artillery immediately followed it. Dunsterville had to spend the occasional night in the hotels because the rumour had got round that he was deserting his troops by sleeping aboard his ship. When he did patronize the hotels, he was amused to find that a man was sent round daily to check that he had really slept in the bed.

Meanwhile Dunsterville was receiving a number of undercover visits by Russian businessmen and others in the town with whom it was dangerous to appear to be too friendly, as they were labelled by the rest of the town as 'bourgeois' and 'counter-revolutionary'; at the same time Tarters living the town, excellent people as they were, had to be visited in secret at dead of night, unaccompanied apart from a guide. Deputations from other quarters were safer and could be entertained in public, even on board the *President Kruger*. Spies abounded, including a representative of the Russian Legation in Teheran who openly took notes at these functions.

Steamers were now leaving daily for Krasnovodsk crowded with refugees, which at least eased the problem of supplies in Baku. Dunsterville was anxious to keep on good terms with the dictator of Krasnovodsk, one Kuhn, as he was fairly certain that he would have to evacuate Baku, and it would be useful to be able to cross the Caspian and recommence operations there, linking up with General Malleson's mission.

On one occasion, Commodore Norris was invited by the Baku Bolshevist fleet to accompany one of their gunboats to shell Turkish trains on the line south of Baku. The line was within a thousand yards of the coast and the trains on it offered a splendid target. When within range the guns opened fire but the shooting was inaccurate and the results poor. The Commodore suggested to the Russians that he should stand in closer to the shore, shorten the range and make it easier for the gunners.

Orders were given to this effect and crews' spokesman promptly appeared on the bridge. 'The crew wish to know what is the meaning of this change of course?'

'The English admiral thinks you would make better shooting if we got closer in to the shore.'

The spokesman replied, 'The ship is to be put back at once on her former course and no change made until the committee have discussed the matter.'

After the original course was resumed, the meeting was held and it was concluded unanimously that, as the Turks were known to have a field battery somewhere on this part of the coast, to stand closer in might bring the gunboat under fire from the shore. The decision was taken that the ship should at once return to Baku, the captain was informed and the ship put about.

A similar situation occurred when the Turks shelled the waterfront at Baku and the crew of the *President Kruger* decided that it would be safer to change the berth – without even a committee meeting. The ship was moved and the captain and Dunsterville informed; it turned out to be not only safer, but in a quieter part of the town where an evacuation, if needed, would be easier to organize without attracting too much notice.

All this time the Turks were pressing closer to the city. British troops in the front line beat them back but it was impossible to stem the tide since the local army, although large enough to put up an adequate defence, was not keen on fighting and was content to leave it to the British whenever possible. A new line was taken up closer to the city but Dunsterville was convinced that Baku was doomed unless the local soldiery changed their attitude.

He sent a letter explaining this to the provisional government of Baku and stating his determination to withdraw his force. In answer he was invited to a committee meeting which went on until Dunsterville left at one o'clock in the morning. What resolutions were passed eventually he never knew but next morning he discussed the situation with General Lewin, on a tour of inspection from Baghdad, and they agreed that withdrawal was the only option.

Dunsterville called his own committee meeting of the town officials and their committees, and gave them the news. They went away thunderstruck and sent Dunsterville a letter stating that the Provisional Dictatorship would only allow the British to leave at the same time as their own troops and after the town had been evacuated by non-combatants. Another letter demanded that the British transfer more troops to the town from Persia or Baghdad which, of course, was not possible.

The British continued to train the Baku forces, although Dunsterville was convinced the town was doomed and that the best way for the authorities to save the lives of the townsfolk was by negotiation with the enemy. On 12 September an Arab deserted from the Turkish Army with the information that a great assault was being prepared for the 14th.

The 14-mile front was strengthened with all available men, including those who were on the point of leaving for a raid on the Tiflis railway, and a contingent of 500 men with ten machine-guns sent by General Bicherokov. The aircraft reported that on the Turkish side, large numbers of reinforcements were arriving by train.

On the eve of the Battle of Baku, the front line was held by a mixture of British (7th North Staffords, 9th Worcesters, 9th Royal Warwicks, an Armoured Car Squadron and the 8th Battery, RFA), Armenians, Russians and the Baku troops.

The Turkish attack began at 0400 hrs on 14 September 1918. The Turks immediately broke through the part of the line held by the Baku troops and took over the heights on the left, but 900 riflemen of 39 Brigade – the Warwicks and the Worcesters on the right, and the North Staffords on the left – managed to stop the Turkish advance by 0800 hrs, when counter-attacks were attempted by the Baku units who were heartened by a false rumour that Bicherakov's troops were arriving in strength.

Dunsterville went to see the Russian Commander-in-Chief, General Dukuchaiev, at 1100 hrs and found his headquarters in a state of chaos. Making sure that the orders for a counter-attack were being issued – not that they were likely to be obeyed – he came away convinced that it was time to start the preliminary steps for evacuation.

Back at the port he ordered that cotton bales from the wharf be hauled on board the *President Kruger* to protect the bridge against rifle fire and the two smaller ships, the *Kursk* and the *Abo*, were made ready to accommodate the wounded. The *President Kruger* would take the bulk of personnel of the Mission.

Up to 1600 hrs Dunsterville hoped that by some miracle the town might be saved, but finally gave orders for the withdrawal which was to start at 2000 hrs, with the troops on the right of the line moving out first, covered by the left, the North Staffords, who would have to hold on for another hour until 2100 hrs. He was fairly sure that as soon as the retirement was known in the town, the British would be regarded as enemies and fired on.

As the sun set, the fighting died down. Dunsterville had already notified the dictators of his decision and loading started. By 2200 hrs all was ready and another small steamer, the *Armenian,* was taken over and loaded with as much of the arms and ammunition as possible to follow in the *President Kruger*'s wake.

With the lull in the fighting, the dictators woke up to what was happening. Two appeared on the deck of the *Kruger* with the order that the British were to return to the front and not attempt to sail, otherwise they would be fired upon by the gunships. Dunsterville got rid of them. The gunships were some distance away and there was a guardship at the exit to the harbour, but Dunsterville decided to chance it and gave the order to cast off.

They had only gone a few yards when a sailor suddenly rushed on deck shouting, 'My wife, my wife, I've left my wife behind. O, save my wife!'

The crew immediately dropped anchor, the ship turned round, pulled up the anchor, and went back to the wharf where it manoeuvred close enough for the lady to be passed on board. The second attempt to leave the wharf was interrupted by a second female voice that belonged to another forlorn wife who was hoisted up on deck.

By this time it was well past midnight as they set a course for the harbour entrance. All went well until they were creeping past the guardship when some clever ill-wisher amongst the crew turned on all the lights.

The signal came: 'Who are you? Anchor at once!'

In response the convoy put on full speed, the guardship opened fire and the shot whizzed past the bridge. The helmsman fled but the captain seized the wheel and steered the ship to safety, although it seemed likely that the *Arcadian* would not be so lucky.

By daylight, they were well out in the Caspian Sea with the troops feasting on bread, hard-tack biscuits and tea, all that there was on board. Total casualties in the fight for Baku had been 180 killed, wounded or missing.

Towards sunset Bandar-e-Anzali was in sight with the two smaller ships, the *Kursk* and the *Abo,* carrying casualties, already safely anchored and their cargoes comfortably in the hospital ashore. Twelve hours later the *Armenian* appeared, having received six hits from the guardship's shells. Before he left the quay, Colonel Rawlinson, in charge of the ship, had been visited twice by commisars. The first was made a prisoner and locked in a cabin, the second said that he could provide a pass if he was allowed to have his wife and family travel on the boat. Rawlinson agreed at once.

He then visited the *President Kruger* to have a final word with Dunsterville but when he got back to his ship he found the gangway besieged. At the point of the bayonet his few British soldiers threatened all these on board to prevent them giving the alarm and cast off. The anchor could not be hauled up because somebody had sabotaged the chain so it was abandoned. Rawlinson stood by the captain on the bridge with drawn revolver. When the guardship signalled the *Armenian* to stop, the captain signalled that was going to turn to starboard.

Rawlinson's revolver convinced him to hold his course and Rawlinson sent an officer down to the engine room with the same argument, whereupon the speed markedly increased. When the guardship opened fire the captain tried to do a runner but Rawlinson grabbed him and posted four armed soldiers, who stood around the bridge with their rifles trained on the trembling officer.

By this time the spokesman of the ship's committee arrived to announce that the crew would not allow the ship to be taken out. He was quietly apprehended and a bit later Rawlinson told him that he would reward the crew when they arrived in Enzeli – a proposal that he placed before his Committee in such an inviting manner that Rawlinson had no more trouble with them.

At Bandar-e-Anzali Dunsterville received a written petition from the revolutionary sailors on the *Kursk* which read as follows:

We, the Committee and Crew of the SS. Kursk have witnessed with intense admiration the heroic conduct of your brave British soldiers in the defence of Baku. We have seen them suffering wounds and death bravely in defence of our town, which our own people were too feeble to defend. It is wonderful to us that these fine fellows from that distant island in the North Sea should have come all this way to the Caspian and have given up their lives there in the cause of honour and glory.

We are so much impressed by their bearing and valour and by the whole episode of the British endeavours to save Baku from the Turks that we wish to be at once taken over as a body and granted British nationality.

After the arrival at Bandar-e-Anzali on 16 September, Dunsterforce was stood down and regular troops from the 14th Division took their place.

Although Dunsterforce was no more and Baku was in the possession of Nuri Pasha, the British were determined to keep control of the Caspian Sea itself. Commodore Norris and Captain Washington were therefore sent by the Admiralty to acquire ships. These officers were followed by naval personnel, whilst 6-inch guns and mountings, ammunition and armour plating were conveyed by motor lorries over the 700 miles of mountainous road separating Bandar-e-Anzali from Baghdad. The ships they acquired were turned into passable imitations of cruisers and Norris became the commander of one of the strangest navies in the world. Krasnovodsk, garrisoned by the 1/4th Hampshires was held on to and became the dockyard for the new British Caspian navy.

Chapter Thirteen

The End of the Campaign

(Maps 25, 26, 27 & 28)

During this time, General Marshall had been carrying out actions further up the Euphrates where the Turks were rumoured to be massing for an advance from Hit under the thrusting commander of their 50th Division, Nazim Bey. General Brooking marched towards the town and the Turks promptly abandoned the place. Bitumen wells were scattered over the desert around the town – the bitumen was used for roofing the houses, for waterproofing boats and baskets, and in places lay unexpectedly and surprisedly in congealed lakes, as flat and hard as pavements standing a foot above the ground. (Candler)

On the approach of General Brooking, the Turks had retreated further upstream to Khan Baghdadi, 20 miles off, so the British force advanced towards them from Sahiliya on 25 March 1918, with 50 Brigade leading, 42 Brigade 4 miles further back, and the reserve and a mobile column of Ford vans 5 miles behind them. The Turkish first line was captured by a fine rush of 50 Brigade who waited for 42 Brigade to come up before tackling the second line. Meanwhile the cavalry managed to make a forced march and get behind the second line, thus cutting off the Turks' retreat.

After a bombardment for half an hour the attack started at 1800 hrs. One thousand prisoners were taken and when the retreating Turks ran straight into the cavalry, another thousand surrendered. Just before dawn a further 2,000 surrendered to the armoured cars on the Aleppo road. Brooking was still not satisfied and continued

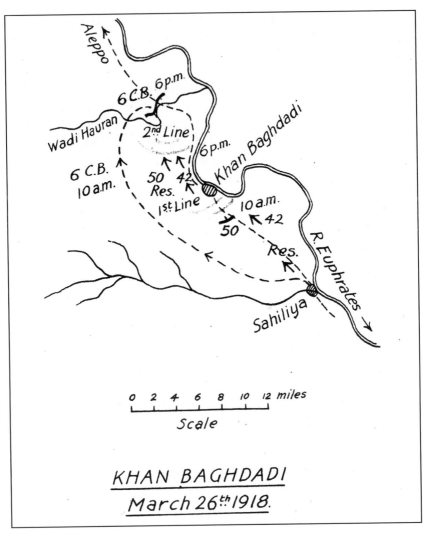

Map 25. Battle of Khan Baghdadi

the pursuit until he caught up with Nazim Bey, the unfortunate commander of the Turkish 50th Division, and two British officers who had been captured the night before. The push continued until the town of Ana was also in the bag.

Thirty-two miles beyond Ana, armoured cars, sent forward for the purpose, came upon Lieutenant Colonel Tennant, the RFC commander, and Major Hobart, who had made a forced landing in

210

the desert after their petrol tank had been holed by machine-gun fire a few days before. Under guard, they were on their way to Aleppo. Tennant tells the story of their rescue from their Turkish guards:

But there, a hundred yards along the road, as large as life, was an armoured car with others behind. I howled it to Hobart, and we went with heads down as if all the devils of hell were behind us. The Turks scattered behind the rocks under the machine-gun fire; we never looked round. The officer commanding the cars, Captain Tod, leapt out and dragged us into the turret, the men yelling with excitement. It was beyond one's wildest dreams. We lay and panted and talked till the open plain was reached, where sniping would be impossible; whiskey and bully-beef were produced – the most wonderful meal of one's life.

Candler sums up General Brooking's achievement:

The endurance and rapidity of the troops were extraordinary. The infantry were marching two days and two nights with little or no sleep, and fighting all day and part of two nights. The cavalry covered something like ninety miles in the first two days and the armoured cars 170 miles apart from detours, between Hit and the farthest point of the pursuit . . . Khan Baghdadi was a crushing blow to the Turk.

After the extensive destruction of the stores that the Turks had gradually amassed along the Euphrates for their projected offensive, it was clear that any danger from that quarter had been finally extinguished.

Marshall now needed to do something to protect the communications of Dunsterforce through Persia, so he decided to capture and hold the area Kifri–Tuz Khurmatli (called Tuz for short). The Turkish XII Corps had its 6th Division in the Mosul–Kirkuk area and the 2nd Division from Kirkuk to Qara Tepe.

General Egerton, who was to lead the advance, devised an ambitious plan. A converging attack on Qara Tepe was to be simulated in the hope of inducing the enemy to fall back on Kifri, but the real attack was to be a wider one, and was to include Tuz, some 20 miles north-west of Kifri. So while the Turks were congratulating themselves on having once again carried out a sly withdrawal and escape, the line would be cut 20 miles beyond them.

Thirteen hundred MT vans were used to carry troops to the area. By now, motor vehicles were common in the Army and armoured cars were being used in the fighting in conjunction with the cavalry, 'wheels' being the commonly used slang term for them. Tuz lay beyond the Jabal Hamrin on the River Aq-Su, the name given to the Adhaim river beyond the mountains.

The columns moved forward on the night of 26/27 April, meeting with little opposition. In Qara Tepe the Turks had slipped away for the thirteenth time, and it was the same at Abu Gharaib. The 'wheels' were sent off to capture Kifri which they did with little trouble, while the rest of the force continued the advance and came upon the enemy just short of Tuz at Kulawind. With the motorized battery and Lewis guns putting down fire on the enemy force from the front, the cavalry attacked from the right in a charge over 500 yards of desert plain. Two hundred Turks were killed in this action, 565 were taken prisoner and the rest fled.

The horsemen continued on towards Tuz but it was too late to mount an attack. Next morning, 28 April, Tuz and Yanija on the other side of the Aq-Su river were found to be occupied by the enemy, but a ford was discovered 3 miles off which the cavalry and 'wheels' crossed during the day and occupied a knoll nearly a mile further north.

That night the infantry crossed the river and by 0700 hrs next morning they had captured Yanija Buyuk with few casualties. A few miles further on they entered Tuz at 0900 hrs and took a considerable number of prisoners, while the cavalry to the north were charging down the Turks who were making a stand at Yanija Kuchuk on the Kirkuk road. This was the signal for a general surrender of Turkish soldiers all over the battlefield.

The summer of 1918 was a quiet period in Mesopotamia. The pandemic of influenza which appeared in Europe in the spring of 1918 spread northwards and eastward to India and began to appear in Basra in September. The death rate rose sharply and spread outside the town to decimate the Bakhtair, Lur and Qashtai tribes; within a few months it caused a greater loss of life than had been suffered in four years of warfare in the whole of the country.

General Marshall was proving to be a more congenial colleague than Maude had been for Arnold Wilson, the Political Officer, for he had a concern for the people of the country that Maude had never displayed. One of his concerns was for improvement in the

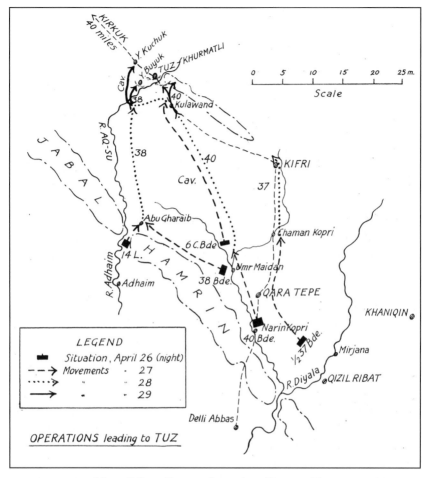

Map 26.   Operations leading to Tuz

agriculture of the Baghdad vilayet (province). Wilson invited the most important sheikhs in the area to a reception held for them in the Baghdad Soldiers' Club gardens. During their stay in the city they were shown a model farm, cotton experimental cultivation and what Marshall described as 'various classes of military engines of destruction such as guns, howitzers, armoured cars and aeroplanes'. Clearly the C-in-C was also concerned to improve the shining hour by emphasizing the offensive power of the British Army. As far as the cotton was concerned, experiments had shown that Mesopotamia could produce a better class of cotton and heavier

213

yield per acre than Egypt, the main producer of raw cotton for the European market.

The many canals that led off the Diyalah were taken in hand by the Irrigation Directorate and a new regulator was installed to get a better head of water so that more acres could be brought under cultivation. Experiments had also been done with crude oil for cooking purposes rather than wood, all of which had to be imported from India. Another Indian import that could be dispensed with was soap since they were now making their own.

In September, an American Mission, styling itself 'The Persian Famine Relief Commission' arrived in Baghdad and Marshall received instructions to give it every assistance. He did so, although he was not quite convinced that famine relief was the principal objective of the Mission. He tells us that some members did really help to fight famine but the leaders, having been sent up into Persia, entered into negotiations with the government there and eventually secured concessions in the north-west of the country on behalf of the Standard Oil Company.

Also in September news came that Bulgaria had asked for an armistice. It began to be rumoured that after their defeat in Palestine by General Allenby the Turks would soon follow suit. The British Government decided to take advantage of the situation to strike another and probably last blow in Mesopotamia, by proposing two operations: to advance on Mosul (Al Mawsil), and also up the Euphrates. Marshall objected to the second plan – after sending so much transport to Dunsterforce, he had only enough for one enterprise, and he favoured Mosul.

The way led through Tikrit and then traversed a deep gorge formed by the passage of the Tigris through the mountain ridge which to the south is the familiar Jabal Hamrin, and to the north is given the name of Jabal Makhu. Further upstream beyond the hills the river is joined at Humr by a considerable tributary augmenting it from the east, called the Little Zab. It is the only obstacle in the flat land north of the Jabal Hamrin and east of the Tigris.

Turkish defences had been constructed at Fat-Ha, the village in the gorge between the Jabal Hamrin and the Jabal Makhu, and, 20 miles further north, on the right bank of the Tigris at Humr. Two other defensive lines were located north and south of Sharqat which is on the Tigris 25 miles north of Humr.

On 24 October a force led by Lieutenant General Cobbe

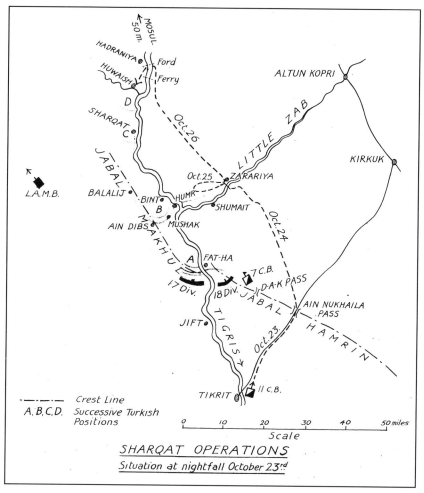

Map 27.   Sharqat Operations

approached Fat-Ha only to find that the Turks had decamped
during the night having blown the roads on both sides of the gorge
into the river. 11 Cavalry Brigade crossed the river to the wider left
bank, marched north and forded the Little Zab, so that and by the
26th they had reached a point on the Tigris well beyond the
Turkish line north of Sharqat. Here they proceeded to make a
further river crossing and established themselves at Huwaish, 5
miles away from the Turks. By dawn on the 28th, 53 Brigade, who
had made a forced march to assist the Cavalry Brigade, were on the

215

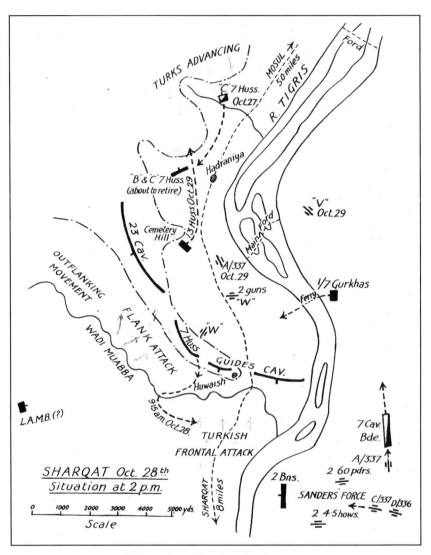

Map 28. Battle of Sharqat

left bank of the river. A battalion of Gurkhas from the Brigade started to cross, a slow business since there was only a raft and a small boat available.

During the day the Turks began a series of probing attacks, all of which were driven off. More reinforcements began to arrive and the Cavalry Brigade's defensive line was now firm. But they were anxious to see the 17th Division which was supposed to be advancing up the right bank of the river in the lee of the Jabal Makhul mountains to attack the southern Turkish line. But there was no sign of them. It had been a difficult day for the infantry division against strong opposition and they were tired, but General Cobbe was merciless, driving them on throughout the night of 28/29 October.

The Cavalry Brigade spent a disturbed night. The Turks had established some artillery on a bluff on the north side of the British position and were shelling the reinforcements attempting to cross the river. This battery was finally destroyed in one of the last British cavalry actions, by the 13th Hussars, who galloped across the flat to the foot of the bluff, dismounted and climbed it. The Turks were already discomfited by incoming artillery fire and the appearance of the dismounted cavalry, lances in hand, was the last straw – they fled. The 730 Turks by the guns were made prisoner, while those fleeing were captured by a squadron of the 14th Lancers. Meanwhile, as the day wore on there was still no sign of the 17th Division.

The reason for this was that they had been stopped beyond the Turkish defences south of Sharqat and held up by a muddle over the supply of field artillery ammunition. Poor communications and inept staff work over whether all the ammunition had been expended produced the confusion and it was not until after daylight on 30 October, when it was discovered that there were still 1,000 rounds in hand, that General Cobb could advance with his whole force.

But the Turk had shot his bolt. For six days he had been harried from pillar to post and allowed scarely any rest. Though he had conducted his series of retirements with all his customary skill, he had reached the end of his tether. As Cobbe approached his southern redoubts at break of day, loud explosions were heard in the Turkish lines opposing the Cavalry Brigade and white flags began to appear. The battle – and the war – had come to an end.

Ismail Hakki, the commander of the Tigris force, surrendered in person. The fugitives were chased northwards by the 18th Division but when the pursuers had reached a point 12 miles south of Mosul, news came that an armistice had been signed and the war was over.

The Turks sent out a flag of truce with a letter requesting Major General Fane, Commander of the 18th Division, to withdraw to the position he had held at the moment when the armistice was signed. Fane refused and his troops bivouacked outside the town, being serenaded every day by a Turkish military band whose main offering was many (unintended) variations on the tune of 'God Save the King'.

Marshall went up there with Arnold Wilson for a conference with Ali Ihsan, the Turkish Commander-in-Chief. As the terms of the armistice had been very clumsily drawn up Ali Ihsan attempted to play the lawyer and argue his way through them. Marshall saw the funny side of the proceedings but told the Turk clearly that he was determined to take over the Mosul vilayet and that if he resisted by force he would be held responsible for any blood that might be shed.

Ali Ihsan was furious and turned bright red, but eventually signed a document that Marshall had drawn up that listed the terms which he thought were appropriate.

Next morning Turkish flags were flying from every public building, the Turkish army stores were being sold off and Colonel Leachman, who had been appointed as Political Officer for the region, was obstructed when he tried to take over in the town. Marshall wrote to the Turkish general who sent back a long and animated answer that he did not recognize Marshall's authority and had sent in his resignation to the Minister of War. Marshall told him to leave and provided an escort of two armoured cars to help him on his way to Nisibin. Things then began to go smoothly and Marshall returned to Baghdad.

The Turkish resistance in the last days had showed no signs of slackening. Although short of men and material, blind with no air force, cavalry or armoured cars, deaf with no communications from the outside world, and dumb with no means of communicating their situation to anyone, they had fought an obviously losing battle with courage and skill right up to the end.

The British and Indian soldiers could look back on the campaign with mixed feelings of sadness and satisfaction that affect all winning armies. They had left behind them some 60,000 of their comrades in graves strewn the length of the Tigris and Euphrates and, as with all wars, but particularly in the case of Mesopotamia, they must have wondered whether this sacrifice, in the context of the whole war, was worthwhile.

Marshall ends his book with a comment that would be unfashionable nowadays:

The sweeping-up after a campaign is always an arduous and tiresome operation and in our case was complicated by political questions. President Wilson's Fourteen Points and his twaddle about self-determination and the rights of small nations were the parrot-cries of the moment. Instructions were received to canvas the various districts to find out from the Arabs whom they wished to govern them, whether Turks, British or one of their own people. Generally the answer came pat, and the local 'Cokkus' or political officer was at once nominated as their future ruler. The intelligentsia were different and, being mostly Mohammedans, they ipso facto voted for a ruler of theit own religion.

Chapter Fourteen

Consequences

It is not usually realized that the numbers of casualties suffered in the Mesopotamian Campaign were, in terms of percentages of soldiers involved in individual battles, as high if not higher on occasions than those on the Western Front. This was not only due to the ferocity of the fighting, but also to the poor evacuation facilities and medical care that they received.

Two of the most important factors in the campaign were undoubtedly the administration and the effect of the terrain. The effects of the administration, or rather the lack of it, were most critically felt in the earlier part of the campaign up to 1916, and mainly in the field of transport – river transport – for little else was of use for long-distance carriage.

When General Barrett captured Basra with the 6th Division in November 1914, his river transport consisted of three river steamers, seventeen lighters and a number of *mahailas*, which were usually towed but were capable of sailing under favourable conditions carrying 25–39 tons when the river was at its lowest. Large numbers of native craft had to be hired but their carrying capacity was not very great although they provided good service throughout the campaign.

In May the river fleet was increased to ten steamers, four tugs and nineteen lighters that were usually lashed either side of a steamer. The following year new steamers from Burma arrived that were either stern-wheelers or screw driven and drew 5 feet, which made it difficult for them to operate in the Narrows, the stretch of river above Qurna. In June 1916, paddle steamers began to arrive, one year after they were ordered. They arrived in sections and the order was finally completed in January 1917. Attempts were made to tow craft over from India, but in the process 3 steamers, 22 lighters, 17 sternwheelers, 2 rafts and a floating dock foundered.

This deficiency in river transport was detrimental to the performance of the Force from the outset. In November 1915 when the daily tonnage available was 150 tons, the troops' daily requirements were 208 tons; in April 1916 the daily tonnage available was half what was required.

As a result, on 21 January 1916, when the Battle of Hanna was fought, there were 10,000 infantry and twelve guns left in Basra. On 8 March, when the force at Dujaila was desperately trying to push forward and relieve Kut, 12,000 men and 26 guns were idle downriver. This inadequacy weakened or even paralysed the attacking capabilities of the force in the early part of the campaign.

In due course the Inland Water Transport (IWT) run by the Royal Engineers took the matter in hand and by the time of the Armistice there were 446 steam tugs and launches, 774 barges and 414 motor boats on the Tigris; the number of sappers involved was 4,300. These figures do not include the native craft of which there was always a swarm around the riverside settlements.

To keep this great river fleet – by far the largest of its kind in the world – in operation, an immense organization had to be built up at the shortest notice. Many craft were constructed at Basra in purpose-built yards, manned by labour from the United Kingdom and India, although there were many delays, some inevitable, others due to lack of foresight and mismanagement in Britain. Drawings and construction plans, for example, were not sent out with the first shipments of materials, only arriving after a lapse of several months. Instead of being carried by a special messenger or courier, in at least one instance they were packed in a wooden box which lost its paper address label and made one trip to England and back to Basra before its contents were accidentally discovered.

Quarters for the construction and dockyard staff had to be built on land reclaimed for the purpose; slipways had to be laid down, workshops erected, and heavy machinery for the repair of every class of river steamer installed.

To transport oil fuel, special barges had to be obtained from India or built on the spot, and large tanks erected upriver. The variety of stores needed to keep the flotilla in service was bewildering, collected as they had been from all over the world, so that no kind of standardization was possible. Every type of engine, every known form of propulsion, every brand of paddle and screw was represented. To man this heterogeneous collection of craft, sailors and craftsmen arrived from all over the world. Jamaicans and men from Barbados were much in evidence; Hong Kong volunteered 6,000 carpenters and mechanics; stokers from Somalia, boatmen from Zanzibar and mechanics from every part of India and Burma all worked under the supervision of foremen from English, Scottish and Irish shipyards.

The clerical work was enormous and it was efficiently carried out by Indian clerks at twice the pay they would have received in India – they included Brahmins, Goanese and Bengal Christians, Moslems, Madrasis, Sikhs, Mahrattas and Buddhists, all working together in reasonable harmony. Pig farms were established both at Baghdad and Basra to meet the demands of Chinese labour and the British soldier. At Basra only one landowner protested against the scheme. He was under the impression that the pigs would be wild boars, the only kind that he knew of, and he was afraid they might break loose and eat his children as the wild pigs of the marsh were reputed to do.

Nor were the responsibilities of the IWT restricted to the efficient management of the river flotilla. The Tigris soon became over-crowded and to prevent collisions and groundings an elaborate system of river controls became necessary. The Tigris was buoyed from Basra to Baghdad, the buoys being shifted as the channels changed. In 1917 a system of river-training works was instituted known as 'bandalling'. This involved the construction of temporary fences of hurdling to direct the water at its lowest into a particular course, so as to narrow the stream and increase its depth. It was enormously costly and not always effective, but like the buoyage service was amply justified by the results. An extra six inches of water at half a dozen difficult places during the autumn meant an extra hundred tons of cargo a day at the river ead.

A great deal of the work on the Tigris was performed by the Royal Indian Marine, the Royal Navy and the Royal Naval Reserve, assisted by the Army who often delegated soldiers to supervise and control the native vessels which were the main carriers of supplies up the Tigris. Starting with the Royal Indian Marine steamer *Lawrence* and three old sloops (*Espiègle*, *Odin* and *Clio*) that the Admiralty had intended for destruction, the Royal Navy gradually expanded its fleet to include a great variety of vessels including tugs, launches and the 'Fly' and 'Insect' gunboat classes that were especially built during the campaign, under the cover name of 'China' gunboats, to conceal their destination and whose shallow draught allowed them to operate much further upriver than the sloops.

But even if river transport had been adequate, the port of Basra was for a long time incapable of dealing with the inward flow of stores. Queues of ships had to anchor in mid-stream and were unloaded into native boats so that even as late as July 1916 it was usual for a ship to spend 39 days in port at Basra before being free to return on its homeward voyage. Sir George Buchanan, who later took charge of the facilities at Basra, said on his first visit, 'The military expedition to Basra is, I believe, unique inasmuch as in no previous case has such an enormous force been landed and maintained without an adequately prepared base.' Between December 1915 and March 1916, 129,500 troops, 33,000 animals, 4,800 vehicles and 71,500 tons of cargo had been disembarked there in that primitive fashion.

Even then, the river was no better than an inefficient single-track railway and had to supply an army of 120,000 men more than 200 miles from the Basra base. General Barrrett first asked for a real railway in February 1915, but India refused on grounds of expense and it was not until after the fall of Kut, when the War Office took over the control of operations, that the first railway was built. Finally, Baghdad was linked to Basra by rail in a journey of twelve hours in August 1917.

The control by India of the early part of the campaign proved to be a mistake for there was no co-ordination between the civilian and military authorities. This was probably the legacy of Kitchener's autocratic and secretive ways of running the military machine, an attitude which he later displayed very clearly in his dealings with the Gallipoli Campaign.

Apart from this, the Indian Government was not fitted to control a large expedition overseas; the Directorate of the Royal Indian Marine was not satisfactorily organized, for example. The civil executive did not understand the difficult climatic conditions in Mesopotamia and the military did not properly insist on the necessary requirements to cope with them. This disunity of purpose can be seen in other British campaigns in which at first the government is learning what co-operation means, followed by a period when it is forced to make such co-operation effectively possible, then the time of success when the hard-learned and expensive lessons are put into effect.

But the change needed a spur. For the Nile Campaign, another 'river war', Gordon's death at Khartum was the spur. After that, transport, material and troops were collected and this methodical preparation finally resulted in Omdurman. In Mesopotamia, the fall of Kut was the spur.

The terrain enormously favoured defence. Because of the open landscape, the attackers moving across it were subject to the full effect of small-arms fire at long ranges. This never happened even on the Western Front. The result was that again and again attacks were brought to a halt with heavy casualties at ranges between 1,000 and 1,500 yards. In contrast to the Western Front, the decisive weapons were not artillery, but the rifle and machine-gun, and to a lesser extent, the cavalry whose swan song on the military world stage it was, together with the armoured car and the aeroplane.

Numerous irrigation channels, some thousands of years old, the lack of landmarks, the mirage and the ease with which digging could be carried out all favoured the defenders. Vast distances, the feature-less plain, the lack of adequate cover, the inundations that could be controlled by the enemy upstream all added to the difficulties of attack. Movement was handicapped by lack of local information and maps and, away from the river, the complete absence of drinking water for both men and animals in the hot weather; in the cold weather, the plain was transformed into a morass of sticky mud.

The rivers Tigris and Euphrates were the most important features in the landscape not only as obstacles but, in the case of the Tigris, as a line of supply and, above all, as the source of water to which, therefore, all troops were tied. The result of this was the one weak-ness of the defence – except under the unique conditions afforded by the Suwacha Marsh, and, later, by the angles between the Hai and the Tigris, there was always an open flank. An open flank means that there is room to swing wide of the enemy's line and get behind it to tackle it from the rear. Commanders like General Townshend took advantage of this fact and his operations at Es Sinn and Ctesiphon are good examples of bold night operations in which, unseen by the enemy, he turned their flank. Later in the campaign most of the battles like Ramadi and Tikrit were based on outflanking movements.

One feature that the campaign demonstrated was the advantage of night operations. In the desert, obstacles like built-up areas, railways, woodland and so on that get in the way in a European country are practically non-existent, and direction is no more difficult to maintain than by day. There being no landmarks, compasses had to be used both by night and by day. Communication was hardly more difficult than by day, while surprise was easier to achieve, movement could be on a broad front and the supremacy of the rifle and machine-gun was devalued. It was used occasionally earlier in the campaign but it was not until the later stages that we find it fully successful as at Shumran, Tikrit and Khan Baghadi.

Infantry attacks by day in the open desert were very costly. The standard pre-war method of troops advancing in a series of rushes and providing their own covering fire did not work in a bare countryside. 'Somme-style' attacks were as suicidal as they were in France, and the use of artillery to provide a moving barrage could not be carried out because of the shortage of guns. Smoke was used on the Western Front to hide advancing infantry but it was never tried in Mesopotamia, although the mirage substituted for it on occasions. Units were hampered as far as firepower was concerned by having only four machine-guns per battalion, compared to the Turkish six.

During the middle of the day in the summer the war practically stopped. Marching in great heat was enervating and the men quickly became dehydrated so that 8 miles a day was as much as could be covered. Marching by night was much to be preferred.

The great disappointment of the years before the capture of Baghdad was the poor performance of the cavalry, which often seemed to move at their slowest pace, and hung behind the infantry. Perhaps this was because the regular Indian cavalry brigades had been sent to France whereas the brigade sent to Mesopotamia was a scratch one. But they learnt on the job and in the final year of the campaign they performed well and provided the final burst of brilliance that foreshadowed the demise of their role in the military world.

A striking difference between the tactics of the two opposing forces was in the use of ships. Both sides used them for conveying troops and supplies, but the Turks restricted them to that role; they never used them offensively. The British, on the other hand, had Royal Navy and Indian Marine vessels on the river playing a vital part in supporting the Army's forward movement – using their guns on Turkish units during battles, pursuing them in retreat and, in some cases, taking the leading role and spearheading a British advance. It is fair to say that if the naval forces had not been present, progess northwards would have been much slower and in particular sitations, impossible. They certainly upheld the Senior Service's reputation for enterprise and gallantry and, together with the Imperial land forces, were part of one the most successful combined operations in the history of modern warfare.

One of the problems encountered by the whole army, but in particular by the artillery, was the mirage. After early morning, unless the guns were already ranged on their target, they had to cease firing until the late afternoon brought clearer visibility. Aircraft were becoming the necessary adjunct to the artillery for finding targets, ranging on them and spotting the fall of shot, but they were very few and far between at the beginning of the campaign. Townshend had four, Maurice Farmans and Martynsides, later increased to one flight. By December 1916 the Royal Flying Corps had No. 30 Squadron, later joined by No. 63 Squadron, operating with the Tigris Corps using BE2s and Bristol Scouts under the command of Lieutenant Colonel J.E. Tennant.

Like the armies on the Western Front, the Tigris Force had to enter a learning curve that took it from an ill-equipped frontier expeditionary force to the nucleus of a modern army with armoured motorized columns lacking only tanks, strafing aircraft, efficiently-used artillery and, under the command of General Marshall, smaller, mobile, independent columns. One of the most obvious outcomes of the campaign was the coming of age of the Indian Army as a world-class military force, a reputation that it has continued to maintain to this day.

The British were never able to control the dissident and intractable elements amongst the desert tribesmen. This was as true after the British Government had accepted the mandate for Iraq from the League of Nations as it was during the war. During the war they had never been subdued and the punitive expeditions occasionally undertaken by the army of occupation were more likely to emphasize the Army's limitations rather than demonstrate the British ability to govern. This had also been the situation in Turkish times. After the war aircraft were often used to keep order amongst the itinerant tribesmen.

In every direction in Iraq uncharted marshes and networks of canals serving great areas of irrigated lands proved to be impassable obstacles to the punitive army column. But this did not mean that it was possible to follow the example of the Turkish rulers and ignore these tribemen altogether. Attempts had to be made to collect taxes as was done in the settled parts of Iraq, otherwise it would store up difficulties for future governments of the country. The policy adopted in the Basra vilayet, with a fair amount of success, was to appoint the sheikh of each tribe as the Mudir or representative of the government in his area. A salary of £15 a year was attached to the job but the prestige that it brought was out of all proportion to its monetary worth. Their duties were to collect taxes, maintain order, settle minor disputes and provide tribal labour for public works such as the clearance of canals or the construction of roads. Some sheikhs abused their powers, prosecuting ancient family quarrels or amassing wealth, and the system required careful handling and a great deal of patience, but some proved to be capable administrators and future leaders in a larger sphere.

The Mesopotamian Commission had been established in March 1916 and reported in May 1917. It was set up to enquire into the origin, inception and conduct of operations, the supply of drafts, reinforcements, ammunition and equipment, and the medical provision. Because they reported before the end of the war their findings were influenced by the fact that the struggle was still going on and the outcome still to be decided. The medical conditions described to the Commission members after Ctesiphon and Sheikh Saad have already been set out, and their strictures had an immediate and dramatic effect for the better, a turn of events that was greatly speeded up by the decision of the British Government to take over the campaign.

On the conduct of the military operations, they were less than fair to the Indian Government which did not have the means to support anything more than a minor expedition, a fact known to and agreed by the British Government early in 1914. The responses to their requests to London for reinforcements were niggardly since they were received and attended to by Lord Kitchener, who had been responsible for the parsimonious policy in the first place and now resented having to divert a single man away from the Western Front.

However, it is true that the Indian Government showed little knowledge and understanding of Mesopotamia throughout the campaign. This is demonstrated by the fact that the Commander-in-Chief, Sir Beachamp Duff, never visited Mesopotamia, and ignorance about the conditions in the country amongst the Indian higher command was almost total. This explains a good deal about relations between India and Mesopotamia, and the way in which they were enthusiastic about advances like that of Townshend's from Kut, for example, basing their support on the speed of the movement prior to that time, whilst knowing nothing of the conditions that were to be faced further north.

Not enough was known of the difficulties presented by the climate or the Tigris. In summer, it was usually too hot for proper operations; in winter, it was often too wet. Spring and autumn were the best times of the year for campaigning but these optimum conditions did not last for very long. Much of the equipment was often not suitable for the fluctuating seasons. A good example is the single-fly tent: during the summer it did not provide sufficient protection for the troops in the torrid conditions, and in winter was simply inadequate against the cold and the wet. Many other examples could be quoted.

As far as individuals were concerned, the Commission came to the conclusion that blame should be shared. Sir John Nixon received the weightiest share for his disregard of the supply problems. This was unfair, because he could not actually solve them – that could only be done by those in India. In India, others responsible, in the Commission's view, were the Viceroy (Lord Hardinge) and the Commander-in-Chief (Sir Beauchamp Duff), who resigned; in England they blamed the Military Secretary of the India Office (Sir Edmund Barrow), the Secretary of State for India (Mr Austen Chamberlain), who resigned, and the War Committee of the Cabinet.

By the time the Commission had reported, most of the inadequacies had been made up, or very soon would be, but it is probably true to say that the discussion that ensued centring around the relationship between Britain and India began to strengthen doubts about the future viability of that arrangement, at least in the form in which it was then operating, and provoked a discussion about the very future of the Imperial link.

Chapter Fifteen

Aftermath

What of the subsequent careers of the chief actors in this drama?

General Nixon gave evidence before the Mesopotamian Commission and came in for a good deal of the blame as we have seen. He was not employed again and died in December 1921 after suffering ill health for several years.

Charles Townshend returned to Paris after the Armistice was signed and then to England to be faced with hostility from the Press about his presumed complacency over the treatment of the British and Indian prisoners of war after the fall of Kut. He was never really given credit for his successes earlier in the campaign. He resumed the old habit that so annoyed his colleagues and seniors of writing letters to all and sundry who might help him in his career. Earlier in his life he had barely been given a new post before he was angling for something better. But he was disappointed both in further promotion and in employment. He was placed on half pay and despite his indignation was never employed again. Another disappointment was when his hopes of succeeding to the title of Marquis Townshend were dashed when his titled cousin unexpectedly had a child. He entered Parliament, visited Turkey against the wishes of the government and wrote his book *My Campaign in Mesopotamia*. He died in Paris in 1924, aged sixty-three.

Sir Percy Cox became acting minister to Persia after the war for a short time and later Iraq's first high commissioner where he was universally known as 'Suposi Kokus'. He spent five years there and ended his public career in the country. He was President of the Royal Geographical Society in 1933 and died in 1937.

William Wassmuss, German agent. Towards the end of the war he was captured by the Persians and handed over to the British but was finally allowed to return home to Germany. Some years later he returned to Tangistan to teach modern farming methods. The experiment failed and he went back to Germany where he died penniless and friendless aged fifty-one.

First Baron Hardinge of Penshurst, Viceroy of India. His resignation after the sweeping censure in the Mesopotamian Commission was not accepted and in 1920s he became British Ambassador in Paris, but unexpectedly resigned in 1922 and died in 1944 at the age of ninety-six.

Sir Beauchamp Duff was recalled from India in 1916, nominally to give evidence before the Mesopotamian Commission and was not employed again. He died in 1918.

Sir Fenton Aylmer retired from active service after the war and became Colonel Commandant of the Royal Engineers. He died in 1934.

Sir Percy Lake was not employed again after his retirement from command of the Mesopotamian Force in 1916. He died in 1940.

General Nicolai Baratov. After the defeat of the White Russian forces, he emigrated to France where he became President of the Fédération Général des Invalides Mutiles de Guerre Russes à l'Etranger. He died in Paris in March 1932, aged sixty-seven.

Major General L.C. Dunsterville. Retired from the army and became a writer, mainly of his reminiscences and autobiography. Died in 1946, aged eighty-one.

Major General Sir William Marshall. Posted to Southern Command in India after the war. Retired from the Army in 1924. Died in 1939 aged seventy-four.

Sir Arnold Wilson. He continued in Iraq until relieved by Sir Percy Cox and continued in government service, being admired for his obvious abilities and drive, but disliked by some for his reputation as a pusher and for his abrasive tongue. During the Second World War, although well over age, he joined the RAF as a rear gunner and was shot down and killed over France on a bombing mission.

'Official Eyewitness' (Edmund Candler). The only correspondent nominated by the War Office and given this title; so referred to by the army in Mesopotamia. Nowadays we would say that he was embedded in the Force. He wrote reports for the London newspapers which were heavily censored at Basra, a practice against which he was continually complaining without success. After the war he wrote his own account *The Long Road to Baghdad*. He died in 1926.

Victoria Cross awards

Six members of the Indian Army won the highest award for bravery during the campaign. They were:

Chatta Singh, Sepoy in the 9th Bhopal Infantry. On 13 January 1916, during the Battle of the Wadi, he left cover to assist his officer who was lying wounded and helpless in the open. Chatta Singh bound up the officer's wounds and then dug cover for him with his entrenching tool, being exposed all the time to very heavy rifle fire. For five hours until nightfall he shielded the helpless casualty with his body and then, under cover of darkness, went back for assistance and brought him to safety. Chatta Singh ended the war with the rank of Havildar.

Lance Naik Lala, 41st Dogras. On 21 January 1916, at El Orah, finding an officer lying close to the enemy lines, Lance Naik Lala dragged him into a temporary shelter. After bandaging his wounds, the lance naik heard calls from his own adjutant who was lying wounded in the open only 100 yards from the enemy. Despite being told to remain where he was, Lala insisted on going to help. He stripped off his own clothing to keep the adjutant warm and stayed with him unril just before dark. After dark he carried the first casualty to safety and then returned with a stretcher to rescue his adjutant. Lala ended the war with the rank of Jemadar.

Naik Shahmad Khan, 89th Punjab Regiment. On 12/13 April near Bait Ayeesa, Naik Shahamad Khan was in charge of a machine-gun covering a gap in a new line within 150 yards of the entrenched enemy. He beat off three counter-attacks and worked his gun single-handed after all his men, except two belt-fillers, had become casualties. For three hours he held the gap and when his gun was knocked out, he and his two belt-fillers held their ground with their rifles until ordered to withdraw. With the help of his two men, he then brought back his gun, ammunition and one severely wounded man and, finally, the remaining arms and equipment. Shahamad Khan finished the war with the rank of Jemadar.

Captain John Alexander Sinton, Indian Medical Service. On 21 January 1916, at Orah Ruins, Captain Sinton attended the wounded under very heavy fire and, although he was shot through both arms and the side, refused to go to hospital and remained on duty as long as the daylight lasted. In three previous actions he had also displayed the utmost bravery. Sinton finished the war as Brigadier.

Major George Campbell Wheeler, 9th Gurkha Rifles. On 23 January 1917, at Shumran on the River Tigris, Major Wheeler, together with one Gurkha officer and eight men, crossed the river and rushed the enemy's trench in the face of very heavy fire. Having obtained a footing on the far bank, he was almost immediately counter-attacked by the enemy with a party of bombers. Major Wheeler at once led a charge, receiving in the process a severe bayonet wound in the head. In spite of this, however, he managed to disperse the enemy and consolidate his position. Major Wheeler finished the war as a Lieutenant Colonel.

Major George Godfrey Wheeler, 7th Hariana Lancers. On 12 April, at Shaiba, Major Wheeler took out his squadron in an attempt to capture a flag which was the centre point of a group of enemy who were firing at one of the British picquets. He advanced, attacked the enemy's infantry with lances, and then retired while the enemy swarmed out of hidden ground to make an excellent target for the Royal Artillery's guns. Next day, Major Wheeler led his squadron to the attack on the North Mound. He was seen far ahead of his squadron, riding straight for the enemy's standards and was killed in the charge. Buried in Basra War Cemetery.

(These accounts are taken from Mike Chapman's website (www.victoriacross@chapter-one.com).

Other VC winners from the British Army and Navy were:

Lieutenant Commander E.C. Cookson RN. Buried in Amara War
    Cemetery.
Lieutenant Commander C.H. Cowley RN. No known grave.
Sergeant D. Finlay. No known grave.
Lieutenant H. Firman. No known grave.
Private J.H. Fynn. No known grave.
Lieutenant Colonel G.S. Henderson. No known grave.
Corporal S.W. Ware. Amara War Cemetery.

And the future of Mesopotamia?

General Maude promised in his proclamation that the British had come to liberate them from the Turks, and that the British wished the people of Iraq to regain their past prosperity. This prosperity was a long time in the past.

After the Armistice, Britain accepted a mandate for Iraq under the League of Nations. In 1920 the Arab government in Damascus encroached on the Euphrates boundary, as a result of which rebellion broke out in the north of the country around Mosul and peace had to be restored, only for another agitation, this time against the British mandate, to break out in the middle Euphrates and Baghdad.

At this point an article on Mesopotamia was written for the *Sunday Times* and was published on 22 August 1920. Its author was T.E. Lawrence, the Arabs' self-appointed spokesman in Britain, and it turned out to be an attack on the military administration which was controlled from Baghdad by Sir Arnold Wilson. Lawrence's response to the rebellions, in which he asserted that 10,000 Arabs were killed, was to describe the government as being more bloody and inefficient than the British public knew, since the communiqués from the Baghdad authorities were belated, insincere and incomplete. He went on to say that the reason for the latest rising was given by the Mesopotamian Government as political, but that they did not say what the people of Iraq were demanding. Certainly they were hanging Iraqis for what they called political offences. Perhaps they did not know what the agitators wanted; perhaps it was even what the Cabinet had already promised them.

He suggested that to reduce the number of 90,000 troops that were stationed in Iraq, together with aircraft, armoured cars, gunboats and armoured trains, some 7,000 of the Iraqis who formed the old Turkish force of occupation could be enrolled, instead of the three extra brigades that had recently been sent from India and further denuded the troops that guarded the North-West Frontier.

Perhaps as a result of this article from an individual who was a cult figure at the time, the British Government announced that Sir Percy Cox would be appointed High Commissioner with power to create both a Council of State under an Arab president and an elective assembly. This led to the whole of central Iraq rising in arms and the massacre of 300 young soldiers of the Manchester Regiment, together with British officials who were either murdered or taken prisoner. Even more troops were rushed from India and Sir Percy Cox invited the Naquib of Baghdad, the religious head of the Sunni community, to form the Council of State. As the agitation subsided it was learnt that the French had occupied Syria, driving out King Faisal.

Lawrence had come to know Faisal, one of the sons of Sherif Hussain, the ruler of Mecca, during the Arab Revolt and it was due to his persuasion that Faisal was proposed as ruler of Iraq. He journeyed to Iraq and after a referendum on the rival claims of himself and Ibn Saud, Faisal was proclaimed king and called upon the Naqib to form a cabinet. Wilson was against this development, warning that Faisal was looked upon by the majority Shia population of Iraq as a foreign Sunni king and that risings would surely follow.

It seemed then that Britain had fullfilled its mandate and could relinquish responsibility for Iraq, but it was not to be, for some attempt had to be made to educate the people of Iraq into the ways of Western institutions and democracy.

The period 1921–2 was a time of further disturbances in the north and south-west of the country. It was suspected that they were fomented by Turkish agents with whom the Allies were still theoretically at war. Brigandage was rife and refugee desert tribes were creating difficulties by moving into Iraq to escape the punitive activities of Ibn Saud, the Sultan of Najd, whose forces followed them into Iraq and attacked the Iraqi Camel Corps and the shepherd tribes not far from the railway that linked Basra to Baghdad.

At this time both King Faisal and his Prime Minister were agitating for the complete abrogation of the British mandate, since it was inconsistent with Iraq's sovereign independence, and for its replacement by a treaty. Britain, however, preferred to have the treaty within the mandate and described the difference as being merely technical. Faisal, urged on by the agitation, refused to sign it so Sir Percy Cox assumed sole authority and by vigorous methods that included the use of motorized columns and aircraft, restored order in the country. The treaty was at length signed but the mandatory obligations still carried on. In return for the signature, Britain undertook to secure Iraq's admission to the League of Nations.

A dispute had arisen in the north of the country with Turkey over the line of the northern Iraq border. The League of Nations appointed an International Commission to adjudicate and the outcome was that Mosul was given to Iraq. In 1932 Iraq became a member of the League of Nations and Britain's mandate came to an end. The subsequent history of Iraq has been by no means untroubled, but that lies beyond the scope of this narrative apart from a brief note concerning the most recent events.

Faisal died in 1933 and, purely as a postscript to the above, it is worth recording his assessment of the people over whom he was called to rule, which he made shortly before his death: 'unimaginable masses of human beings, devoid of any patriotic idea, imbued with religious traditions and absurdities, connected by no common tie, prone to anarchy and perpetually ready to rise against any government whatever'.

The second invasion of Mesopotamia, or Iraq, was that by the British and American Coalition in 2003 and was more or less all over in four weeks. They had the use of mobile columns that could operate far out in the desert, a technique developed by the British Long Range Desert Group in the Second World War in North Africa, and they had the advantage of overwhelming air power and aircraft that could be used as artillery. Helicopters could bring parties of troops to given spots at short notice and be used to attack troops and tanks very effectively. But supply was a difficulty, just as it had been in the First World War, despite the fact that they did not have to depend on the inefficient communication systems offered by the rivers.

In both wars the invading powers had difficulties in controlling Iraqis. During the first war it was less of a problem for the British took the precaution of accompanying the military force with political officers, whose particular job was to ensure that ordinary life returned to the towns and cities after the passage of the military – but after hostilities ceased the difficulties multiplied as they also did in 2003. It does seem strange that the Coalition forces did not anticipate the disorder and looting that would follow their arrival in a town. In the First World War there was some looting, as at Amara, but it was dealt with firmly within a few hours by shooting any looters on sight.

In 1914, Mesopotamia, like most parts of the far-flung Turkish Empire, was completely undeveloped with no modern amenities like roads or railways, and everything had to be provided for the Army and the contingents of auxiliaries that followed it to allow them to function. This was not the case in 2003 since the Allied army carried its world around it in a cocoon, but the civilian amenities that were in place in Iraq by that time were disrupted by their activities and this meant that those who depended on them, like doctors in the hospitals, administrators, the media, public transport and so on, who are essential to the functioning of life in a modern state, were not able to operate. Life more or less came to a standstill in 2003, which did not happen in the First World War since life then was lived much closer to the subsistence level and people did not depend on systems that could be so easily disrupted. Fewer people lived in towns in those days and those who did were accustomed to fending for themselves and providing their own basic necessities like lighting, food and water. The much larger town populations in 2003 could not do this and expected electricity, food and water to be provided.

Bibliography

Bell, Gertrude, Letters edited by Lady Bell (1987)

Burne, Lieutenant Colonel A.H., *Mesopotamia: The Last Phase* (1938)

Candler, Edmund (Official Eyewitness), *The Long Road to Baghdad*, 2 vols (1919)

Evans, Major R., *A Brief Outline of the Campaign in Mesopotamia 1914–18* (1926)

Halil Bey, Memoirs (nd)

Herbert, Aubrey, *Mons, Anzac and Kut* (1919)

Hopkirk, Peter, *On Secret Service East of Constantinople* (2001)

Jones, E.H., *The Road to En-dor*, Pan Books (1955)

Marshall, Major General Sir William, *Memories on Four Fronts*, Ernest Benn (1929)

Mousley, E.O., *Secrets of a Kuttite* (1922)

One of its Officers, *With a Highland Regiment in Mesopotamia 1916–17* (1918)

Shakeshaft, A.J. (2nd Norfolk), Personal diary quoted in Moberley's Official History, Vol II, pp. 534–6

Sherson, Erroll, *Townshend of Chitral and Kut* (1928)

Sykes, Sir Percy, *A History of Persia*, 2 vols (1930)

Tennant, Lieutenant Colonel J.E., *In the Clouds above Baghdad* (1920)

Townshend, Major General Sir Charles, *My Campaign in Mesopotamia* (1920)

Tuohy, Ferdinand, *The Secret Corps* (1920)

Wilson, Sir Arnold T. *Loyalties – Mesopotamia 1914–1917* (1930)

Yeats-Brown, Captain Francis *Lives of a Bengal Lancer* (1930)

Official Publications

Kearsey, A., *A Study of the Strategy and Tactics of the Mesopotamia Campaign 1914–1917* (nd)

Moberly, Brigadier General F.J., *The Campaign in Mesopotamia*, vols I–III (1923)

Officers of the Staff College, Quetta, *Critical Study of the Campaign in Mesopotamia up to April 1917* (1928)

Cd 9208 *Report on the Treatment of British Prisoners of War in Turkey* (1918)

Cd 8610 *Mesopotamia Commission Report* (1917)

Index

240

241

242